The Theme Is Freedom

D0684933

The Theme
Is Freedom

RELIGION, POLITICS, AND
THE AMERICAN TRADITION

M. Stanton Evans

REGNERY PUBLISHING

A Salem Communications Company

www.Regnery.com

Copyright © 1994 by M. Stanton Evans

All rights reserved. No part of this publication may be reproduced or transmitted in any form or by any means, electronic or mechanical, including photocopy, recording, or any information storage and retrieval system now known or to be invented, without permission in writing from the publisher, except by a reviewer who wishes to quote brief passages in connection with a review written for inclusion in a magazine, newspaper, website, or broadcast.

Library of Congress Cataloging-in-Publication Data

Evans, M. Stanton (Medford Stanton), 1934–
The theme is freedom : religion, politics, and the American
tradition / M. Stanton Evans.
  p.   cm.
Includes bibliographical references and index.
ISBN 0-89526-497-8 (alk. paper)
1. Liberty—Religious aspects—Christianity.   2. United States—
History—Religious aspects—Christianity.   3. Conservatism—
Religious aspects—Christianity.   4. United States—Religion.
I. Title.
BR517.E83 1994

322'.1'0973—dc20   94-528
                                                                CIP

Published in the United States by
Regnery Publishing
A Salem Communications Company
300 New Jersey Ave NW
Washington, DC 20001

Manufactured in the United States of America.

10 9 8 7 6 5 4 3

Books are available in
quantity for promotional or premium
use. For information on discounts
and terms, please visit our website:
www.Regnery.com

Distributed to the trade by
Perseus Distribution
250 West 57th Street
New York, NY 10107

For my father,
who kept the faith

Acknowledgments

THIS BOOK HAS BEEN a long time coming, and would never have appeared at all without the help of many people. Foremost among those whose assistance must be acknowledged are the Regnerys, *père* and *fils*: Henry, for his longtime friendship, unfailing kindness, and example—as well as for specific encouragement on this project. Al, for urging me to go ahead with the book, steering it to completion, and exhibiting Stoic patience with my recastings and revisions.

Equally patient and consistently wise has been my editor, Patricia Bozell, whose thoughtful guidance and gimlet eye have saved the author (and thus the reader) from many obscurities and errors. Two others who must be acknowledged on this account are my highly efficient production editor, Jennifer Reist, and the indefatigable Christina Sobran, who typed and retyped (and retyped) the manuscript as I struggled for greater clarity of expression.

Others who assisted in most material fashion are Malcolm Kline, whose research aid was always timely, effective, and highly valued; Claire Chatelin, Alexandra Gural, Denise Laugesen, and Katarina Spears, who helped out with the typing; and my other colleagues at the office: Fred Mann, Mary Jo and Billy Buckland, Piper Lowell, Courtney Chamberlain, Irma White, Peter Spencer, Guy Murdoch, and Michael Chapman. All had a heavier load to bear because of my preoccupation with this project.

Among those who have encouraged and supported this endeavor are David Jones and Roger Ream of the Fund for American Studies, Ron Robinson and James Taylor of Young America's Foundation, Ken Cribb and John Lulves of the Intercollegiate Studies Institute, and the officers, members and diligent staff of the Foundation Endowment. Thanks are also owing to the Liberty Fund of Indianapolis, and the many publications it has made available, a dozen of which, at least, are cited in my discussion.

A word also needs saying about those who have helped to shape the contents of this volume through years of friendship and discussion: Ralph Bennett and William Schulz, Tom Winter and Allan Ryskind, Frank Meyer and William Rusher, Don Lipsett and John Ryan, Frederic Andre and Jim McClellan, Vic Milione and E. Roy Smith, Don Cope, Lew Uhler and Andy Gollan, and many others, who know that faith and freedom go together.

Finally, these pages are not only dedicated to the memory of my father, but also reflect the many conversations I had with him across the decades about the religious basis of our society, and countless other issues. A man of prodigious learning, his faith, integrity, and love of family never failed him, or me. The same may be said about my peerless mother, a classics scholar whose knowledge of ancient and English history has greatly aided my researches, and who has helped me in so many other ways. This book is for them both, the best of parents.

—Hamilton, Virginia, June 1994

Contents

Introduction

FRIENDS WITH WHOM I have discussed the topic of this book propose a racier, hence more commercial, title. Something like, "The Secret History of the United States," "The Civilization They Tried to Hide," or (the all-purpose, most inclusive version) "Everything You Were Ever Taught Was Wrong."

Though a bit casual for the gravity of the subject, these would be accurate summaries of my thesis. Most of what will follow is an attempt to set straight accepted but in my view mistaken notions about our country, its institutions, and its freedoms. In the usual case, I argue, such teachings are not only off the mark but tangible inversions of the record; this despite the fact that all of them are promoted on a regular basis by well-known and seemingly learned people who instruct us on such questions.

It is astonishing to think that our immensely powerful country, having reached the heights of worldly grandeur, should know so little about its past, or about the sources of its greatness. Yet this all too obviously is the case, as reflected in many surveys that test us for historical information. It is even more astonishing to reflect, no doubt, that we have been plied with misleading comment on the subject—that authors and teachers and media pundits have misrepresented the nature of our system, and the values it embodies. Yet such, it is suggested in these pages, is precisely our condition.

Under no illusion that this modest counterhistory is going to change things, I thought it important to make the effort, for reasons that will be noted as we go along but probably need some definite statement at the outset. It is perhaps apparent on general principles that we ought to have a factual treatment of our ideas and institutions, rather than making do with fables. That, presumably, is why we want histories to be written in the first place, and have courses of historical study conducted in our schools. Granted a certain leeway for ancestral legend (definitely not the current problem), one would assume, people are entitled to a truthful record of their country.

Our need for accurate data becomes the more compelling when we note that things of practical moment are riding on the outcome. We are not dealing, after all, with merely antiquarian topics. According to our understanding of these questions, principles are espoused and actions taken at the present day, and decisions are arrived at that have tremendous consequences for the future. Knowing where we come from can tell us something, maybe a lot, about where we should be going. Among other things, our history shows us the kind of people we are (or were), the sort of country that we have (or had), the measures that are appropriate to the political order, and a great deal else.

The connections between our subject and issues of the day, indeed, are many, and appear throughout the course of the discussion. Most obviously, there is ongoing conflict over the role of religious teaching in our discourse, schools, and public institutions. Few issues reveal as clearly the cultural warfare that divides our nation, and that will be a recurring topic in these pages. This has been a source of legal combat and political rancor for many years, and nothing suggests that trouble on this front will be abating. The usual history leads to one conclusion on such questions, a different view of the historical record to another.

A second point of connection, tied closely to the first, is the place of conservatism in American life, and its relation to the political values of our culture. This is chiefly of interest to self-described conservatives, of course, but has relevance for many others, since it raises the question of what, if anything, Americans should be conserving. There are those who argue, based on the alleged lessons of our past, that "American conservatism" is an oxymoron—that nothing by this name makes sense in our society, the supposed prototype of modern revolution. Only by going to the record can questions of this sort be answered.

Closely related to these topics is the matter of governing methods in our system: Most notably, the degree to which political and economic power may be collected safely in one center, the boundaries to which that power should be subject, and the linkage of these political problems to matters of religion. This involves not only the much-disputed legal issue of church-state relations, but the more encompassing question of how our freedoms generally connect up with our faith. The standard teaching is very emphatic on the subject, with implications that shall be considered from several angles in this volume.

Our topic is also tied in, though indirectly, with the "multicultural" movement in the schools. The premise of this agitation is that we are so immersed in Western "Eurocentric" notions that we have short-changed other cultures and the insights that they offer. Accordingly, the educational system is to be revamped (and in many cases has been) in favor of Afrocentric, feminist, gay, and other counterculture teachings that challenge the usual "canon" of white, male-dominated, European studies.

A threshold problem with this issue is that much of what is being called for has precious little to do with other cultures— the Sumerian or Inca civilizations, Japan or China, or the achievements of the Arabs, all of which might usefully be studied. What we typically observe instead is a bold attack against *our* culture, as this has generally been understood, based on neoMarxist and other radical doctrines (themselves derived, in many cases, from Western sources). Even so, the basic complaint is that Western culture is too much with us, and needs to be supplanted.

As might be guessed from what is said above, my take on this is basically the other way around. The argument here is that, far from being steeped in Western culture, we know almost nothing about it, and what we think we know is commonly in error. There is a great deal not to like about the "canon," as shall be seen, but what is wrong will be made substantially worse by yielding to the multicultural clamor.* All of us could benefit from knowing more about the varied cultures of the world; but multiculturalism, like charity, begins at home.

The facts on all of this are "secret," not in the sense that they are especially cryptic, but rather in that almost no one bothers to inquire or talk about them. The records are there in histories from a bygone era, in long-forgotten documents and journals, in scholarly researches—but these are passed over in current discourse. Much of what will be mentioned in this discussion should be available in any good-sized reference library. But except for the specialists themselves, it seems to be seldom read, less frequently expounded, and almost never pulled together. The present essay is thus a kind of archaeological dig, trying to unearth a cultural record buried out of public view by multiple generations of modern teaching.

Though religion is a central focus, this book makes no pretensions as a work of piety or theological doctrine. It is an effort to trace, conceptually and as a matter of historical fact,

---

* A fairly typical rendering of the "canon" lists "Plato and Aristotle, Machiavelli and Rousseau, Hobbes and Locke, Nietzsche and Freud, Marx and Mill, Jefferson and Dewey." The problem with this sequence is not that the authors are dead white European males, but that most of them have nothing to do with our free institutions—indeed, promoted doctrines profoundly hostile to Western freedom. And, as shall be discussed, the two that are connected to American liberty—Locke and Jefferson—are routinely misrepresented in the usual teaching. Such problems won't be corrected by reading Maya Angelou or *The Color Purple.* (The quote is from Irving Howe, "The Value of the Canon," in F. E. Beckwith & Michael E. Bauman, eds., *Are You Politically Correct?* Prometheus, 1993)

the nexus between religious values and the rise of our political system. Nothing deeper is attempted. As it is, I am acutely conscious of my limitations. The subjects covered range from ancient kingship to medieval statecraft to modern-day free-market economics. Any of these could properly be, and often has been, the lifelong study of the most able scholars. Knowing my inadequacy for the job in question, I have often wished that someone better qualified would do it. But since that person, so far as I can tell, has not stepped forward, I have persisted in the project.

In handling these materials, I begin with the intellectual problems involved, as these are posed in the conventional teaching, and thereafter move to chronological treatment. The book is divided, roughly speaking, between these two approaches. The reason for this is that only if the main conceptual questions are spelled out plainly from the start will the relevance of the history be comprehensible in the modern era. From an accurate reading of that history, I believe, we can deduce the key political principles of our system, see why they became such, and thereby gain an understanding of our freedoms.

These principles can be in turn a source of present guidance, and in my opinion should be—though no systematic application is attempted. The links (and differences) between theology and the rule of earthly law, the dilemmas posed by contractual theories of the state, the line between encouraging virtue and trying to compel it, and other subtle questions, are touched on but not developed. My original idea was to pursue these matters rather fully, but to do so would require another book as long as this one. The reader has, at least for now, been spared that burden.

Two further disclaimers, or explanations, are needed by way of opening comment. One is that my aim is to come up with a synoptic picture, which means the narrative must generally keep moving (such, at any rate, is the hope). This is a strategy fraught with peril. Detail that might have brought out some aspect in more telling fashion has been omitted or drastically compressed—while sidebars to the main development (e.g., the vast political derailment of the Renaissance) get only passing mention. In almost every case, the topics dealt with cry out for more extensive treatment than I could give them.

The principal danger in this method, of course, is that of merely skimming—of hitting a lick here and another there, relying on paraphrase and assertion, and thus not presenting sufficient data to back up what is being said. I have tried to guard against this by offering enough by way of historical fact and relevant citation to document the accuracy of treatment. The object is to have a sensible discussion, properly grounded in the record, but avoiding academic density and jargon. Whether I have steered successfully among these shoals is for the reader to determine.

Also, to change the metaphor, I am trying to follow an institutional thread—to track beliefs and customs from one stage to the next, and to highlight matters that are ignored in the conventional teaching. The resulting emphasis may seem to neglect some other elements in the story—such as (to pick a prominent case) the role of Locke in propagating social contract, of which our Declaration of Independence is so notable an expression. Since Locke's influence is stressed repeatedly in the usual treatment, my version focuses on the countervailing data. This doesn't mean that Locke had nothing important to do with social contract, but rather that his writings should be assessed in a completely different philosophic setting.

Likewise, in my analysis of the American Revolution, I focus on data that show the conservatism of the Founders, and their effort to hang on to their existing institutions, rather than seeking radical changes. This does not preclude the notion that many changes resulted *from* the revolution, as of course they did. Or, to pick a last example, when I discuss the influence of religious precept in our culture, I am aware, *e.g.*, that eighteenth-century ideas of "natural theology" were not the orthodox position, for reasons that will be addressed in several places. The point is not to gauge the orthodoxy of people's views, but rather to see where their opinions came from.

My debt to many intellectual sources is great—too much so to be stated properly in this introduction (a bibliographical section is added for this purpose). I simply note at this point that study of these sources has confirmed for me, not only the greatness of our country, but the impressive nature of our forebears. Granted all their human frailties, the clerics and statesmen who framed our institutions were amazing people, armed at the critical moments with wisdom and intrepid courage. May this survey contribute its mite to rendering them, and their achievements, a measure of historical justice.

The Theme Is Freedom

1

The Liberal History Lesson

WE WHO SURVIVE into the final years of the twentieth century have witnessed an astounding moment in the biography of the human race: The collapse of communism's despotic rule in Eastern Europe and the Soviet Union. It would be hard to overstate the significance of this immense development, for the affected nations or the world in general.

With the demise of the evil empire, myriad states and subject peoples that suffered the yoke of Soviet bondage have been given a chance to breathe the air of freedom. In the brief period 1989–91, some 400 million captives staged a colossal jailbreak, along the way demolishing a tyrannical system once considered immune to challenge. This surely ranks among the greatest changes in human status, and global fortune, that have ever been recorded. The analogies that come to mind are the fall of Rome, the Reformation, the founding of our country, World War II—in secular terms, about as big as such events are capable of getting.

The lessons that may be learned from this transition are many, and profound. To date, however, there is little to indicate that we have learned them, or are about to. While there were rejoicings in America at the end of Soviet communism, these were mixed with expressions of befuddlement and concern, if not outright regret. Our official sympathies had been with the "reform communism" of Mikhail Gorbachev, and only reluctantly did we accept the more explicit anticommunism of Boris Yeltsin. Government and media spokesmen alike have since deplored the absence of stability in the region, the lack of "someone to deal with" in the former satellites, the complexities of a world without our long-familiar foe, and so on.

In keeping with such notions, our response to the fall of communist power in Europe has been groping and uncertain; when the *Götterdämmerung* arrived, we had no plan to cope, nor is there one to speak of at this writing (two years after the Yeltsin revolution). All too obviously, we didn't understand what was occurring there, or why, and don't understand it now. It is viewed as a great, mysterious business, full of riddles, surprises, unknown players, and baffling causes. Yet these events are fraught with meaning, not only for Eastern Europe, but for America and its people.

Much that is involved in assessing the problems of the Eastern states is, of course, a difficult matter of unraveling knots, creating institutions, and dealing otherwise with the specifics. Yet there are certain overarching respects in which the moral is clear enough, and from which we ought to be drawing some conclusions. These have to do, precisely, with the ideas and practices of freedom. At this level, the lessons could hardly be much plainer, or more urgent. The communist system in the Soviet bloc and elsewhere has been a huge experiment in collectivist planning, with governments wielding total power in an attempt to build a godless Eden. That experiment has been a failure, in every way that could be imagined.

Like other totalitarian movements of the era, the communists proposed a hard-nosed bargain: People would exchange their liberty for security and economic progress; all-knowing experts would organize society by "scientific" methods, making decisions that private parties were incompetent to manage. (As late as 1989, this was described by one Western pundit as a

Marxist version of "social contract."[1]) What happened instead was a debacle, on both sides of the ledger: mass murder and enslavement in the political realm, chaos and privation in terms of economics. In essence, people ruled by communist planners gave up their freedom for a mess of pottage—and then were told the pottage wouldn't be delivered.

From this unhappy outcome, a number of things should be apparent. One is that zealots with plans for making over the world by fiat are a deadly menace, and should be resisted wherever they show themselves, on whatever pretext. This has been seen repeatedly since the French Revolution, and applies most notably to the ideologies of the modern epoch. If we have not yet learned to doubt would-be messiahs, human engineers, and supposedly scientific planners of the lives of others, it appears that we shall never learn it.

The fact that all these horrors happened on our intellectual-cultural watch should also be a cause for bleak reflection. Measured by such basic standards as respect for human life and personal freedom, ours has been the most barbaric era in the history of the planet. More than 100 million people have been exterminated by the totalitarian powers, with millions more locked up in slave camps or subject to other organized repression. If this is an age of enlightenment and progress, as we have so often been assured, how did these enormities happen? And where did these despotic movements come from? These are questions that deserve attention, and will be considered in the ensuing pages.

Beyond this, there are some more immediate points, with more obvious relevance to our condition. The communist misadventure teaches, most of all, the dangers of concentrated power, devoid of checks or limits. Because the Soviet commissars controlled all the levers and hinges of the system, there was nothing to impede tyrannical rule in any way whatever, other than their own discretion or internal struggles: no constitutional safeguards, no free speech or press, no independent legislature or judiciary—merely the relentless, grinding power of the ruling faction. Such methods, all too plainly, are fatal to the cause of freedom.

Likewise, the end of the Soviet Union shows that running a complex society by command just doesn't work, resulting in the most daunting problems for the rulers, and unspeakable hardship for the people. Economies set up in this fashion don't have the incentives needed to encourage work and output, don't know what to produce, or when, can't get materials to the places where they are wanted. As pointed out long ago by Mises, and confirmed by all experience since, such problems are inherent in any collectivist regime. In this respect at least it doesn't seem to matter whether the planners are psychotic tyrants or mild-mannered civil servants; the trouble is built in to the nature of the system.

All this being so, one might have supposed the Cold War end-game would have deepened appreciation of our free market institutions, and spurred a renewal of interest in our other freedoms. Beyond the most bromidic comment, however, this hasn't happened. We were amazed and relieved by what we saw, celebrated briefly, then went back to our usual pastimes. The total collapse of the most elaborate scheme of collectivism ever known has been treated almost as an incidental matter—absorbing drama, to be sure, creating problems and opportunities, but with no other connection to our behavior.

This lack of awareness appears not only in our vague response to events in Europe, but also in our conduct on the homefront. Again, there is little to suggest we have gleaned anything worth knowing from the Soviet fiasco—concerning power, free markets, or deeper aspects of the subject. One need only note in this regard the vast authority wielded by our central government, affecting every sector of economic life and many other important matters. On recent estimates, Washington now absorbs some 40 percent of our Gross National Product, through tax and spending programs, mandates and controls, and efforts are constantly being made to up the ante. No day elapses without some new demand for bigger subsidies and steeper taxes, expanded schemes of regulation, investment directed by official foresight, and the like.

At this writing, to take the obvious case in point, our political leaders are gravely weighing a proposal to turn one-seventh of our economy, the health care system, over to a regime of national planning. The measure favored by the ruling party closely resembles collectivist schemes that have prevailed abroad: a "national health board," which would decide how much 250 million people ought to spend on health care, compulsory enrollment, a network of minute constraints, punishments for noncompliance, and a great deal else. Connect the dots, and the resulting picture is quite familiar: we are being asked to adopt the style of top-down rule that proved calamitous for Eastern Europe.

Consider also a last specific, the case of price controls, which destroyed all hopes of economic calculation in the Soviet system, and must do the same in any other. Few lessons are clearer from global history than that such controls lead on to dearth, misallocation, and economic meltdown. Yet we have compulsively dabbled in these interventions, and more are suggested on a continuing basis. This has most recently been the case with health care, but has occurred as well with energy, housing, cable TV, insurance rates, and many other consumer prices. Our public debates reflect no glimmer of understanding that the collapse of communism into economic rubble has any bearing on these topics.

Thus, by a strange inversion, the U.S. and the USSR seem intent on trading places. As the formerly communist nations struggle to escape the toils of collectivism and establish the institutions of the market, we blithely adopt collectivist practices of our own, albeit in gradual *ad hoc* doses, including measures that a voluminous record shows to be not only feckless but preludes to disaster. Santayana warned us about people who failed to study history; Franklin's version was more succinct, and less polite: "Experience keeps a dear school, but fools will learn in no other."[2] We are on course to verify both statements.

One explanation of our collectivist drift is the myopia that prevails, in most opinion-moulding circles, concerning economic subjects. It sometimes appears, indeed, that ignorance of economics is a precondition for holding office in our country, or discoursing on policy questions in the media—a secret pledge somewhere that must be signed before the novice is granted entry. The trouble, however, goes beyond the realm of economics. At a deeper level, it is fair to say, there is little or no attention to more fundamental issues, concerning the origin, nature, and workings of a free society. Above all, we seem to have no idea of what it takes to bring such a political order into being, or what is needed to sustain it.

A comparatively innocent source of this default is that we take our liberties for granted. Since our freedom has always been there, more or less, it appears completely normal—something we can rely on and not have to think about unduly. To most Americans, it seems routine that we can say what we want, go to whatever church we please, or move about the country as we wish. It also appears to be entirely natural that we can walk into a supermarket and find it full of produce, that there are stores at every crossroads, cars and houses and consumer goods of all descriptions. That's the way it generally has been, for as long as most of us can remember.

But, as events both past and current plainly tell us, none of this is "natural" or "normal" at all—if by that we mean the common and usual condition of the species. Quite the contrary. The collapse of the Soviet system, while spectacular and huge, is far from being the only instance. Haiti, Cuba, Somalia, Ethiopia, and Sudan are cases that have appeared in recent headlines, and many others could be noted. Most people at most times and places have not enjoyed the freedoms we find prosaic, nor have they known the comforts that are provided by our system. Measured by previous standards or those of the world around us now, our freedom is among the rarest achievements in human history.

The point of these reflections is not merely to count our blessings, which we should certainly do, but also to understand them. Clearly, our freedoms didn't simply happen; they were the result of deliberate precautions and provisos, acts of statecraft which it behooves us to study and remember. If we want to grow orchids instead of weeds, it is well to know what kind of climate, soil, and nurture are congenial to orchids; ignorance of or indifference to these matters will predictably result in failure. Ignorance of or indifference to the safeguards needed for the growth of liberty will issue in a like result, but with effects more baleful to consider.

Were these our only hazards, the outlook for maintaining a regime of freedom would be problematic. There is, however, a further and more serious obstacle to be surmounted: The fact that powerful elements in our society are actively opposed to the idea of limited government and free markets, as is apparent from the measures we have cited. These are the people known to our politics as liberals, whose reflexive answer to almost any problem, real or imagined, is to consign more power to the state. Though linguistically confusing, the fact that "liberalism" now means the concentration and use of top-down power hardly needs much proving. How it got this way, after starting out as a creed of freedom, will be examined in a later chapter; suffice it here to note that expanding government power, especially over economic matters, is the liberal cure for anything that ails us.

Given this obvious fact of record, it is hardly to be expected that liberal elements in our politics will be attentive to the rules of liberty, at home or elsewhere. It is not surprising, for example, that liberal analysts in the United States were unable to grasp the massive, systemic problems of the USSR and Eastern Europe, to foresee the utter chaos into which these regimes would tumble in the 1990s, or to draw any useful lessons from that outcome. With their own belief in controls and planning, our liberals were ill equipped to spot the fallacy of such arrangements behind the Iron, or Bamboo, Curtain.

If space permitted, we might rehearse the amazing tale of liberal-left astigmatism on this subject—the recurring but unrequited passion for such as Stalin, Mao, Castro, Ho Chi Minh, the Sandinistas, the African National Congress. Even after the record was in concerning the genocide and other infamies of the communists, which were of course deplored, many liberal academics remained effusive about the "growth rates," health care, education, and other supposed achievements of these tyrants. This learned ignorance was still being spouted in the 1980s, when Marxist systems were imploding, and their harried masters scuttling for survival.* No one in the communist countries believed a word of it, but this nonsense was given credence in the West, encouraging our respectful posture toward a disintegrating Kremlin.

If the liberals are unable to figure out the case for freedom, this task would appear to fall to the main opposing faction in our politics, the conservatives. On first appraisal, the outlook here would seem to be more promising, and to some extent it has been. American conservatism has historically preached a doctrine of limited government and free markets (among other

---

* In 1984, to pick one notable offender, John Kenneth Galbraith was proclaiming: "That the Soviet Union has made great material progress in recent years is evident both from the statistics (even if they are below expectations) and, as many have reported, from the general urban scene. One sees it in the appearance of solid well-being of people on the streets, the close to murderous traffic, the incredible exfoliation of apartment houses, and the general aspect of restaurants, theaters, and shops—though these are not, to be sure, the most reliable of indices." (Quoted in the *Washington Times*, January 15, 1992) Likewise, economists Paul Samuelson and William Nordhaus, in the 1989 edition of their standard text: "The Soviet economy is proof that, contrary to what many skeptics had earlier believed, a socialist command economy can function and even thrive." (Quoted in Mark Skousen, *Economics on Trial*, Business One Irwin, 1991, p. 208)

things), and generally speaking does so now. This viewpoint, moreover, has been featured by the Republican party of the present era, chiefly through spokesmen such as Barry Gold-water and Ronald Reagan. Here, if anywhere, should be the people who grasp and state the case for liberty that urgently needs making.

Yet even in these precincts there is confusion. Most notably, there is a school of thought suggesting that American conserva-tism isn't, or shouldn't be, the party of individual freedom. Such notions, it is contended, are really a form of "classical liberal-ism," dating back to the eighteenth and nineteenth centuries, and have nothing to do with conservative theory. In this anal-ysis, conservatism is a creed of virtue, order, hierarchy, and tradition, stressing the need for moral authority in the state. These ideas, supposedly, run counter to notions of free mar-kets, limits on official power, and letting people make their own decisions.

Although other factors enter in, the central issues in this critique involve the question of religion. By and large, conserva-tives are religious, and religion is widely considered hostile to personal liberty. Belief in moral absolutes, adherence to the long traditions of Judaic and Christian teaching, and a pessimistic view of human nature are common attributes of conservative thought, and these allegedly translate into author-itarian practice. Conversely, notions of individual freedom are said to have an irreligious or at least a nonreligious basis: Skepticism about moral absolutes, a rationalist approach to social problems, and an optimistic view of human nature are considered essential features of a libertarian outlook.

The people who tell us these things are fairly numerous, and also highly influential. They include, most obviously, the aca-demic and media critics of conservatism, always prompt to sow discord among the opposition. These have produced an endless stream of books and articles arguing that American conservatives are a motley rabble without a philosophic leg to stand on. Over the years, we have been variously informed that American conservatism does not exist, is not "true" conservatism, is old-fangled liberalism in disguise, or—even worse—a front for robber barons, a form of mental illness, a coalition of cranks and bigots. Whatever the particular angle, a dominant message has always been that conservative precept is opposed to freedom.

These aspersions have been so profuse that almost any academic treatment might supply the text. Fairly typical are the statements of Clinton Rossiter, a supposed authority on such matters, who deplored the fact that many so-called conservatives in the United States "asserted the primacy of the individual over society," that the American Right had grievously sinned through "the unthinking zeal with which it first embraced and still cherishes the principles of economic liberalism," and that too many conservative stalwarts professed a species of morality and religion that "served Mammon as often as God."* Other opinions in this vein could be provided at endless length.[3]

Such comments might be discounted as *parti pris*, but they draw strength from the fact that many on the Right say something not too different. There are philosophical libertarians, for example, who reject the "conservative" label, and some who specifically disown its religious connotations, emphasis on tra-

---

* These words were written thirty years ago, but the more it changes in this regard, the more it remains the same. Witness this recent journalistic version: "There was no clear body of conservative doctrine ... with the exception of Senator Taft, conservative politicians in Congress were not an intellectually gifted lot [unlike, apparently, liberals in Congress—MSE]. Insofar as the intellectual leadership of the Right came mainly from the business class, both its motives and its prescriptions were suspect ... [Some] embraced the liberal idea ... in the nineteenth century sense, as opposition to all forms of statism and as support for free market economics above all else ... Post war conservatism was thus conceived in contradiction." (E. J. Dionne, *Why Americans Hate Politics*, Simon & Schuster, 1992, pp. 151–157)

dition, and ideas of human nature. More conspicuously, there are "big government" conservatives who argue that the state should be in the business of instilling virtue, making welfarism more efficient, promoting "populist" blue-collar interests, or otherwise using government power for right-wing causes.* All of which would seem to support the view that conservatives can't be, and aren't, defenders of the limited state, free market economics, or libertarian policy in general.

This line of argument has an interesting effect, which the attentive reader may have noticed. Whatever its other supposed merits, *it precludes the very idea of resistance to big government, since nobody has proper grounds for stating an objection.* On the one hand, liberals who *used* to believe in limited government no longer do so, and take their stand for state coercion. On the other hand, conservatives who *want* to resist big government are told they can't or shouldn't adopt that view, since their real philosophy is also in favor of the intrusive state, in one fashion or another. Both left and right,.therefore, reject the concepts of limited government and free markets; all are statists, and all shall have big government proposals.

This result, as may be seen, is highly convenient for those who support expansive federal power, since it enlists both major schools of political thought in the United States, and both political parties, in favor of the program. That conclusion by itself should be enough to arouse a bit of skepticism among the wary. Why, after all, should *both* major tendencies in our politics be in favor of bigger government, albeit for somewhat different objects? How does it happen that a country founded

---

* Such views, though presented in terms of theoretical argument, obviously draw sustenance from more practical considerations: The fact that Republican candidates (and hence to some degree conservatives) have shown a marked ability in modern times to win the White House, having triumphed in five of seven presidential elections since 1968. This has contributed greatly to the change in theoretical position, especially as regards executive power (matched by a corresponding re-think on the left).

on the concept of the limited state has no strong political interest to defend that concept now—when it so obviously requires defending? On the face of it, this seems to be a most peculiar outcome.

As a little inquiry will determine, skepticism in the matter is amply borne out by the record. It is the argument of this essay, indeed, that all such notions are mistaken, at least as they apply to the historical and theoretical aspects of the subject. (Pragmatic political disagreement is another question.) In point of fact, as shall be shown in some detail, there is a strong conservative tradition in the United States, rooted in the still longer tradition of our English forebears, and more broadly speaking in two millennia of Western culture. The key political insight of this tradition is, precisely, the idea of *imposing limits on governmental power*, in the interests of protecting freedom—a doctrine that became the core and essence of American theory at the epoch of our founding.

The net meaning of this sequence, it shall be argued, is that libertarian statecraft has a long and honorable pedigree in the religious/cultural history of the West, and in the experience of our nation. Even more to the point, perhaps, this libertarian view, at all the stops along the way, has been dependent on religious values and traditional practice for its survival. Accordingly, there is indeed a case to be made for personal freedom and limits on the power of the state—and conservatives are the very people who should make it.

Such a demonstration, it should be apparent, would gainsay the usual charges of incoherence directed at the Right. It would suggest, for one thing, that the limited government, free-market stress that has marked conservatism in the United States is not in conflict with conservative values, as Rossiter and so many others have contended, but an expression of them. It would further suggest that the traditionalist and libertarian strands in conservative thought are congruent instead of contradictory— even if individual spokesmen choose to play up one against the other. Most relevant to current discourse, it would argue that conservatives of the present day should not accept big government nostrums, however these are bottled and labeled.

It should be apparent as well that the matters involved in such discussion transcend parochial debate about the "conservative movement," traditionalists vs. libertarians, or even the policy squabbles that divide conservatives from liberals. *What is at issue is the very nature of American society, the sources and intended functions of our institutions, and the provenance of our freedoms.* To consider these topics we must engage the most basic questions about the political order in which we live, the values it embodies, and the connection of these to the beliefs and habits of religion. The point to be decided is not which side of some factional quarrel is going to triumph, but what kind of country America is, or should be.

Confusions about these deeper issues, in my view, stem from a common source—a widely held but mistaken thesis about the intellectual progress of the West. This teaching, based on the ideologies of the modern era, purports to give a history of our freedoms. So far as I can tell, it is in every major respect a misstatement of the data—concerning the sources of free government, the libertarian safeguards embedded in our system, and the relationship of these to our religious culture. It is nonetheless pervasive in academic and media treatment of all the subjects that have been mentioned.

For want of a better term, I call this way of viewing things "the liberal history lesson," since it is coterminous with liberal thinking. The basic notion is, exactly, the supposed clash between religious precept and the practices of freedom. Our religion and our liberty, we are informed, have always been in conflict. Freedom, democracy and intellectual inquiry allegedly flourished in the pagan era, only to be crushed to earth in the Christian Middle Ages. This regime of clerical oppression supposedly ended when "humanist" scholars of the Renaissance and Enlightenment threw off the shackles of religion, rediscovered the learning of the ancients, and set modernity on the path to freedom. It appears to follow that a regime of liberty requires a secularist, anticlerical view of religious questions.*

As usually treated, American history is a subset of this larger teaching. In numerous texts and essays, we are told that our founding fathers were devotees of the Enlightenment, hostile or skeptical toward ideas of religion. The Founders are often portrayed as "radicals" who overthrew established institutions, broke with the past, and gave expression to Enlightenment notions in declaring independence from Great Britain. Thereafter, in the Constitution and Bill of Rights, they carefully guarded the workings of political society from the influence of religion—most notably in the opening phrases of the First Amendment, forbidding "an establishment of religion." Our break with England and constitutional founding are thus depicted, with variations, as cognates to the French Revolution: a venture in radical innovation, rejecting the authority of religious faith, basing our new republic on secular assumptions.

Despite the efforts of some excellent scholars, this formula is so widespread in modern thought as to constitute a kind of reflex. It is argued by liberal theoreticians who are themselves

---

* This thesis has been stated so often and in so many different ways that it is doubtless familiar to most readers. The following is a sample, selected more or less at random, from a popular intellectual history: "They discovered [in antiquity] a great authority for their break with the medieval spirit, and out of the conflict of authorities eventually rose freedom ... All this meant, of course, a revolt from the Christian ethic; in place of love, joy in the exercise of man's God-given powers; in place of obedience to the will of God, freedom and responsibility under reason; in place of faith ... the fearless quest of the intellect." (John Herman Randall, *The Making of the Modern Mind*, Riverside Press, 1940, pp. 220 *et seq.*) A more elegant source is Jacob Burckhardt: "In the Middle Ages ... human consciousness ... lay dreaming or half awake beneath a common veil. The veil was woven of faith, illusion, and childish prepossession ... In Italy, this veil first melted into air; an *objective* treatment of the state and all things of the world became possible. The subjective side at the same time asserted itself ... man became a spiritual *individual*." (Italics in original.) (*The Civilization of the Renaissance in Italy*, Modern Library, 1954, p. 100)

the heirs of the Enlightenment, is taught in treatments of Western culture generally, and forms the backdrop for almost all discussions of politics and religion.* It is, for instance, the premise of numerous Supreme Court decisions on prayer in the public schools. According to the Court—and countless liberal authors—America's founding fathers constructed a "wall of separation" between our religious and political institutions, fearing any mixture of the two would endanger fundamental freedoms. Hence prayer or Bible-reading in the schools must be forbidden, along with other kinds of public backing for religious value or observance.

Likewise, the supposed conflict between faith and freedom has been the basis for nonstop denunciation of the "religious right" and its involvement in the political system. Efforts to bring religious conviction to bear in electoral or legislative battles, we are informed, transgress the most basic principles of the republic—violating the cherished wall of separation. To judge from media accounts of recent years, this activity is a growing menace to our freedoms. Similar notions are expressed in battles about abortion and other "social issues," such as pornography, homosexuality, or "value-free" sex education, and sporadic proposals in the states to balance the teaching of Darwinian evolution with "creationist" instruction.

Indeed, this way of thinking breeds dispute about cultural

---

* Again, two comments must stand duty for countless others: "The long night of faith was over; the new day of reason had arrived; a decent respect for the rights of man and the opinions of mankind now replaced reliance on religious authority . . . it was only as the works of the European Enlightenment found their way piecemeal into the libraries of Harvard and Yale, and thence into the hands of the curious few, that the new modes of thought gradually took root in the American mind." (Robert C. Whittemore, *Makers of the American Mind*, Apollo, 1964, pp. 49–50) "[The Founders'] task was to establish the framework within which the natural rights announced in the Declaration of Independence would be protected. . . . Their authority was founded not on tradition or revelation but on nature grasped by reason. This was a new beginning . . ." (Allan Bloom, *Confronting the Constitution*, AEI Press, 1990, p. 1)

matters of all sorts, embracing many long-familiar issues: the generally adversarial posture of the learned toward supposedly ignorant religious folk; disparagement of the "Bible Belt" and its religious habits; the promotion of secular, permissive themes in media entertainments; the strong presumption, among our intellectual classes, that religious doctrine entails repression and stagnation. These notions suffuse our literature and social comment—all reflecting the influence of the standard history, and all suggesting that liberty and religion are everywhere at swords' points.

Against this pervasive backdrop, the idea that one can favor both religious belief and individual freedom must inevitably seem a hopeless contradiction. Choose our republic and its values, and you accept the secular-Enlightenment doctrine on which it all was based; choose the religious tradition of the West, and you reject the premises of our nation. You may have one or the other, but may not consistently have both. Hence the alleged impossibility in our system of "real" conservatism, with its foundation in religious precept; and hence the supposed confusion of those who try to link up faith and freedom. Given the standard version of our history, there is no other way to see it.

In the pages that follow, we shall examine various aspects of this teaching. Among the topics to be considered are the conceptual relations between religious value and ideas of freedom, the role of tradition in a free society, and the political implications of religious thought concerning human nature. While the conventional wisdom says conservative views about these matters are hostile to ideas of freedom, my analysis is entirely different. In fact, it will be argued, conservative doctrine on these questions is not only compatible with free institutions, but essential to them; conversely, secular liberal notions that supposedly conduce to liberty do the reverse, and must in the end be lethal to our freedoms.

Also to be considered is the accuracy of the standard treat-

ment simply as a matter of information. Here there is an astonishing story to be recited, since the liberal exegesis misstates
material points at every stage of the discussion, from antiquity
to the era of our founding. In many cases, the errors are so
glaring (concerning, for instance, social contract, the nature of
the American Revolution, or the place of religion in our system)
as to suggest that the conclusions were established first, the
data hustled up to fit the thesis *ex post facto*. Whatever the case
in that regard, much of what we have been taught about these
subjects distorts the facts beyond all recognition.

These are, of course, extremely strong assertions, and the
reader is entitled to ask by what authority I make them. My
answer is the historical record, which will be set forward as
clearly as I can do it, given the constraints of space and vast
scope of the subject. The evidence of this record, in my view,
is overwhelming, so much so that our survey must resort, time
and again, to samplings and compressions, rather than extended treatment of any single matter. Even so, I think it will
be apparent that there is a tremendous quantity of material
out there which goes directly counter to the standard version.
The major problem in this respect is an embarrassment of
riches.

But if this be true, a second question is in order: How could
so many people get it so completely wrong? This is a puzzle
that will recur throughout these pages, and to which a
couple of tentative responses should be addressed before proceeding further. Foremost among these, I believe, is simply the
mindset of the era, which has long been both secular and statist.
As none other than Darwin aptly put it, "the force of impressions
generally depends on preconceived ideas."[4] An age intensely
hostile to religion sees events through secular lenses, ignoring
the role of biblical precept in Western institutions, American
institutions most of all. The historian surveys the evidence (at
least sometimes), but fails to see it; or rather, sees it as something else, congruent with the initial thesis: the influence of

Greek or Roman models, doctrines of the Renaissance or Enlightenment, "radical" theories of one sort or another—anything, that is, but our religion.

Compounding the problem is the necessary but often misleading specialization of such studies. It is impossible, for example, to understand our revolution or constitutional founding without some knowledge of the original settlers and their faith, the English common law experience that lay behind them, and the medieval background from which all this developed. Typically, these are glossed over or ignored entirely in our histories, which portray ideas of popular sovereignty, limits on royal power, or the right of resistance as "radical" concepts invented in the modern epoch. In fact, however, all these ideas had been expressed with utmost clarity (and repeatedly) in the Middle Ages. This is commonplace for students of the earlier era, but seems unknown to those who write the history of our nation.

Finally, there is the influence of what might be called "the verbal fallacy"—to which all writers, and academics most of all, are naturally prone. Their bias is toward words and documents, rather than settled institutions, accustomed practice, and everyday existence. The assumption is that some theorist invents ideas and writes them down on paper, that other people read these thoughts and then repeat them, and that this transmission of words and phrases is what political history consists of. It is all a matter of tracking parchment formulations, especially when these can be somehow strung together to fit the central thesis.

Obviously, words and phrases are important and influential, and no sensible person would argue otherwise; many such will be examined in our discussion. However, document-hopping in this fashion obscures the fact that political words are always uttered in a cultural setting, and relate to many nonverbal matters—the real world problems people face, the history they have known, their laws and customs, and most of all, their religious values. The notion that people read some theoretical statement, then rush off to act according to its doctrines, is not the way it happens; the document is always a product of the other things, which led the authors to believe what they were writing, and caused other people to accept it. Unless these other things are noticed, there is not much chance that we shall understand our freedoms.

2

In Search of Freedom

IF WE WANT TO FIND the sources of our freedom, we first need to know what freedom is, as Americans have historically defined it. Odd as it may seem to devotees of simple common sense, different people mean different things by the expression, and confusion at this level defeats all hope of clarity at any other.

We need only note in this respect that the communists themselves made copious use of words like "freedom" and "liberation" to describe what they were doing. Partly, of course, this was a propaganda measure to baffle credulous people in the West, a ruse that all too frequently succeeded. But it was also a function of communist "dialectic" thought in general, which routinely inverted the meaning of words and phrases. The Marxists were always saying things like, "freedom is the appreciation of necessity."* To the communist mind, "liberation" *actually meant* the triumph of the proletarian vanguard by violent methods, followed by the murder, enslavement, and ruthless persecution of helpless victims.

While this is the most notorious case of freedom's being defined out of existence, there are many other instances on record. Sir Robert Filmer, more than three centuries ago, argued that "the greatest liberty in the world" was the privilege of

* This is Friedrich Engels'—approving—paraphrase of Hegel.

living under an arbitrary monarch—a privilege that Americans have been quite pleased to do without. More familiar is Rousseau's idea of freedom as subjection to the "general will," a concept bearing obvious similarity to the usage of the Kremlin. Then there are the New Deal slogans of "freedom from want," "freedom from fear," and many other examples that might be cited, in which freedom gets transmuted into reasons for compulsion.

Whether these notions are seen as quixotic, subtle, or merely vicious, they are not the concept we are discussing. Our definition, by comparison, is completely unsophisticated. Freedom in these pages means *the absence of coercion*—to the extent that this is feasible in organized society. It means the ability of human beings to act in voluntary fashion, rather than being pushed around and forced to do things. This formula has the benefit of being clear and simple, and of using language in its ordinary context. It is what people generally mean when they address the subject: Someone who does something of his own volition is free; someone forced to act at gunpoint isn't. This seems an obvious enough distinction, and, in an age disgraced by the totalitarian horror, a useful one to keep in focus.

Also, for those who like to think and speak with some precision, this formula has the merit of defining freedom on its own account, rather than merging it into something else. It means, for instance, the ability to decide things on a voluntary basis, but says nothing at all about *what* will be decided. This gives freedom a status of its own, a helpful feature if we want to compare or contrast it with other values.* Even so, it comes

---

* Liberty defined this way, as Hayek notes, "does not mean all good things or the absence of all evil. It is true to be free may mean freedom to starve, to make costly mistakes, or to run mortal risks . . . But if liberty may therefore not always seem preferable to other goods, it is a distinctive good that needs a distinctive name . . . it describes the absence of a particular obstacle—coercion by other men . . . It does not assure us of any particular opportunities, but leaves it to us to decide what use we shall make of the circumstances in which we find ourselves." (*The Constitution of Liberty*, Chicago, 1960, pp. 18–19)

attached with a proviso: Liberty to act on one's own behalf must be fenced off by the equal liberty of others, so that freedom for one individual doesn't become oppression for a second. Freedom in this sense must be mutual, so as not to contradict the basic premise.

Most important for our discussion, freedom thus defined also entails a certain kind of governing system. If a regime of liberty is to exist, some agency must forestall the use of force or fraud by which one person invades another's rights, render justice in doubtful cases, and provide a zone of order in which people may go about their affairs in safety. This agency is the government. Its basic job is to maintain the equal liberty of the people, by preventing various species of aggression. Likewise, for identical and fairly obvious reasons, government also must be precluded from violating freedom. Taken together, these concepts add up to the notion of the order-keeping state, which protects its citizens from hostile forces, but is itself restrained in the exertion of its powers.

As students of these matters will have noted, this is pretty much the "classical liberal" view of freedom. Indeed, the definitions and provisos just set forward reflect discussions of the topic provided by John Stuart Mill and Herbert Spencer,* and before them, in more rough and ready fashion, Locke and Adam Smith, as well as others who have grappled with the issue. How this agrees with conservative belief and religious values is, of course, another question, which will need to be examined. (Since the formula doesn't say anything about the way that freedom is *used*, for example, it is subject to the charge of

---

* Thus Mill: "The only freedom which deserves the name is that of pursuing our own good in our own way, as long as we do not attempt to deprive others of theirs or impede their efforts to obtain it." (*Essential Works of John Stuart Mill*, Bantam, 1961, p. 266) Spencer's version was: "Every man has freedom to all that he wills, provided he infringes not the equal freedom of any other man . . . We must . . . adopt this law of equal freedom in its entirety, as the law on which a correct system of equity is to be based." (*Social Statics*, D. Appleton and Company, 1897, p. 55)

ethical indifference. It is for this reason, among others, that Rossiter says conservative and libertarian notions are in conflict.)

Establishing such a regime of freedom is no easy matter, as it requires a proper balance between the requirements of liberty and those of order. Government needs sufficient power to do its job, but not too much—which would endanger freedom. The dilemma was summed up by Burke: "To make a government requires no great prudence. Settle the seat of power, teach obedience, and the work is done. To give freedom is still more easy. It is not necessary to guide; it only requires to let go of the rein. But to form a *free government*, to temper together these opposite elements of liberty and restraint in one consistent work, requires much thought, deep reflection, a sagacious, powerful, and combining mind."[1]

Similar thoughts about the topic were expressed by the Founders of our republic. Indeed, Americans will have no trouble recognizing the view of government we have been describing, since in general outline it is our own: an emphasis on voluntary action, safeguards for individual rights, limits on the reach of power. The core ideas of American statecraft have been, precisely, that government exists to provide an arena of ordered liberty, but that government in turn must be prevented from violating freedom. "In framing a government which is to be administered by men over men," as Madison phrased it, "the great difficulty lies in this: you must first enable the government to control the governed; and in the next place oblige it to control itself."[2]

If this is our idea of freedom, then the issue to be examined is where it comes from, and what kind of preconditions and institutions are needed to sustain it. To the extent that liberty defined this way is thought desirable, this is a question of the greatest moment. Fortunately, it is also a question for which there is a definite answer. In fact, the major clues that will help us solve the mystery have already been noted in our discussion:

the great fragility of freedom, the problems involved in getting it and keeping it, and its consequent scarcity in the experience of nations. While deplorable for the vast majority of the human race, the atypical nature of free institutions makes our task a good deal simpler. There aren't that many cases to be considered.

Free societies have certain features in common that set them apart from other systems, and a comparison of these differing traits and outcomes is the obvious starting point for our investigation. There is, for instance, the curious fact that in the ancient world ideas of liberty as we conceive them quite simply did not exist. No such concepts were expressed, much less put in practice, in Babylon, Egypt, imperial Rome, the Persian monarchy, or the Asiatic kingdoms. The preferred regime in these societies was all-powerful kingship, under one label or another, with no conception of individual freedom. A closer approach to our ideas in some respects occurred in Athens and Republican Rome, but even here, as shall be seen, our notions of personal liberty and the limited state were missing.

In the modern era, examples of free government are also notable for their absence. Quite apart from the totalitarians with their Gulags and Gestapos, the norm of twentieth-century statecraft has been anything but libertarian. In the decades since the end of World War II—supposedly an age of democracy and freedom—most of the Orient, Africa, Latin America, and the Middle East have lived under some species of repression, mostly revolutionary despots and military strongmen. Even with the demise of the Soviet Empire, because of problems arising in other regions, the general situation in this regard does not appear to be improving.*

---

* According to an estimate by Freedom House, as of early 1993, the percentage of human beings in the world who live in free societies had diminished in the preceding decade, from one-third or so of the global population to approximately one-quarter. At year's end, this group concluded that the situation had deteriorated even further, and that fewer than one-fifth of the world's inhabitants lived in freedom. (*Wall Street Journal*, December 16, 1993)

Accordingly, when we look for our idea of freedom, we find it in a narrow range of times and venues: The continent of Europe, before and after the totalitarians; the United Kingdom and its dominions; and the United States—commonly grouped together as "the West." To these have been added in recent years some parts of Latin America and the Pacific rim, and a state or two in Africa—to which ideas of limited government have been to some degree exported. That is the lot. In this respect as in a number of others, Rousseau had the situation backwards: Man is almost everywhere born in chains; only in a limited number of places has he been free. Why this has been the case will be the object of our study.

As our sequence obviously suggests, the concepts and institutions of freedom are of European origin, though capable, on occasion, of being transplanted elsewhere.It is in Europe, also, that we find other attributes of free societies—economic progress and expansion, the application of new technologies, the development of systematic science. All are aspects of the modern outlook that tend to go with freedom, and all came to the fore in Europe. This specific provenance of our ideas and values has in recent discourse been disparaged. It is, however, of the essence. If this is where freedom and related notions come from, then obviously we need to know the reason. Why should such conceptions emerge from Europe, rather than, *e.g.*, from the otherwise impressive culture of Confucian China? Why did these things take root in one particular civilization, but not in others?

To raise such issues, be it noted, it is not required that we presume or argue the "superiority" of European culture. As the multiculturalists are fond of saying, there are all kinds of societies in the world, each with its own distinctive beliefs and values and important contributions. In this view, no one is better or worse than another, only "different." Far be it from us to sit in judgment of other people's customs. We shall revisit this notion in a moment, but for now conveniently accept it:

The point is, exactly, that European culture *is* different from other cultures—and one of the ways in which it is most strikingly different is in its concept of personal freedom.*

Any serious consideration of these issues must bring us back, eventually, to the topic of religion. Every culture reflects the influence of religious precepts of one kind or another, and this is decidedly the case with Europe. As all authorities on the subject are agreed, the entity known as "Europe" was chiefly a product of Christianity—so much so that Europe and its off-spring were once described as "Christendom." As the church for many ages was the only universal institution, this should not be surprising. In a society divided by language, custom, ethnic background, and territorial ambition, it was religion that supplied the elements of unity: An accepted matrix of belief and value, art and symbol, the administrative mechanisms of the church, and—in the clerical and official use of Latin—a common argot that bridged the linguistic differences of the region.

Christopher Dawson, the principal student of such matters, expresses the connection this way: "Without Christianity, there would no doubt have been some kind of civilization in the West, but it would have been quite a different civilization from that which we know; for it was only as Christendom—the society of Christian people—that the tribes and people and nations of the West acquired a common consciousness and sense of cultural and spiritual unity. . . ."[3] Granted that many other elements such as Teutonic custom and Roman legal practice were folded into the final product (not always in beneficial fashion), it was religion that suffused the whole with a common outlook and gave to Europe its distinctive view of statecraft.

---

* Nor does this perspective mean that Western society has always adhered to the ideas of freedom that we have stated; all too obviously, it hasn't. The litany of exceptions and violations is long, from religious persecutions to wars of conquest to the long-continued existence of slavery in our own society. The moral is otherwise: *Not that the West has always adhered to its ideals, but rather that these ideals are of its making.*

Even when this religious unity was fractured at the Reformation, the power of Christian doctrine in moulding European institutions would continue. Though Catholics and Protestants battled fiercely among themselves, the political and cultural notions of the modern European states still received the imprint of Christian teaching, albeit in several different guises. It was on this ground of underlying unity that the Protestant Burke sprang to the defense of Catholic France against the secularism and atheism of the Jacobins—arguing that the civilization of the West was "virtually one great state having the same basis of general law," founded chiefly on the precepts of religion.[4]

That biblical teaching was the formative influence in the creation of Europe, and that Europe was the nursery of freedom as we know it, are both established facts of record. Taken separately, these are prosaic statements of common knowledge, hardly worth the trouble of assertion. Put them together, however, and the result is intensely controversial. This is not the linkage, after all, suggested by the usual story; the notion that Christianity equals Europe equals freedom is, indeed, the reverse of what should be expected. If Christian doctrine is opposed to freedom, then liberty ought to flourish where Christianity has had the smallest degree of influence, and languish where that influence is the greatest. That a general survey *prima facie* says the opposite suggests that something in the conventional history is mistaken.

As shall be seen, this correlation of Christianity with the rise of freedom is anything but accidental. In fact, the precepts of our religion provided the conceptual building blocks for the free societies of the West—including the very idea of liberty as we know it, limits on the power of the state, and institutions that gave these practical expression. Much of our discussion will be devoted to the particulars that show this; here we note only some general features that raise perplexing questions about the standard theory. Consider, for instance, the notion of *voluntary behavior* as the core idea of freedom, with which we started our discussion. Those who imagine that such ideas were invented by Locke or Mill (or that the Middle Ages were a time of mental slumber) might weigh the following passage from Aquinas:

". . . voluntary is what proceeds from the will . . . a man may be dragged by force, but it is contrary to the very notion of violence that he be thus dragged of his own will . . . if this were by compulsion, it would no longer be by an act of will . . . nor have external acts any measure of morality, save in so far as they are voluntary . . . if we speak of the goodness which the external act derives from the will . . . then the external act adds nothing to this goodness . . . The involuntary deserves neither punishment nor reward in the accomplishment of good or evil deeds . . ."[5]

St. Thomas thus expressed quite plainly our distinction between what is voluntary and what is not, which is central to any kind of libertarian theory. Nor is this all. Along with its emphasis on volition, there arose in Christian thought a reciprocal concept of limits on the state—since its compulsions dealt only with externals. Again St. Thomas is our guide (though we could show the same from St. Augustine): ". . . man is not competent to judge of interior movements that are hidden, but only of exterior acts . . . Consequently, human law could not sufficiently curb and direct interior acts . . . Human law cannot punish or forbid all evil, since while doing away with evils, it would do away with many good things, which would hinder the advance of the common good. . . ."[6]

This idea of *limits on state compulsion*, obviously, is also integral to the free society. It is distinctly biblical in origin, and was pervasive in the medieval era—and not merely as a concept. At the period when Aquinas was writing, limits on political power were the norm in Europe, though you could never guess it from the usual teaching. Representative institutions at this era were vigorous and growing, and the power of kings accordingly constrained—up to and including ideas of popular sovereignty, social contract, and resistance to tyrannical rulers.

At the high noon of the Middle Ages, the *cortés* in Spain, Estates General in France, *Reichstag* in Germany, and Parliament in England were wielding powers of taxation and sharing otherwise in state decisions—the prototype of free government as we know it.*

Generally speaking, in point of fact, the Middle Ages were a time of waxing freedom—growing protection for private rights, expanding urban liberties, and increasing commerce. The elective principle was pervasive, from aldermen and mayors to the conduct of the papacy and empire. Rule by unilateral edict was unknown. All of this was in keeping with the precepts of the church, which taught that earthly power should be subject to a higher law, and also held accountable to the governed. As the clerical spokesman Gratian put it, ca. 1140, "the law of princes ought not to prevail over natural law . . . princes are bound by and should live according to [the] laws."[7]

These comments are so different from what is commonly believed that they will require a fuller exposition on their merits. Pending that, Lord Acton's summary suggests the neglected realities of this Christian era: "Representative government, which was unknown to the ancients, was almost universal. The methods of election were crude; but the principle that no tax was lawful that was not granted by the class that paid—that is, that taxation was inseparable from representation—was recognized, not as the privilege of certain countries, but as the right of all . . . Slavery was almost everywhere extinct and absolute power was deemed more intoler-

---

* To pick the most prominent example: the *cortés* of Spanish Aragon, roughly contemporaneous with St. Thomas, included representatives not only of the clergy and nobility, but also deputies from the towns. Among them, we are informed, they "had practically complete control of legislation and of the collection and use of funds . . ." The king at his accession swore an oath that recognized the coordinate authority of the *cortés*, acknowledging that he could not govern without its concurrence. Other European legislative bodies at this period enjoyed similar, if less extensive, powers. (Edward P. Cheyney, *The Dawn of a New Era*, Harper, 1962, p. 81)

able and more criminal than slavery. The right of insurrection
was not only admitted but defined, as a duty sanctioned by
religion . . ."[8]

From an American standpoint, what is most relevant about
the medieval period is the experience of England, since this
was the proximate source of our ideas and institutions. English
and continental politics of the Middle Ages had much in common, but differed sharply at the outset of the modern era.
On the continent, far from advancing the cause of freedom,
Renaissance ideas of kingship and related institutional changes
almost destroyed it. In France and Spain, the chiefly German
"Holy Roman Empire" and the city-states of Italy, neopagan
concepts of absolute authority came to the forefront, denying
the medieval view that there were, or should be, limits on the
secular power. In England alone, the struggle would produce
the opposite verdict.

We are used to thinking of England as the home of representative government; less familiar is the idea that England enjoyed free institutions at the on-set of the modern age because
it had *retained* them from the preceding era. While Renaissance notions were triumphing on the continent, the English
experienced, in Maitland's phrase, "a marvellous resuscitation
of the medieval law."[9] That they did so was in large measure,
again, the doing of the church, which in Britain produced a
remarkable series of statesmen/clerics—from Becket and John
of Salisbury in the reign of Henry II to Langton, Grosseteste and
Bracton in the century to follow. The doctrine that they imprinted on English constitutional theory was that "the king is
under God—and under the law," and not entitled to rule by
personal edict. This was the essence of Christian teaching
about the state and it became the guiding precept of England's
common lawyers.

By far the greatest challenge to this doctrine was the conflict
between the Stuarts and the Parliaments of the early 1600s,
which sealed the English verdict against divine-right kingship.

In this contest, religious motives were again conspicuous, as opposition to the Stuarts was led by intransigent Puritan squires, zealous believers in the higher law who conceded little to the power of kings. They were, as James I correctly noted, "ever discontented with the . . . government, and impatient to suffer any superiority." Should they have their way, he said, "I know what would become of my supremacy."[10]

James is often described as a foolish king, but on this point he obviously knew whereof he spoke. These religious-political quarrels indeed destroyed the supremacy of the Stuarts, and had other historic consequences also. Most notably, they led to the first substantial emigration of Englishmen to America, and thus to the creation of our country. The people who came over in the 1600s were among the most devoted partisans of the Puritan interest, adherents to Christian doctrines of the higher law and consensual authority. They accordingly planted the medieval view of limited, constitutional government in the colonies from the outset. The significance for our institutions may be glimpsed in the statement of John Cotton, chief theologian of early Massachusetts:

"Let all the world learn to give mortal men no greater power than they are content they shall use, for use it they will . . . It is . . . most wholesome for magistrates and officers in church and commonwealth never to affect more liberty and authority than will do them good, and the people good; for whatever transcendent power is given will certainly overrun those that receive it . . . It is necessary, therefore, that all power that is on earth be limited, church power or other . . . It is counted a matter of danger to the state to limit prerogatives; but it is a further danger, not to have them limited."[11]

It was on the basis of such doctrine that the Puritans established their church and civic institutions, thereby creating many practices of free government with which Americans are familiar. Our indebtedness to these religious sources for numerous features of our statecraft is one of the most remarkable aspects of the record, which we shall examine in a later chapter. It is, however, a debt that is disparaged or ignored in the conventional teaching. According to the standard history, the views of these initial colonists were at best irrelevant to our ideas of freedom. The Founders of the eighteenth century, it is said, were *philosophes* and secularists, and created our republic on this basis; so the religious opinions of the early settlers are nothing to the purpose.

If we consult the record of the revolutionary/constitutional era, however, once more we see a different picture. In the early history of the republic, the dominant thesis was that free government depended, precisely, on the teachings of religion. While many details about this topic will have to be deferred, we may at this point note some of the general attitudes of our Founders, in which ideas of personal liberty and free government were routinely grounded on religious value. Here, for instance, is Washington's formulation of the subject:

"Of all the dispositions and habits, which lead to political prosperity, religion and morality are indispensable supports . . . The mere politician, equally with the pious man, ought to respect and to cherish them . . . Whatever may be conceded to the influence of refined education on minds of peculiar structure, reason and experience both forbid us to expect that national morality can prevail in exclusion of religious principle. 'Tis substantially true, that virtue or morality is a necessary spring of popular government . . . Who that is a sincere friend to it can look with indifference upon attempts to shake the foundation of the fabric?"[12]

Washington made many other statements to this effect throughout his long career in public life—urging his troops, e.g., "to live and act as becomes a Christian soldier." Nor were his opinions in this matter unusual in the founding era. John Adams remarked, for instance, that America was established on "the general principles of Christianity," as well as on the "general principles of English and American liberty." As he put it on the eve of independence, a free government "is only to be supported by pure religion or austere morals. Public virtue cannot last in a nation without private, and public virtue is the only foundation of republics."[13]

Similar views were held by other Founders, from stalwart Puritans such as Samuel Adams and Roger Sherman to arch-Federalists like Jay and Hamilton. Indeed, the hardest thing to discover in the annals of our founding is the type of hostility toward Christian faith that would prevail in revolutionary France. Even Jefferson, often cited as a *philosophe* and secularist, believed that freedom was grounded in religion. "Can the liberties of a nation be thought secure," he asked, "when we have removed their only firm basis, a conviction in the minds of the people that these liberties are of the gift of God?"[14]

The reasoning of the Founders in this regard was identical to that provided by Burke contemporaneously in England: Self-government required observance of the moral law, respect for rights of others, restraint upon the passions. Virtue was thus a necessary precondition to a regime of freedom, and a nation that lost its religious moorings was considered ripe for tyranny. Conversely, since religious belief and ethical conduct were matters of volition, the Founders also believed that liberty was integral to ideas of virtue. While they did *not* hold strictly "separationist" views about this subject, they believed that the political state was incompetent to deal with spiritual concerns, and should tend chiefly to the job of keeping order.

From what we know about the founding era, the ideas expressed by such as Washington, Adams, and other leading men reflected common opinion in the country. Americans generally were raised on Scripture, accustomed to institutions that embodied Christian precept, and instructed by pastors attentive to the political meaning of religious doctrine. (Tory spokesmen repeatedly complained that their main antagonists were the "black regiment" of the New England clergy.) Throughout the founding epoch, the emphasis was on the unity, not the opposition, of faith and freedom, and this remained a feature of our statecraft for many years thereafter.

"There is no country in the world," Tocqueville would write in 1835, "where the Christian religion retains a greater influence over the souls of men than in America . . . Religion in America takes no direct part in the government of society, but it must be regarded as the first of their political institutions; for if it does not impart a taste for freedom, it facilitates the use of it . . . I do not know whether all Americans have a sincere faith in their religion—for who can search the human heart?—but I am certain that they hold it indispensable to the maintenance of republican institutions."* [15]

Thus, on a first reconnaissance of the subject, we note a recurring pattern, completely different from the usual teaching. Rather than finding political freedom rising in opposition to the religious values of the West, we see exactly the reverse: ideas of personal liberty and free government emerging in Christian Europe; institutional development of such ideas in the Middle Ages; vigorous defense of these in England, on the basis of medieval doctrine; the translation of such ideas and institutions to America by a religious people, and the persistence of this connection in our life and thought long past the founding era. If religion is the enemy of freedom, how are these matters to be explained?

Applied to more recent controversies in our politics, this overview raises some other intriguing questions. Consider, for instance, the notion that our ideas of liberty were invented by rationalists of the modern era. How is this thesis to be recon-

---

* A similar verdict was rendered two generations later by Lord Bryce, whose acuteness as an observer of our institutions ranks second only to that of Tocqueville. Bryce noted the proliferation of churches in America, the piety of the people, the widespread knowledge of the Bible, the prevalence of religious literature, and the general harmony among the many sects and denominations. All of this bears little resemblance to a purely secular republic set up on the principles of the French Revolution; it suggests instead a remarkable continuity, at a distance of 250 years, with the religious impulse of the early settlers.

ciled with the religious *leitmotif* so obviously interwoven with our political history, and what is the reason for this repeated linkage? How do we get from the medieval order described by Acton to the American founding, from the Puritans to the federal Constitution, or from Aquinas to Mill and Spencer? These are questions the standard history not only fails to answer, but in the usual instance doesn't ask.

Other questions come to mind as well. If our founding fathers believed so strongly in religion as a support for our political institutions, why would they have adopted measures barring religion from public life? The conventional wisdom does have an answer here, of course, but it is very far from the reality of our founding—as shall be discussed in some detail. Consider also the case of the "religious right." If Washington, John Adams, and the rest believed religious precept was essential to a regime of freedom, why is it unthinkable that proponents of Christian value now should say the same? How did the idea develop that involvement of religious people in our public discourse is such a menace?

Finally, similar questions will arise if we consider the usual critique of conservatism in our politics—that its effort to unite religious value with ideas of limited government makes it incoherent. Again, this presupposes a skeptical-irreligious basis for our freedoms. If personal liberty and limited government are based on the secularist themes of the Enlightenment, then a "conservatism" that adopts such notions would appear to be a hopeless contradiction. But if our freedoms are in fact derivative from our religion, then it would seem the charge of incoherence should be directed elsewhere.

Such, in brief compass, is the argument of this essay: Not only that faith and freedom "can" go together, but that they have to do so. The point is argued on a twofold basis: that religious belief and its associated values are conceptually indispensable to a regime of freedom; and that, as a matter of historical fact, our institutions of free government were developed on the basis of religious precept. Considered either way, the evidence shows that freedom is coterminous with faith— precisely as the founding fathers, along with such as Burke and Tocqueville, so frequently contended.

In some past debates conducted on this topic, the notion that religious virtue and political freedom go together has been described as "fusionism." While in the present essay the concept is affirmed, the label is emphatically rejected. The term assumes the point at issue—that liberty and virtue are incompatible and can be brought together only by some *tour de force* that links them arbitrarily together. This, in my view, is an inaccurate and prejudicial statement of the question, since it accepts the liberal thesis that faith and freedom are naturally in opposition. The point is not that liberty and religious value can be "fused" by some ingenious method, but rather that they are a necessary unity—hemispheres that form a whole, thematically and in the development of our institutions. Western freedom is the product of our faith, and the precepts of that faith are essential to its survival.

3

The Age of the Despots

SOURCES OF HOSTILITY to religious belief in modern thought and politics are not far to seek; familiar enough, we may assume, not to require a long discussion. A summary of the principal causes, however, would include the following:

—The idea that religious absolutes by their nature, and the Christian religion in particular, are congenial to oppression. This was the defining attitude of secular philosophers of the Renaissance and Enlightenment, and has since become a common axiom of our thinking. Antagonism to Christian doctrine on these grounds was notable in the French Revolution and its radical offspring, but has also been evident in the other main political movements of our era.

—A more generalized view that strong belief in anything translates into a desire to impose it on other people, so that the way to ensure a regime of freedom is to avoid the development and advocacy of strong beliefs. Spokesmen for this idea in Western intellectual history have included Lucretius, Montaigne, and Bertrand Russell. It draws support from the obvious fact that zealots of all descriptions (including irreligious ones) have indeed attempted at various times to impose belief on others.

—The slightly different notion that religious faith is merely superstition and thus irrelevant to the world we live in, since its precepts have been supplanted or discredited by "science." All religions, in this view, are mystical efforts to explain things that have natural causes not yet deduced by reason. This too has been a leading feature of modern thought in virtually all its aspects. Such thinking is powerfully aided by the belief that Darwinian evolution offers scientific answers to questions about human life that were previously sought for in the counsels of religion.

—The historical thesis, already noted, that freedom and limited government in point of fact developed from the denial of biblical faith; that liberty and other admirable qualities existed in ancient Greece and Rome, were submerged by the rule of the Catholic Church in the Middle Ages, and recovered only with the decline of Christian influence at the era of the Renaissance. Freedom in the modern world, American freedom most of all, is depicted in this teaching as the offspring of skepticism and irreligion.

Given this cluster of ideas, an aversion to religious influence in our public life—not to mention explicitly Christian involvement in elective politics—is virtually automatic. For those who see matters in this light, the idea of conducting civil affairs on a religious basis is both absurd and dangerous; it violates all the historical lessons and accepted practice, mixes church and state, goes against the premises of our system. Hence angry opposition to the activities of the Christian right, those who oppose abortion on religious grounds, or anyone else who thinks our politics are, or should be, founded in religion.

Equally to the point, all these assumptions converge into a central thesis: *If belief in religious absolutes implies repression, it follows that denial of such absolutes will lead to freedom.* A stance of moral relativism is accordingly viewed as the proper outlook for a free society. No concept, indeed, is more pronounced in modern thinking. We see it daily in talk of pluralism, diversity, and alternative lifestyles, held out as guidelines for our conduct. The supposed lesson is that there are no universals, that one opinion is as good as the next, that nobody can say for sure that one point of view is right and another mistaken.

While this pop-culture doctrine draws on all the notions we have listed, the scientific-rationalist bias of modern thought has arguably been the leading factor. Since science has supposedly cast down religious doctrine about the origin of life, the moral teachings of religion have tended to share in the resulting disrepute. Science, after all, knows nothing of moral absolutes; it can tell us how things work, how one thing leads to another, general laws of physical or even human nature. But being purely descriptive and analytical, it can't tell us what ought to be; only what is. For logical positivists, pragmatists, and behaviorists of the present age, the *locus classicus* is Hume's disdainful maxim: "Let us ask: Does it contain any abstract reasoning concerning quantity and number? No. Does it contain any experimental reasoning concerning matter of fact and existence? No. Commit it then to flames. For it can contain nothing but sophistry and illusion."[1]

This value-free approach is supported by other fashionable doctrines of the modern era. Kindred theories that undermine the idea of absolutes are historical and cultural relativism, also widespread in academic thinking. The first teaches that, since people believe different things in different epochs, it is impossible to render judgments between one period and the next. The second says that because different cultures view ethical issues in different ways, we are disarmed from saying one is better than the other. All we can do, as one famous sociologist put it, is affirm the reality of "coexisting and equally valid" systems of belief.

It is widely supposed that notions of this type must lead on to freedom—implying a stance of suspended judgment, and therefore tolerance toward others. Historian Peter Gay, for instance, describes "the policy of toleration and the associated idea of cultural relativism" as follows: "Relativism is a way of looking at the world, the recognition that no single set of convictions has absolute validity. Eclecticism is the philosophical method consequent on relativism—since no system has the whole truth, and most systems have some truth . . . Toleration . . . is the political counterpart of this world view and this method; it is the policy for a large and varied society."[2]

This equation of relativism with tolerance, and thus with liberty, is a commonplace of modern wisdom—reinforcing the view that religious belief must be adverse to freedom. But is it accurate? A survey of the record, and a little independent thought, will tell us that it isn't. It should be fairly obvious, indeed, that moral relativism, however derived, must undermine the very possibility of freedom. *No system of political liberty has ever been created from such notions, nor is it theoretically conceivable that one could.* On the other hand, the most brutal forms of despotism, from the age of the Renaissance to our own, have been developed exactly on this basis.

The reason for this is apparent the minute that we actually think about it: For freedom to exist, there have to be certain assumptions about the intrinsic worth of the individual, the respect that is owing to all human beings, the need to limit the compulsions that can be used by one person against another. When such assumptions are firmly held and embodied in political institutions, freedom to greater or lesser degree can flourish. Where they are rejected, freedom will never come into being in the first place, or else will be progressively lost where once it has existed.

What is common to these libertarian precepts, of course, is that all of them are axiomatic, *moral* statements. They aren't "scientific" in the sense required by Hume, nor is such a worldview congenial to their existence; the political implications of scientific relativism, indeed, are quite the opposite. As for ideas of historical or cultural relativism, the negative outcomes are equally apparent. There are numerous periods of history, after all, and many cultures, that have practiced despotism and relished the idea of slavery. If no epoch or culture is preferable to another, then freedom also must be a matter of indifference.

Anyone who has even nodding acquaintance with the history of the twentieth century will know that these are not abstract or captious questions. On the contrary, they are questions that have been asked, and answered, in the most practical way that could be imagined—in the conduct of nations that founded their politics on a denial of revealed religion. What these have shown us, without exception, is that in the absence of clear standards of right and wrong, there is no basis for affirming the dignity of the individual, or for placing limits on the rule of force, and thus no hope for freedom.

These implications have been widely evident in the modern era, but nowhere more so than in the terrible despotisms created by the totalitarian movements. All of these began by rejecting the religious heritage of the West, denying objective standards of moral conduct, devaluing the very concept of humanity. The end result, in every case, was to place total power over the individual in the hands of an autocratic state, to be wielded without restraint or mercy.

The degree to which totalitarianism has made war against the idea of freedom, and the practical meaning of this conduct, are well known. Indeed, in the case of communism, the phenomenon continues—in mainland China, North Korea, Vietnam, Cuba. We know that such regimes deny the elementary liberties of their people, and have routinely jailed and murdered their opponents. Also known, in a general way at least, is that communism is irreligious—formally atheist, antagonistic to all faiths, alert to stamp out the influence of synagogues, mosques, and churches. Less understood, perhaps, is that this stance is integral to the system—as to other totalitarian movements—and directly linked to its despotic practice.

That the original doctrine was hostile to religion may be seen throughout the writings of Marx and Engels, and was in fact the major premise of their theory. Most to the point, it was the basis for denying standards of right above the tide of history or flux of power.* As Engels put it: "We . . . reject every attempt to impose on us any moral dogma whatever as eternal, ultimate and forever immutable moral law . . . We maintain on the contrary that all former moral theories are the product, in the last analysis, of the economic stage which society had reached at that particular epoch. And as society has hitherto moved in class antagonisms, morality was always a class morality . . ."[3]

One obvious implication of such notions—arguably the most obvious—is that if there are no objective standards of right, if "morality" is merely an expression of dominant interests, then there are no limits on what you may do in seeking to advance your own. We see this transition in the thought of Lenin: "We repudiate all morality derived from non-human and non-class concepts. We say it is a deception, a fraud in the interest of the landlords and the capitalists. We say that morality is entirely subordinated to the interests of the class struggle of the proletariat . . . We say: morality is what serves to destroy the old exploiting society and to unite all the toilers around the proletariat, which is creating a new communist society. . . . We do not believe in an eternal morality."[4]

If all of this is accepted, then there is no reason whatever to observe normal standards of truth, to refrain from murder and violence, or to respect the rights and liberties of anyone. An appeal to *force majeure* is accordingly pervasive in Marxist doctrine. Consider the implications of these statements, gleaned from various of Marx's writings: "For the creation on a

---

* Marx stated the basic notion this way: "Man makes religion, religion does not make man . . . Religion is the sigh of the oppressed creature, the heart of the heartless world, just as it is the spirit of an unspiritual situation. It is the opium of the people. The abolition of religion as an illusory happiness of the people is required for their real happiness . . . Religion is only the illusory sun, which revolves around man as long as he does not revolve around himself. The task of history, therefore, once the world beyond truth has disappeared, is to establish the truth of this world . . ." And so on. (Lewis Feuer, ed., *Marx & Engels*, Doubleday, 1959, pp. 262–263)

mass scale of the communist consciousness, it is necessary for men themselves to be changed on a large scale, and this change can only occur in a practical movement, in a revolution." "Force is the midwife of every society pregnant with a new one." "Without revolution, socialism cannot develop." "[The proletariat] can only in a revolution succeed in ridding itself of all the muck of ages and become fitted to found society anew."[5]

Such appeals to violence are often matched in Marxist theory by demands for brutal coercion once the revolution has succeeded. As Marx famously put it, "there will be a political transition period in which the state can be nothing but the revolutionary dictatorship of the proletariat." Engels' version was that "the state is only a transitional institution used in the struggle to hold down one's adversaries by force." And again: "A revolution is the most authoritarian thing there is; it is the act whereby one part of the population imposes its will upon another . . . if the victorious party does not want to have fought in vain, it must maintain this rule by means of the terror which its arms inspire in the reactionaries."[6]

In these assertions we are but a step away from the Gulag and the show trials of a Stalin, the genocide of a Mao or Pol Pot—the killing fields where political power grows from the barrel of a gun. All of which goes to suggest that, rather than "perverting" the weighty teachings of Marx and Engels, Stalin and Mao put them quite faithfully into practice.[7]

The communist case considered by itself would be enough to show the connection between denial of religious value on the one hand and the rise of despotism on the other. As it happens, however, this is but a single example from the record of atrocity and suffering that stains the pages of the twentieth century; the other totalitarian movements also contributed to this appalling story, and exhibited the identical traits in terms of value theory and political outcomes. Since the conventional treatment portrays these as "right-wing" movements, the extent of this resemblance needs to be examined.

Neither fascism nor Nazism was anything like a coherent doctrine—having arisen from a stew of racial, neopagan, and occultist speculations. While there is no single founder of this way of thinking, the author who comes the closest is Nietzsche. Writing mostly in aphorisms and invective, and professing his disdain for systems, Nietzsche nonetheless produced a discernible system of his own: A merciless creed expressing to the fullest the brutality inherent in the negation of religion.

Nietzsche's worldview was premised on a hatred of Christianity and its works, and on the denial of any objective measure of right and wrong; hence his "nihilism" and repeated description of himself as an "immoralist," "atheist," and "the Antichrist." From his rejection of moral absolutes and standards of intelligibility, he concluded that nothing mattered except "the will to power," a system in which "great men" or "supermen" assert dominion over others. His writings glorify strength, aggression, and unmitigated cruelty. Here are some samples:

"Dead are all the gods, now do we desire the superman to live . . . The great man is necessarily a skeptic . . . Freedom from any kind of conviction is part of the strength of his will. . . . the many distresses of the small constitute only a sum in the feelings of powerful human beings . . . to derive advantage from the disadvantage of many; this can be . . . a sign of a great character who manages to master his compassionate and just impulses . . . he wants not sympathetic hearts, but servants, tools . . ."[8]

Nietzsche's idols were Alexander, Caesar, and Napoleon—warriors and conquerors who ruthlessly achieved their goals "whatever the cost in men." His rhapsodies to power included praises for the "blond Teuton beast" who struck fear in the hearts of Europe. Contrasted with this was his contempt for the weak or merely average, "a type of man that must one day fall into our hands, that must *desire* our hands." Christianity he saw as the religion of the weak, and he hated it above all for that reason: "The New Testament is the gospel of a wholly ignoble species of men ... These little herd-animal virtues do not by any means lead to 'eternal life...' " And so forth.[9]

Obviously, the writings of Nietzsche are instructive in themselves. He repeatedly makes clear—it is his major, almost his only discernible, thesis—the intimate linkage between the denial of religion and the glorification of brutal force; the one, he says, must lead inexorably to the other. Our case would accordingly be made in adequate fashion if we had nothing more than Nietzsche's repeated statement of it. But there is the further point that all the terrible cruelties he envisioned were actually put into practice by the Nazis—precisely on the basis of the irreligion for which he was the prophet.

The appeal of Nietzschean doctrine to Hitler and his minions should be apparent. The Nazis made a cult of Nietzsche, reprinting his books and producing others that explored affinities between his theory and their practice. The work of Alfred Rosenberg, chief ideologue of the Nazi revolution, is obviously Nietzschean, including glorification of the pagans, hatred of St. Paul, and occultist references to the supposedly Aryan (Persian) beginnings of the Nazi creed. Hitler also was an ostentatious fan, making several visits to the Nietzsche archive, gazing pensively at the bust of the great thinker. That all of this was entirely appropriate may be seen from the pages of *Mein Kampf*, which read in many places like warmed-over *Zarathustra*:

"A man ... filled with joyful determination and will to power is of greater value to the national community than an ingenious weakling ... the immortal spirit and courage of aggression ... the folkish state ... does not build up on the idea of the majority, but on that of the personality ... Organization is putting the heads above the masses and subjecting the masses to the heads ... the selection of these heads is carried out above all ... by the hard struggle for life.... responsibility can and must be borne always only by one man and thus he alone can have the authority and right of command...."[10]

Nor were Hitler and the Nazis laggard in their assaults on biblical religion, Christianity as well as Judaism, and corresponding exaltation of the pagans. "With the appearance of Christianity," Hitler wrote, "the first spiritual terror has been brought into the much freer old world." (This is vintage Nietzsche.) Like August Comte before him, Hitler envied the organizational aspects of the Catholic Church, but fiercely opposed its doctrine and sought to destroy or subvert the influence of all Christian churches on the German people. Rauschning quotes him as saying "the Catholic church is corrupt through and through and must vanish"; the Nazis sought "to eradicate Christianity in Germany root and branch."[11]

As Nazi doctrine was antireligious in the realm of value, so it was radically collectivist in the realm of economic (and other) policy; in this again it resembled its nominal adversaries on the Left, in a way that is usually not brought out in the conventional treatment. Once more we see the coincidence of value relativism with the assertion of statist power against the individual. Here, for example, are excerpts from the original Nazi platform, adopted in 1920:

"The activities of the individual must not clash with the interests of the whole, but must be pursued within the framework of the national activity and pursued for the general good ... Our nation can only achieve permanent well-being from within on the principle of placing the common interests before self-interest ... That [our] demands be realized, we demand the creation of a strong central power in the Reich." (As a later statement also put it: "National Socialism ... undertakes to defend the people as a whole against the individual.")[12]

In pursuit of these conceptions, the 1920 platform further stated: "We demand ... the abolition of incomes unearned by work, and emancipation from the slavery of interest charges ... We demand the nationalization of all business combines (trusts) ... We demand an extensive development of provision for old age ... We demand a program of land reform suitable to national requirements . . . We demand educational facilities for specially gifted children of poor parents, whatever their class or occupation, at the expense of the state."[13]

These specific Nazi demands and the general attitude expressed are not appreciably different from those set forward in the *Communist Manifesto*, or indeed from the welfarist or collectivist maxims common to our era. They are reminders that Nazism, after all, was "National *Socialism*," and that this had a concrete meaning. The *collectivist* character of the Nazi movement is frequently neglected; yet that collectivism, centralizing authority in the Nazi state, was a distinctive feature of the movement, and essential to the tyranny that it created.

It will perhaps come as no surprise at this point to hear that fascism also exhibited the traits we have been discussing, including a high regard for Nietzsche. Mussolini was a devoted student, a fact alluded to frequently by historians, and obviously well known to Hitler.* On Il Duce's fiftieth birthday, Nietzsche's sister described the Italian leader as "the noblest disciple of Zarathustra, whom Nietzsche had dreamed of . . ."[14] To judge from Mussolini's writings, such praises were not mistaken. There is the same denial of universals, the same insistence that values are created by decisive action, and the same outcome in terms of dissolving constraints on what may be done with power. Mussolini stated his credo this way:

"If relativism signifies contempt for fixed categories and men who claim to be bearers of an external objective truth, then there is nothing more relativistic than fascistic attitudes and activity . . . We fascists have always expressed our indifference toward all theories . . . From the fact that all ideologies are of equal value, that all ideologies are mere fictions, the modern relativist deduces that everybody is free to create for himself

---

* When Mussolini was imprisoned in 1943, Hitler sent him an inscribed 24-volume set of Nietzsche's works. (Ivone Kirkpatrick, *Mussolini*, Avon, 1964, p. 552)

his own ideology and to attempt to carry it out with all possible energy."[15]

As with Hitler and the Nazis, a program based on such a doctrine inevitably glorified war and violence, and exalted the authority of the ruler. Thus the fascist catechisms of the 1930s emphasized decisive action, strength, indomitable will.* Likewise, their teachings stressed top-down control of the economy, and the all-encompassing power of the state against the individual. Mussolini the relativist was dogmatic on this topic:

"Against individualism, the fascist conception is for the state ... fascism reaffirms the state as the true reality of the individual ... for the fascist, everything is in the state, and nothing human or spiritual exists, much less has value, outside the state. In this sense fascism is totalitarian ... The state, in fact, as the universal ethical will, is the creator of right ... For fascism the state is an absolute before which individuals and groups are relative ... The fascist state is will to power and government...."[16]

The repeated translation of relativist value theory to ideas of despotic statecraft, and the resemblance of all the totalitarian movements in this respect, are striking. There is another common feature among these modern "isms," however, that needs to be considered further—since it is integral to totalitarian practice. This is the effect of relativist theory in *devaluing the individual*, in denying all grounds for considering the human person worthy of respect. This is the most terrible of the totalitarian doctrines, and it is grounded squarely on a denial of religious absolutes.

Nietzsche once more provides a point of reference, since he

---

* "... the fascist and in particular the soldier must not believe in perpetual peace ... The rifle and the cartridge belt, and the rest, are confided to you not to rust in leisure, but to be preserved in war ... He who advances to the attack with decision has victory already in his grasp ... The fascist revolution has depended in the past and still depends on the bayonets of its legionaries." (Michael Oakeshott, ed., *The Social and Political Doctrines of Contemporary Europe*, Cambridge, 1949, pp. 180–181)

is remorseless in following up the premise. In his view, the only reason our society thought human beings entitled to dignity and freedom was that Christian morality had taught this weak-kneed doctrine down through the ages. Take away Christian morality, he said, and the presumption of dignity, freedom, or equality would collapse; men would simply be phenomena in the realm of nature, where the rule of the strongest was the only standard. Thus:

"[Christian morality] granted man an absolute value, as opposed to his smallness and accidental occurrence in the flux of being and passing away ... Morality guarded the underprivileged by assigning to each an infinite value ... Supposing that the faith in this morality would perish, then the underprivileged would no longer have this comfort—and they would perish ... nihilism is a symptom that the underprivileged have no comfort left."[17]

This means, precisely, that the weakest will perish, and that it is proper that they should do so. Nothing is more shocking in Nietzsche than his violent detestation of the weak, and his insistence that they be sacrificed to the will and pleasure of the strong. He translates this into ideas of eugenics, population control, and euthanasia—all based on a denial of Christian ethics and his own particular brand of Social Darwinism. Here are some representative statements:

"Christianity is the reverse of the principle of *selection* ... In practice this general love of mankind has weakened the power, responsibility, and lofty duty of sacrificing men ... Society, as the trustee of life, is responsible for every botched life that comes into existence ... It should in many cases actually prevent procreation ... The weak and the botched shall perish ... and they ought even to be helped to perish. There is no solidarity in a society in which there are sterile, unproductive and destructive elements—which, incidentally, will have descendants even more degenerate than they are themselves."[18]

The reader of these passages will have no trouble seeing the parallel to Hitlerian concepts of unfettered power, genocide against defenseless people, and eugenic efforts to direct the growth of populations. Such notions, indeed, were fairly prevalent in the intellectual world at the turn of the century*; they resulted from the idea that man, severed from his connection to the absolute, *had been assimilated entirely to the world of nature.* From this it was thought to follow not only that there were no standards other than the rule of force, but also that human beings could be treated as mere phenomena—like animals or objects.

Nietzsche's statements on such themes, again, are frequent: "we have put [man] back among the animals," "nature is not immoral when it has no pity for the degenerate," and more to like effect. Others were not remiss in drawing the reductionist conclusions. In the view of Emil Bergmann, "it is possible to breed not only animals but the man-God." Condorcet had put it that we should "study human society as we study those of the beavers or the bees." Saint-Simon asserted that, in his perfect system, "anybody who does not obey orders will be treated by the others as a quadruped."[19]

As the example of Saint-Simon suggests, this devaluation of the individual is by no means limited to the purely nihilist strain in modern naturalism; it is prevalent as well in the more mechanical, rationalist systems, of which Saint-Simon is the acknowledged father, and from which Comtian socialism and Marxist communism are descended. In these systems too, a denial of religious absolutes leads to the conclusion that man is simply a phenomenon in the natural order, and therefore subject to the manipulations and controls appropriate to the realm of science.

---

* Thus Rilke exulted that "a few men, but great ones, will build a world with their muscular arms on the corpses of the weak, the sick, and the infirm." Pierre Lasserre inquired: "At bottom, is it not the last trick of incurables to set about loving their infirmity and exalting it?" (Henri de Lubac, *The Drama of Atheist Humanism*, Meridian, 1966, pp. 67–68)

This is most evident in the thought of Comte, which John Stuart Mill described as the "completest system of spiritual and temporal despotism which ever yet emanated from a human brain, unless possibly that of Ignatius Loyola." (For the secularist Mill, this was the ultimate insult.) Comte also began from relativist premises, asserting that "there is nothing good and nothing bad, absolutely speaking; everything is relative; this is the only absolute statement." From these assumptions, he went on to argue that liberty of conscience was a hindrance and a myth, and that real freedom was "rational submission to the domination of natural laws."[20]

Such notions, it should be observed, usually come conjoined to the idea of the "superman," though not always expressed exactly in that fashion. That is, while *most* people—the weak, the "botched," the mediocre—are reduced to the level of animals or objects, and thus are suitable stuff for domination and scientific planning, *some* men are exempt from this devaluation. These are the people who will be ruling over the society, doing the planning and controlling, using other people as their raw materials. They also happen, invariably, to be the people drawing up the program. This pattern is common in all authoritarian systems.

The "superman" idea of course was Nietzsche's trademark, but it has been frequently expressed as well by other spokesmen for despotic statecraft. Saint-Simon propounded a doctrine of an elite who "will be directed to guide human intelligence according to my divine foresight." Comte observed "a special tendency toward command in some and toward obedience in others." Hitler's version was that the masses could attain what is best for them "only under the leadership of those whom Nature has endowed with special gifts"; Lenin opined that "the will of a class is at times best expressed by a dictator." [21]

Obviously, any political system that operated on these principles would be as perfect a despotism as it would be possible to invent, and that is exactly what occurred in the totalitarian regimes. The conjunction of all-powerful leaders unchecked by law, and a herd of devalued subjects conceived as having no moral standing whatsoever, is precisely the definition of totalitarian rule. In this respect as well, the service of nihilism or value relativism to the cause of the omnipotent state should be apparent.*

What does all this mean for us? While most people in our society would doubtless agree in condemning the likes of Lenin, Hitler, or Mussolini, the extent to which their way of thinking has intermingled with our own is seldom noticed. The linkages, however, are plainly there—and stem directly from the moral relativism that is said to be the basis of our freedom. There has long been, for example, a cult of Nietzsche in Western intellectual circles, intent on treating him as a great philosopher, playing down some of his more brutal statements, and exalting his role as forebear and inspiration to "existentialists" of the modern era. This laundering of Nietzsche was largely the work of Martin Heidegger, dean of the existentialists, and of Jean Paul Sartre, the other main proponent of atheist-existential doctrine.

Up to a point, this treatment of Nietzsche seems correct. Where it goes astray is in assuming that existentialism itself is a respectable calling, or that it has anything to do with freedom. The main idea of existentialism in this sense is, precisely, that "God is dead," that we are adrift in an empty cosmos, and that man must invent all value and meaning for himself. This is one

---

* Though seldom noted by conventional historians, the views of Marx and Engels bear obvious resemblance in many places to those of Nietzsche, particularly as regarding allegedly lesser races, and the rightness of using force against them. In 1848, for example, Marx and Engels demanded "a war with Russia . . . in which Germany can become virile." Engels asserted that a coming war and revolution would cause the Slav nations "to disappear from the face of the earth. And that too will be progress." The correspondence of Marx, also, is full of racism and anti-Semitism. (Cf. Nathaniel Weyl, *Karl Marx: Racist*, Arlington House, 1979, pp. 111–113)

of the few things the average person can deduce from Heidegger's writings, and it was expressed with utmost clarity by Sartre. All of this seems perfectly congruent with Nietzsche—but not with freedom. The normless world of the existentialists, indeed, is highly conducive to unfree systems.

It hardly seems irrelevant in this respect that Heidegger was a conspicuous fan of Hitler, offering numerous panegyrics to the Nazi leader, all couched in Nietzschean bravado.* Dagobart Runes, who translated and published these fawning statements, thought Heidegger had "betrayed" philosophy by selling out to Hitler. A more logical inference would be that Heidegger simply followed the obvious trend of Nietzschean thought: If God is dead, if men create their values by sheer assertion, if force and not morality is the rule of life, then such as Hitler and Mussolini are natural outcomes of the process.† Given the recurrent nexus between relativism and totalitarian practice, the chief surprise in Heidegger's genuflections to Nazi power is that anyone finds them surprising.

This same conversion from relativism to authoritarian ideology has been evident in the United States itself, most notably in the New Left uprising of the 1960s. This was, indeed, a classic study in how it works: Starting out as an allegedly libertarian faction, the New Left adopted an existentialist position—disdainful of ideas and theories, committed to the "propaganda of the deed." In no time at all it mutated into a dictatorial, neofascist movement that shouted down opponents, seized offices

---

* *E.g.*, "the battle . . . will be fought with all the strength of the new Reich, which Chancellor Hitler will bring to reality. It must be fought by a hard race of men . . . Doctrine and 'ideas' shall no longer govern your existence. The Fuhrer himself, and only he, is the current and future reality of Germany, and his word is your law . . . To the man of this unprecedented resolve, our Fuhrer Adolf Hitler, let us give a threefold 'Heil.' " (*German Existentialism*, Philosophical Library, 1965, pp. 26, 28, 42)

† Mussolini's statement on page 49, for instance, is entirely existential, and reads exactly like something out of Sartre. The latter, for what it is worth, became a notorious fellow traveller of the communists in France.

and buildings (and blew up several), engaged in other violence, and made common cause with revolutionary Marxists. It thus united the themes we are discussing: Nihilism in the realm of value, resort to brutal force in terms of action.

It takes no great feat of analysis to see that here we had some real totalitarians in our midst, following the path marked out by such as Lenin or Mussolini. Nor was the movement lacking in theoreticians to justify its violence. The most famous of these was philosopher Herbert Marcuse, a neo-Marxist scholar well grounded in the art of dialectics. There was such a thing, according to Marcuse, as "repressive tolerance," which allowed regressive right-wing forces to have their say, thereby frustrating the ambitions of progressive spokesmen. This kind of tolerance was to be prevented, the right-wingers to be silenced. True *"liberating tolerance . . . would mean intolerance against movements from the right, and toleration of movements from the left."* (Italics added.)[22] Suppression of dissent against the Left was thus a service to the cause of freedom.

For those who are not committed to Orwellian newspeak, Marcuse's argument is both absurd and vicious. Sad to say, however, it is now entrenched more firmly in our academic and intellectual life than was ever the case in the 1960s. Alumni and/or descendants of the New Left movement are the current avatars of "political correctness" on our campuses, imposing speech codes, confiscating newspapers, banning speakers, bringing recalcitrants up on charges, and revamping curricula to suit the ideology of the Left—"repressive tolerance" at its most blatant. Defenders of these practices, indeed, repeat almost verbatim Marcuse's argument for repressing freedom.[23] Not only can it happen here, it has already done so.

4

From Champagne to Ditch Water

THAT RELATIVIST ASSUMPTIONS lead to authoritarian outcomes has been, of course, denied. Such denial has been a chief objective of the modern intellect since the latter part of the seventeenth century, issuing in ingenious theories that try to develop a case for human freedom or limited government on a strictly rational basis. This has been, in fact, the distinctive feature of liberalism in all its guises, from the Whigs and utilitarians of a bygone era to the welfare staters of our own.

While the various species of liberalism differ widely in details, they are alike in their essential features. Each is an effort to preserve some aspect of human liberty, and/or other by-products of the cultural heritage of the West, from the corrosive effects of relativism and irreligion. In the case of the classical liberal theorists, from Locke to Herbert Spencer, the freedom sought was comprehensive, including property rights and economic liberties. In the case of their modern successors, the idea of economic freedom has long since been discarded, but an attempt has been made to rescue "civil liberties" from the ruin of all value.

Among the Whigs and early proponents of *laissez-faire*, a favored tenet was the idea of "natural right," supposedly deduced on rational grounds from the nature of man and workings of society. Locke's *Treatise of Civil Government* is, of course, the most celebrated effort in this vein; though affected in places by his Christian theism, the central concept is that man's basic nature is such as to lead on logically to a regime of freedom. An even more explicit version is the French Declaration of the Rights of Man, which simply proclaimed the idea of natural right as though it were a self-sufficient doctrine—as did, in different fashion, our Declaration of Independence.*

This natural right approach was vehemently denounced by Bentham, who derided the French assertions as "metaphysics" and the American Declaration as an "absurdity." In Bentham's view, liberty would better be sustained by a utilitarian calculus, through which it could be shown that economic and other freedoms worked out for the "greatest happiness for the greatest number." This was attacked in turn by Spencer, as being itself too hopelessly subjective. Spencer advanced an allegedly more scientific, evolutionary doctrine on behalf of freedom—which suffered its own debunking from other evolutionists in fairly quick succession.

The rapid transition from one of these rationalist arguments to the next, and the general decay of the classical liberal position by the latter part of the nineteenth century, suggest the nature of the problem. Ideas that are perfectly logical and scientific to one emphatic rationalist look very different to another. What seems obvious to me will seem obscure, if not preposterous, to you. Also, as any good historical relativist should have been able to predict, values that are self-evident to one generation become contentious in the next.

What was occurring in these cases is what has continued happening to liberalism ever since. These theorists all took for granted the beliefs and values they inherited from Western culture, imagining that they were not dependent on religious belief for their support. Such concepts were so familiar and so

---

* The resemblances, and differences, between the French declaration and our own will be discussed in Chapter XIII.

widely accepted that they seemed completely obvious, things no intelligent person could fail to grasp if treated to a logical demonstration. And to some degree this was correct—*assuming* the religious-cultural base from which all parties to the discussion were, at least initially, proceeding.

The extent to which this kind of thinking has occurred in Western intellectual history is remarkable. It applies to philosophy, ethics, human nature, techniques of government, science, economics, and a good deal more. In all these categories, liberal theorists have taken ideas or practices resulting from the distinctive religious culture of the West and tried to set them up as self-validating propositions, assuming they could be established solely on an intellectual basis.

Etienne Gilson makes the point in discussing the movement from medieval to modern thought, noting, *e.g.*, that Descartes believed he had deduced the notion of an omnipotent, omniscient Creator God from the operations of pure logic. The more likely relationship, Gilson suggests, was the other way around: *Given* belief in such a Deity, and two millennia of Western thought in which this was incessantly repeated, the idea seemed altogether logical. Prior to that experience, however, it seemed a good deal less so, even to the profoundest intellects of antiquity.

Likewise, on a less exalted plane, with the concepts and practices of freedom. To Frenchmen and Americans of the eighteenth century, the notion that "all men are created equal" and have "inalienable rights" *was* "self-evident," because these people were inheritors of a religious tradition that affirmed this view in no uncertain terms—and in the American case, at least, of a political tradition that said the same. But to the people of the ancient world, before the advent of biblical revelation, such ideas were not self-evident at all. Nor are they to many philosophers and politicians of the modern era.

The slippage in the rationalist approach is exhibited clearly by utilitarianism, which began as an essentially libertarian and free market view and ended by supporting schemes of state compulsion. This effect has been discussed at length by A.V. Dicey, who notes that Benthamism assumed existing benevolent goals of British culture as the starting point for its deductions. Absent these, or even with them, the "greatest happiness for the greatest number" is anything but an objective datum. As every day's political squabbles clearly show, people have very different notions of what the "greatest happiness for the greatest number" might consist of.

This being the case, the formula turns easily into something else—the rule of pure majoritarianism. If we can't determine exactly what the "greatest happiness" is, we can at least determine the "greatest number," by counting heads, and discover what the greatest number *wants*. A system in which arithmetic is the ruling factor, unrestrained by any other, is one where superior force prevails and there are no protections for minorities. And so in fact it tended to turn out—with Benthamism evolving to a rationale for social engineering rather than economic freedom.*

That utilitarianism provided no defense against such slippage is amply illustrated in the career of the most famous nineteenth-century liberal of them all, John Stuart Mill. Having begun as an ardent promoter of free markets and the limited state, Mill became, with astonishing ease, an advocate of socialism. This turnabout is attributed by his critics (and also by Mill himself) to the influence of Harriet Taylor. But the slippage, and the susceptibility to such influences, were there from the beginning.

---

* There is, moreover, a deeper fallacy in the utilitarian view—even if we could get past the criticisms made by Dicey. Supposing that we *could* define the greatest happiness, and also supposing that this were infallibly connected to the idea of freedom, this still doesn't resolve the basic question—raised by yet another famous relativist, Justice Oliver Wendell Holmes: Why *should* we choose the greatest happiness for the greatest number? Why not choose something else? The selection of this (or any other) policy goal, as Holmes observed, is itself a form of ethical decision. This point was also made by Spencer in his *Social Statics*.

Mill's intellectual progress, if it can be called such, reveals the problem with perfect clarity. In his *Autobiography*, he describes his defection from free markets in a textbook display of historical relativism—with a touch of Social Darwinism thrown in for good measure. He came to see, he wrote, "that all questions of political institutions are relative, not absolute, and that different stages of human progress not only *will* have, but *ought* to have, different institutions; that government is always in the hands, or passing into the hands, of *whatever is the strongest power in society* [italics added]; and that what this power is does not depend on institutions, but institutions on it." Hence "the very limited and temporary value of the old political economy, which assumes private property and inheritance as indefeasible fact, and freedom of production and exchange as the *dernier mot* of social improvement."[1]

Mill was within his limits a prodigious intellect, and could hardly have failed to sense the problems inherent in such an outlook. If everything is relative, if the "strongest power" must have its way, how can freedom or any other value be protected? This was a problem Mill addressed, in rather offhand fashion, in his *Utility of Religion*. Whatever the ethical benefit of Christianity, he said, "mankind has entered into the possession of it. It has become the property of humanity, and cannot be lost by anything short of a return to primeval barbarism ... [Christian teachings] are surely in sufficient harmony with the intellect and feelings of every good man or woman to be in no danger of being let go ... That they should be forgotten, or cease to be operative on the human consciousness, while human beings remain cultivated or civilized, may be pronounced, once for all, impossible."[2]

Unfortunately, the values and customs Mill considered the permanent possession of mankind turned out not to be so enduring after all—in fact were systematically and brutally violated on the widest possible scale beginning within two generations of this dogmatic statement. Mill's assertions are typical of the liberal complacency that takes the Western heritage for granted, never dreaming it could be forfeit if its religious-ethical basis were casually subverted. One wonders what he would have thought of the twentieth century, with its tens of millions slaughtered, locked up in death camps, or otherwise oppressed by the totalitarian powers.

Equally cavalier are many statements on such topics by Justice Oliver Wendell Holmes, yet another apostle of Darwinian irreligion. Holmes wore his materialist relativism on his sleeve, but took it in the opposite direction from Spencer's evolutionary market doctrine. In one of his oft-quoted maxims, Holmes wrote to William James, "I can't help preferring champagne to ditch water; I doubt if the universe does."[3] This is sometimes cited as suggesting Holmes' light-hearted libertarian tolerance, but the conclusions he deduced from it were the reverse.

"It has always seemed to us a singular anomaly," he wrote, "that believers in the theory of evolution and in the natural development of institutions by successive adaptations to the environment should be found laying down a theory of government intended to establish its limits once and for all by logical deduction from axioms . . . All that can be expected from modern improvements is that legislation should easily and quickly, and yet not too quickly, modify itself in accordance with the will of the *de facto* supreme power in the community, and that the spread of an educated sympathy should reduce the sacrifice of minorities to a minimum . . ."[4]

This statement, it may be noted, is virtually identical in its general features to that of Mill, and raises all the identical problems. (The reader may have observed that it also sounds suspiciously like Nietzsche.) What it tells us is that where axioms are abandoned, and where relativist naturalism holds sway, the only thing that counts is the "will of the *de facto* supreme power," and we calmly envision the "sacrifice of minorities" to its workings. This is a chill conclusion for a creed that supposedly started with the idea of freedom—but one that, as modern history has shown, is distressingly on target.

As Mill sought a stopping place in the values derived from our religion, Holmes offers the solace of an "educated sympathy." This is his single toehold in the world of moral affirmation. But whence comes this sympathy, and by whom or what is it "educated"? Holmes was a Boston Brahmin, an inheritor of much that is best in Western culture. In the circumstances, it is quite obvious where he got his "educated sympathy"—the religious and ethical heritage that was the basis of Western society in general, and of his native Massachusetts in particular (to be discussed in Chapter XI).

In citing Mill and Holmes, of course, we are taking liberal thought at what is said to be its finest. Both are icons of the modern liberal movement, often praised and quoted—most usually, and ironically, as advocates of civil liberties.* It accordingly should come as no surprise that liberalism in our era has generally followed the mental path marked out · by these sages—migrating away from ideas of freedom and toward conceptions of dominant power, while still professing attachment to the residual values of our culture.

With their intellectual forebears, modern liberals consider certain beliefs and practices natural, obvious, and the like, and suppose that these can be established and defended on a purely intellectual basis. They no longer believe, of course, in free market economics. But they do believe (or claim to) in such things as the dignity of the individual, freedom of speech, equal rights before the law, scientific progress, and other such famil-

---

* Usually glossed over in such praises is the fact that both of them—Mill in *On Liberty*, Holmes in his court opinions—supported ideas of freedom of speech on grounds pertaining to its social *usefulness*, not on any axiomatic (or even constitutional) basis. Such arguments were necessary, of course, given their oft-stated utilitarian and evolutionist positions. All the problems of slippage inherent in such a view are of course as applicable to freedom of speech as they are to any other kind of freedom.

iar notions. All very secular and utilitarian, not having anything to do with ideas of religion. As it happens, however, all of *these* concepts as well, and many others that might be mentioned, are secular by-products of our faith, and subject to the same erosion.

This process has been visible across the decades, as liberals have embraced the leading features of totalitarian statecraft—a buildup of power in the state, and a correlative devaluation of the individual. The first of these effects, as discussed, is quite well known, the chief political trait of liberalism in the modern era. The second is perhaps less so, but demonstrable from the record. Both are the results of abandoning fixed ideas of value that can affirm and defend a regime of freedom.

The collectivist part of this transition is notable in the writings of John Dewey, perhaps the most influential spokesman American liberalism has produced. Dewey was a secularist and skeptic in the realm of value, propounding notions of life-adjustment "progressive" schooling that are still pervasive in our educational system. (His legacy in this regard may be observed in the declining SAT scores of the past generation.) He was also an ardent collectivist who lobbied for economic planning, deplored what he considered the "blind" forces of the market, and expressed his admiration for the economics—if not the politics—of the Soviet Union.

Referring to the communist experiment in collectivism, as of 1930, Dewey opined that it would stir "the admiration of those who had the imagination to see that the resources of technology might be directed by organized planning to serve chosen ends." He thought an American "coordinating council" of government, industry, and labor "to plan the regulation of industrial society, would signify that we have entered constructively and voluntarily upon the road which the Soviet Union is travelling with so much attendant destruction and coercion . . . We are in for some kind of socialism, call it by whatever name we please."[5]

Commitment to government planning and regulation has continued to be a major feature of liberal doctrine ever since. Statements by such as Arthur Schlesinger, Jr., John Kenneth Galbraith, Americans for Democratic Action, and other liberal spokesmen have made the point as clear as can be, explaining and justifying the need for ever more numerous, and more expansive, programs of compulsion. Former Democratic Sen. Joseph Clark, a leader in the ADA, defined a liberal, for instance, as "one who believes in *using the full force of government* for the advancement of social, political, and economic justice at the municipal, state, national, and international levels." Elsewhere Clark rejoiced that, "spiritually and economically youth is *conditioned to respond to a liberal program of orderly policing of society* by government, subject to the popular will, in the interests of social justice." (Italics added.)[6] *

That these opinions are not eccentric in liberal discourse may be seen from many statements by other spokesmen for the cause. Professor Galbraith, for one, has been indefatigable in promoting ideas of concentrated power and top-down control of the economy. Nor has he been reluctant to describe this program as a brand of socialism—sounding, after a lapse of better than forty years, exactly like John Dewey: "The new socialism allows of no acceptable alternatives; it cannot be escaped except at a price of grave discomfort, social disorder, and, on occasion, lethal damage to health and well-being. The new socialism is not ideological; it is compelled by circumstance."[7]

* And further: "They plan well in Russia. There someone decides where little Ivan is going to work. If, at the age of eleven, he seems unresponsive, he goes back to the collective farm. If he shows promise, his education is continued at state expense through technical school and the university . . . How can we [in America] use both the carrot and the stick to get these young people trained and on their way to where they are needed? How can we get more and better teachers, scientists, priests, politicians, rabbis, ministers and social workers? To get them all we will have to settle for fewer brewers, night club proprietors, and lobbyists."

With the collapse of planned economies in Eastern Europe, explicit statements to this effect are less prominent than they used to be. The policy direction they suggest, however, continues as before. "Planning" has nominally fallen out of favor, but the basic idea is now promoted in other guises: "Industrial policy," "public investment," "coordination," "positive nationalism," and the like are euphemisms of the present hour. Consider the following from Robert Reich, a guru of the industrial policy movement (and presently secretary of labor):

"[We need] a positive economic nationalism, in which each nation takes primary responsibility for enhancing the capacities of their countrymen . . . This approach would encourage public spending, in any manner that enhanced the capacities of its citizens to lead full and productive lives . . . Positive nationalism would also tolerate—even invite—public subsidies to firms that undertook within the country's borders high value-added production . . . Other kinds of subsidies would be pooled and parceled out where they could do the most good . . ."[8]

Similar ideas have been expounded in a Reich-connected journal, The American Prospect, which features both Schlesinger and Galbraith on its masthead. During the 1992 election, a single issue of this magazine devoted no less than nine separate articles to "The Logic of Public Investment"; on inspection, this turned out to be the logic of government's taxing and spending more, deciding what technologies shall be promoted, imposing more compulsions on business, and otherwise manipulating the economy. The common assumption is that governments can make decisions better than free markets. The yen for intervention thus continues; the names have been changed to protect the guilty.*

---

* At this writing, the Clinton administration has not yet been in office for a year, but its adherence to these statist precepts is clear enough. This is most obvious in the Clinton health plan, already noted, perhaps the most ambitious scheme of collectivism at a single blow ever proposed by an American administration. Given the normal yen for accommodation in our politics, the Clinton

Issues of this sort are usually discussed in terms of their economic effects, and these are important questions. Even more significant, however, is the meaning of all this concentrated power for our political system, and in particular for the idea of constitutional safeguards in behalf of freedom. There is, after all, a written Constitution of the United States, which supposedly defines and limits the authority of the federal government, in the interest of preventing the abuse of power. To all intents and purposes—despite occasional skirmishing over a restricted set of issues—this arrangement is now defunct. In reality, we no longer have a Constitution, or anything that can be accurately depicted as constitutional law.

The truth of this may be tested by a simple experiment: observe debate about virtually any measure that comes before the Congress, touching any aspect of economic or social policy. In such discussion, the last question anyone thinks to ask will be, *Is it constitutional?* So far as I am aware, indeed, this question is almost never asked at all; it does not occur to anyone to talk about the constitutionality of federal intervention in any zone of daily life—employment, education, child care, disabilities, health care, or the arts. It is simply assumed the federal government has the power to control or subsidize whatever it likes, with the only relevant question being, *Do we have the votes?*

That this is a regime of dominant power and not much else is about as plain as evidence can make it. Equally plain is that such a regime is very far from the design and purpose of our constitutional system, as shall be argued in succeeding chapters. In the reasonings of the liberal legalists, this is contested, with greater or lesser degrees of sophistication. These arguments, if anything, make the situation worse, since the basic

---

White House could conceivably move hereafter in a different direction, and we may fervently trust it will do so. The fact that it should have proposed this plan, however, is anything but reassuring.

idea is to turn the Constitution into its own negation—compounding destruction of the law with a corruption of thought and language.

One favored argument in this vein holds that selected words or phrases of the document—"general welfare," "commerce"—amount to open-ended grants of power all by themselves. Another is that the Constitution may have had a certain meaning in the eighteenth century but has another in our own, evolved to meet the needs of a complex society. Yet another—the ultimate denial of intelligibility in such matters—is that the Constitution actually doesn't mean *anything whatever*, but is simply a vehicle by which judges may make whatever policies they wish.

An amalgam of such views was offered a few years back by Justice William Brennan, who spent three decades on our highest Court advancing the notion of a rubber Constitution. Speaking to the subject of human dignity and judicial safeguards thereof, Brennan asserted that "the precise rules by which we have protected fundamental human dignity have *been transformed over time in response to both transformations in social condition and evolution of our concepts of human dignity*," etc. To this he added that, "because we are the last word on the meaning of the Constitution, *our views must be subject to revision over time, or the Constitution falls captive . . . to the anachronistic views of long-gone generations.*" (Italics added.)[10]

In these assertions we see quite clearly the connection between ideas of liberal relativism and deconstruction of the rule of law. The approach espoused by Brennan, and many other liberal legalists, makes of the law whatever they might happen to choose. It is a maxim of complete discretion—granting freedom where it pleases, refusing to do so where it doesn't. This is the very opposite of a constitutional system in any serious meaning of the term—removing all hope of certitude and fixity in the fundamental law.

Though Brennan was allegedly arguing for civil liberties,* the effect of these ideas must be the opposite of libertarian. If there are no constants in our constitutional system, then there are no effective limits on the power that can be accumulated in the state; the safeguards the Founders thought they were creating do not exist. More generally, if there are no standards by which to measure the rights and wrongs of politics, the only limit on what may be done is simply the will of the "*de facto* supreme power in the community," which has come to mean whatever five justices with their evolving standards can agree on. Such, with marginal exceptions, is precisely the system that we now have.†

While the legal theoreticians have tried to justify these policies by ingenious reasonings about hidden meanings or latent powers, some liberal spokesmen are a bit more candid. Refreshingly honest, if nothing else, is the statement of Rexford Tugwell, one of the early New Deal planners. He gave the game away as follows:

"The Constitution was a negative document, meant mostly to protect citizens from their government, not to define its duties to them or theirs to it . . . It would have been thought fantastic to suggest that individuals ought to be made secure from the risks of their occupations or to be protected from the hazards of life . . . No constitutional amendment had acknowledged the progression from competition to mutuality. None legitimized stability and discipline. It really had to be admitted that it was done irregularly and according to doctrines the framers would have rejected . . . Much of the lagging and reluctance was owed

---

* He was explaining his view that capital punishment is unconstitutional, even though it is explicitly recognized in the written Constitution.

† These exceptions primarily occur in the realm of what is called "preferred rights," meaning rights of speech, press, assembly, religion, etc., that are extended protection under the First Amendment. In terms of our preceding discussion, these may be considered remnants of a free political order that liberalism attempts to rescue from the general decline of liberty.

to constantly reiterated intention that what was being done was in pursuit of the aims embodied in the Constitution of 1787 when obviously it was in contravention of them."[11]

That liberalism has become an ideology of arbitrary power, and that this is linked with and justified by the elastic notions of relativist theory, seems clear enough from these and other items in the record. Thus far the resemblance to the totalitarian movements is apparent. What, however, of the other side of the equation? Totalitarianism, as we have seen, is accompanied by a devaluation of the person. It assumes the individual is incapable of ordering his own existence, unable to live in freedom without a superior to direct him; he is an object of manipulation, a member of the herd, a datum for scientific planning.

Such radical devaluation of human beings is shocking to our sensibility, a development so outrageous that we suppose it couldn't possibly happen here. Notions of this type would likewise be denied, no doubt, by most who back the liberal program, and the denial would be entirely honest. These are people in whom an "educated sympathy" still persists. But there are others who make the obvious deduction from the premise. Consider the following from historian Carl Becker:

"Edit and interpret the conclusions of modern science as tenderly as we like, it is still quite impossible for us to regard man as the child of God for whom the earth was created as a temporary habitation. Rather we must regard him as little more than a chance deposit on the surface of the world, carelessly thrown up between the two ice ages by the same forces that rust iron and ripen corn ... Man is but a foundling in the cosmos, abandoned by the forces that created him ... It has taken eight centuries to replace the conception of existence as a divinely composed and purposeful drama with ... a blindly running flux of disintegrating energy."[12]

This paraphrase is quite representative of modern scientific relativism, as may be shown from many sources. One that is particularly apposite, in view of our previous discussion, is a further statement from Justice Holmes, who wrote to English historian Frederick Pollock: "I see no reason for attributing to man a significance different in kind from that which belongs to a baboon or a grain of sand . . . I don't believe it is an absolute principle or even a human ultimate that man is always an end in himself—that his dignity must be respected."[13]

And here, to provide a last example, is the comment of anthropologist Alfred Kroeber: "Man, to every anthropologist, is an animal in the given world of nature; that and nothing more—not an animal with a soul or destiny or anything else attached to him beforehand, but an animal to be compared, as to structure, and as to function, with other animals; and with the unmistakable conviction that any special traits and qualities which may ultimately be assigned to him are to eventuate from inquiry instead of being supposed."[14]

The logic of these statements is plain enough: If people are really no different from objects in the natural order, why not treat them accordingly? If human beings are mere phenomena, moulded by forces that ripen corn or evolve baboons, why should they enjoy freedom? From such a perspective, indeed, the idea of freedom is an illusion, and a harmful one at that, since it gets in the way of "scientific" treatment. Psychologist B. F. Skinner tells us, for instance, that "the hypothesis that man is not free is essential to the application of scientific method to human nature." It was on this basis that Skinner constructed his behaviorist psychology relying on conditioned reflexes—a system set forward in several books, one quite accurately entitled *Beyond Freedom and Dignity*.[15]

The implications of all this for social policy are profound, though it is important to observe distinctions. Few political liberals, if any, would affirm the views of Skinner—or those of Holmes, at least about this subject—and none that I am aware of has professed the scary ideas of total manipulation mooted so blithely in academic circles. Yet the drift of liberal policy in this direction, viewing human beings as objects of social engineering, is both obvious and growing.

We have noted the vast array of programs administered by the federal government, considered as aspects of consolidated power. But these programs have another dimension as well, particularly in areas of social policy: Welfare and public housing, child development and school busing, rehabilitationist penology, and several others. What is common to these endeavors is something that might best be described as "soft behaviorism." Such programs, that is, don't merely try to help out people by giving them money or other benefits, although this is usually the stated purpose; they also are efforts at *behavior modification by official planners*, aimed at changing the conduct or character of selected people.

While this is not the place to examine these efforts in detail, two specific examples may be cited to make the point. The first is the practice of busing schoolchildren for purposes of racial balance, usually described as an effort to remedy discrimination. This is the legal rationale. If we look to the social science side of it, however, we find the goal of busing is rather different: to change the learning patterns of black children by *getting them away from their families*, thereby supposedly attaining better educational outcomes. This was spelled out by the intellectual father of the busing movement, James Coleman, as follows:

". . . a *more intense reconstruction of the child's social environment* than that provided by school integration is necessary to remove the handicap of a poor family background. It is such a reconstruction that is important—whether it be provided through other children, through tutorial programs, through artificial environments created by computer consoles." Thus: "For those children whose family and neighborhood are educationally disadvantaged, it is important *to replace this family environment* as much as possible by an educational environment—by starting school at an early age, and by having

a school that begins very early in the day and ends very late."
(Italics added.)[16]

While busing is the most explicit example of social engineering in the schools, it is hardly alone in this regard. Recent years have seen repeated attempts to use the educational system as a way of bending and shaping children toward the objectives of the planners: sex education and other types of "affective" learning, various sorts of psychological intrusion, promoting counterculture views on homosexuality, etc. In such cases, the schools are agents of manipulation on behalf of a value-laden program—often if not usually in opposition to the views of parents—rather than a neutral common service provided by the state.

This brings us to our second example, to be noted at this point only briefly, which is the topic of abortion. In the context of the issues we have been discussing, the significance of the abortion question should be evident. Whatever one thinks about this subject in terms of constitutional law or social policy, the fact that abortion is a complete *devaluation* of the unborn child can hardly be disputed. Denial of life to certain categories of human beings for the right and convenience of others is about as clear a case of devaluation as may be imagined; it is also the inevitable outcome of an ethic that denies the religious heritage of the West.

It says a great deal about the drift of modern politics that this subject has become *the* defining issue of the liberal agenda. Abortion on demand, in fact, is the topic above all others on which no dissent whatever is now permitted in the Democratic party—to the point that the pro-life Democratic governor of a major state was refused the right to speak at its national convention in 1992. This grim insistence on the right to kill the unborn child, without restraint or pity, no questions asked, suggests the current status of the liberal ethic.

Nor, finally, is this attitude limited to the unborn; it is increasingly seeking other categories of inconvenient people, most notably the elderly. We are hearing more and more about the supposed merits of euthanasia, and also about the expense entailed by keeping the elderly alive for extended periods in our health care system. Indeed, under existing policies of the federal government—as in other systems where health care has been collectivized—it is now official practice to limit health care to the elderly as a matter of economy.[17]

As in the campaign for abortion, the phrase most often used in arguing for euthanasia is "quality of life"—which sounds high-minded and fairly amiable. Everyone, after all, would like to have a good "quality of life." But what this means in context is something altogether different: It means there is such a thing as a life that is not worth living—*that some people would be better off dead.* It also means somebody else will judge that quality for them, and make the decision as to whether they should live or die. In another place I have documented the similarities between certain liberal views on population control, "quality of life," and related issues, and the views expressed about these matters by Adolf Hitler. These are too lengthy for full inclusion here, and I shall merely summarize them in the accompanying note.* Enough to say that like effects stem from like causes.

---

* Thus one liberal spokesman: "It is within the range of our science to create, very simply, new people physically healthier and intellectually more competent than ourselves . . . we do it regularly, in agriculture and the breeding of livestock, so why not with the human race?" Thus Hitler: "The state has finally succeeded in bringing about that nobler era when men see their care no longer in the better breeding of dogs, horses, and cats but rather in the uplifting of mankind itself." (Quoted in Evans, *Clear and Present Dangers*, Harcourt Brace, 1975, p. 386)

5

The Uses of Tradition

CONFUSION GENERALLY ABOUNDS in modern politics, but some kind of record was established in the summer of 1991—when hardliners in the Soviet Union moved to topple Mikhail Gorbachev and got thwarted instead by Boris Yeltsin.

In that upheaval, the forces pushing for a *coup d'état* were old-line Stalinists and party apparatchiks resisting efforts to move the collectivist, regimented system in the direction of free markets. These hardliners wanted to keep the grinding tyranny of the Soviet state intact, along with their jobs in its bureaucracy. To the extent that there was anybody still around in the collapsing USSR who actually believed in communism, for whatever reason, these appeared to be the people.

Almost as remarkable as this dramatic series of events was the manner in which they were reported in our media. News stories and TV accounts routinely described the last-ditch communists, devotees of a collectivist superstate, as the "conservatives"—a usage that was almost never explained or justified but simply adopted as though it were the most commonsensical and obvious thing imaginable. In reality, it was neither.

For this description to make any sense at all, it had to do so by emptying "conservative" of all value content. In this approach, the word is merely a term of relation—meaning a desire to keep what is. Thus, a hardline communist, a Peruvian drug lord, a Mafia *capo*, or a Democratic senator are all "conservatives," since they want to hang on to the power that they have. Such deployment of terms makes anybody anywhere a "conservative" if he holds power and doesn't want to give it up.

By this logic, for instance, the French Revolution was "conservative" once it got into power, which must mean that Burke and Maistre and others who attacked it were all "liberals." Likewise, it could have been said (and was said in fact) that Lyndon Johnson was the "conservative" in 1964, which would mean that Barry Goldwater was the "liberal." This use of words to signify mere *de facto* power makes political terminology meaningless. (Burke himself knew better. In France, he said, "the master of the house is expelled, and the robbers are in possession.")[1] What was true of revolutionary France, or Lyndon Johnson's America, was infinitely truer of the communist system of violence and enslavement.

Such usage serves to show, among other things, the Orwellian nature of much current discourse. When words are bandied in this manner, sensible discussion of the issues is precluded. It is unlikely we shall learn anything worth knowing about the nature of conservatism, or other topics, from people who can describe the most notorious collectivist regime in human history, steeped in atheism and mass murder, as "conservative."

Stated this way, the mindset suggested by media coverage of the coup may seem hardly worth discussing. It is, however, kin to another and more subtle brand of misunderstanding, which has also served to darken counsel on important topics. This is the notion that conservatives simply want to conserve "tradition," whatever it may be, irrespective of its merits, in blind obedience to the past. Much commentary about American conservatism and its alleged contradictions has focused on this aspect of the subject.

This is more sophisticated than the coup discussion, but comes out in the same vicinity. The argument is that conservatives want to keep things that are long-established, precedented, or customary, rather than casting everything up in the scales of reason. If what is long-established is repressive, conservatives have no basis for opposing it, and will do nothing for the cause of freedom. Simply conserving a tradition for its own sake is thus the opposite of libertarian, and those who cherish the notions of a free society must seek some other standard.

Consideration of such issues raises interesting questions about the nature of tradition, its relationship to religious and other axiomatic beliefs, conflicts among traditions, and the like. For the moment, however, it is unnecessary to enter this terrain, since the immediate point is rather different, and a good deal simpler: namely, that there *are* many different kinds of tradition in the world, and that each of them has some kind of substantive content to it; a tradition is always a tradition *about* something, and it matters what that something is. For American conservatives, this is a very important question, and one for which there is a discernible answer.

Part of that answer is suggested by the account of religious value and political freedom sketched in Chapter II. That discussion was provided to supply an overview of materials that will be examined at greater length hereafter. But it was also offered to show up front, in a connected narrative, the component elements of the tradition from which American ideas and institutions are descended. The leading feature of that tradition, it was argued, is the unity that subsists between religious belief and political freedom. In strictly political terms, what our tradition is "about," therefore, is freedom.

From this fact alone, it would follow that the alleged opposition between "libertarian" and "traditionalist" emphases *in American politics* is an illusion. If our tradition is one of freedom, then that is what conservatives in this country should be trying to conserve. The matter is quite open and shut, and it is of no significance to us if some other tradition somewhere— say, Tibet or Persia—is about something else.

Beyond that rather obvious and generic point, however, other considerations suggest that tradition as it has developed in our society leads on to personal freedom and limited government. In the Anglo-American political experience, three aspects of tradition are important in this regard: The idea of *limits* on the power of kings and magistrates; *the rule of law*, by which all members of a society may regulate their conduct; and *consensual* development of such law, as opposed to top-down decree by the supreme authority of the state. All have been significant in the evolution of our freedoms.

Reliance on tradition as opposed to theoretical schemes of abstract reason is one of the most distinctive features of English law, and efforts to alter this approach have been a famous source of political conflict for many generations. We are used to thinking of this as a quarrel of the eighteenth century between the conservative Burke and English devotees of the Enlightenment, such as Price and Bentham, which of course it was, but it goes back considerably further than that.

Burke certainly stated the rationale for traditionalism in its most elegant form. "I feel an insuperable reluctance," he said, "in giving my hand to destroy an established institution of government, upon a theory . . . I prefer the collected wisdom of the ages to the abilities of any two men living . . . We are afraid to put men to live and trade each on his own private stock of reason; because we suspect that this stock in each man is small, and that individuals would do better to avail themselves of the general bank and capital of nations and ages."[2]

Burke's views to this effect were not mere personal idiosyncrasy, or a species of romanticism, or the protest of some reactionary faction. They happened to be, among other things, an excellent summary of the legal and political tradition of his country, and of the theory that explained it. This was the tradition of the common law, the constitutional and judicial system that had grown up in England across a span of centuries, and in behalf of which the most notable battles for English liberty had been fought.

The essential idea of the British system was that the common law had existed from "time immemorial," that it had been built up by slow accretions down through the ages. It combined unwritten custom, judicial decisions, decrees of parliament, grants and agreements by the kings, adding up to an enormous skein of precedents, diligently studied and applied by English courts and lawyers.

Sir Edward Coke, Chief Justice Hale, and other great expositors of the common law never tired of extolling its traditional nature, arguing that practices developed in this way were more trustworthy than the inventions of a moment. The depths of Coke's traditionalism—and spiritual kinship with Burke—may be seen in this antiquarian passage: "Our days upon the earth are but as a shadow in respect to the old ancient days and times past, wherein the laws have been by the wisdom of many excellent men, in many successions of the ages, by long and continued experience, fined and refined, what no man (being of so short a time), albeit he had in his head all the wisdom of the world, in any one age would ever have been effected or attained to."[3]

Coke's point, like Burke's, was that reliance on tradition in many respects is much *more reasonable* than reliance on unaided reason. Tradition offers the collected knowledge and experience of many generations, which are more likely to be wise than the speculations of any individual, or group of men, at any given time. In doubtful matters, the presumption should therefore be in favor of tradition, even when theoretical speculation can't grasp the reasons. The point was driven home by Hale (responding to the theories of Hobbes):

"There are many things in laws and government that are reasonable to be approved, though the reason of the party does not presently or immediately and distinctly see its reasonableness. It is reasonable for me to prefer a law by which a kingdom hath been happily governed four or five hundred years than to adventure this happiness and peace of a kingdom upon some theory of my own, though I am better acquainted with the reasonableness of my own theory than I am with that law . . . Long experience makes more discoveries touching convenience or inconvenience of laws than it is possible for the wisest council of men at first to foresee."[4]

That this doctrine is traditional to the *nth* degree is obvious enough. That it is also libertarian may seem less so. Such, however, is the case. It may be said, in fact, that this old-fashioned approach to legal matters is the proximate source of Anglo-American freedoms. Behind the ramparts created by custom and tradition, defended by such as Coke and Hale, the political and economic liberties of the subject were able to take root and grow in England, when they were being trampled elsewhere.

The reason for this libertarian effect is that the common law created a tremendous obstacle to the *workings of unchecked power in the state*. For if the law grew up by way of custom and tradition, over great intervals of time, then it was not the work of any individual and could not be changed at anyone's discretion. It was outside the ordinary workings of the process, pre-existed the powers of the day, and would survive them. This made it superior to the will of any king, or group of legislators, and gave it independent status.

The political implications of all this were well understood by the combatants in the constitutional history of England. The foes of arbitrary power in the crown were tenacious advocates of the common law and its procedures, and looked to it as their chief defense against excessive taxes, seizure of property, and other species of oppression. The common law was their constitution, bill of rights, and code of procedure rolled into one, as well as a political-legal record of the English state. Magna

Carta, other charters and concessions of the kings, the rights of parliament and the church, taxation by consent, trial by jury, and so on, were all embedded in its vast mosaic.

Because of its intricacies and haphazard evolution, the common law would become a favorite target of reformers seeking something uniform and "rational." Such as Hobbes and Bentham rang the changes on the inequities and anomalies in the system, citing many features that did not commend themselves to reason. It was indeed an unwieldy business. But its intractable, drawn-out nature was what made it effective as a *rule of law*, with all the benefits for freedom that this entails. It meant "a government of laws, and not of men," in which kings and others in authority could not do whatever they wished. The rules that governed their behavior—and that of their subjects—were therefore solid, ascertainable, and above all not changeable at anyone's discretion.

The importance of this concept to the development of freedom can hardly be overstated. Under a rule of law, not only are there exterior limits on the power of the state, but citizens have some definite idea about what the political authorities may or may not do, and benchmarks by which to measure official conduct; equally important, the citizens have a definite idea of what *they* may do, and can plan their lives accordingly. Hence opposition to *ex post facto* laws, violation of known procedure, or efforts otherwise to change the rules of the game against the subject. Hence also a further motive to rely on precedent, by which such rules have been established, and can be discovered.

The need for certitude about these matters was constantly stressed by the traditionalists and common lawyers, from Glanville and Bracton in the medieval gloaming, to Coke and Hale in the age of the Stuarts. Coke put it this way in conference with James I: "The law was the golden met wand and measure to try the causes of the subjects, and which protected his Majesty in safety and peace; with which the king was greatly offended, and said then he should be under the law, which was treason to affirm, as he said: to which I said that Bracton saith, *quod rex non debet esse sub homene—se sub Deo—et lego* [the king should not be under man, but under God and the law.]"[5]

As the example of James suggests, such doctrines were not to the taste of ambitious monarchs, or to others in authority who wanted to do as they pleased when wielding power. English history from the earliest periods is replete with kings who viewed the matter otherwise—such as John, reproached with violations of the feudal law, or Richard II, accused of saying the "laws were in his mouth." Kings and supporters of their power were always inclined toward more expansive notions, which could be used to override the limits of the system.

Just such a doctrine came to them at the era of the Renaissance, with the widespread revival of the Roman-Byzantine view of kingship, derived from the *Institutes* of Justinian. This concept, which matched the theory and practice of imperial Rome, said *the king was the law speaking*, directly contrary to English precepts. "Whatever has pleased the prince," according to the *Institutes*, "has the force of law, since the people by the *lex regia* enacted concerning his *imperium* have yielded up to him all their power and authority."[6]

The background and development of this idea will be discussed in a later chapter. Suffice it to note that such a concept would prove appealing not only to absolute monarchs on the continent—and to the Stuarts—but to all proponents of top-down power in the state. In the modern era, variations on the theme have been many, nominally having nothing whatever to do with kingship. All of them boil down to one highly recognizable precept: *That the law is the edict of the political sovereign of the moment.* It is therefore limited by no exterior principle, but is exercised at the discretion of whoever happens to be in power, and thus can be changed at will when some new ruler gets on top.

That the traditional English view was congruent with limited government and personal freedom, and that this top-down doctrine was the reverse, is evident enough. The common lawyers, however, didn't leave the matter to surmise, but spoke out early and often on the subject. Among the most comprehensive of such statements is that of Sir John Fortescue, the Lancastrian chief justice, ca. 1470. In a comparison of English and continental views of kingship, Fortescue attacked the Roman doctrine in explicit fashion:

"The laws of England admit of no such maxim, or anything like it. A king of England . . . is obliged by his coronation oath to the observance of the laws, which some of our kings have not been well able to digest, because thereby they are deprived of . . . free exercise of dominion over their subjects . . . [An English king] cannot, by himself, or his ministry, lay taxes, subsidies or any impositions of what kind so ever, upon the subject. He cannot alter the laws, or make new ones, without the express consent of the whole kingdom in parliament assembled . . ."[7]

The collision of these differing views would convulse the politics of seventeenth-century England, leading to the downfall of the Stuarts. Coke and the common lawyers in the Parliament argued "that the king hath no prerogative, but that which the law of the land follows." The Stuart position, as stated by James, was that he "desired and commanded as an absolute king," and that "the absolute prerogative of the crown . . . is no subject for the tongue of a lawyer."[8] The first was the traditional view, the second—from an English standpoint—a thoroughgoing innovation. Libertarians of the present day may ponder which is more congenial to freedom.

The common law idea defended by Coke and his allies in Parliament was a species of constitutional doctrine, approximating medieval notions of a law above the state. But it was also a highly practical matter, involving political and legal protections that gave the theory definite expression: the rights and privileges of Parliament, taxation only by consent, defense against arbitrary imprisonment, legal rules and court procedures for defending private rights. It was this system of definite legal protections to which Burke referred when he contrasted the British system to French notions of abstract and purely theoretical freedom.

Such, in brief, was the tradition from which England fashioned limits on the power of kings, and such was the tradition that nourished the institutions of America. It is often forgotten that the people who first settled on these shores were products of the common law experience, and for that reason, among others, staunch opponents of absolutism in the state. They departed England precisely when the struggle about these issues was at its zenith, and when advocacy of the traditional view by Coke and others in the Parliament was most intense. That background would have lasting consequences for the politics of our country.

Not, to be sure, that the colonists imported all of the English law when they came over, nor could they feasibly have done so; conditions were different, there was a wilderness to tame, other influences were at work—chiefly the theological doctrines that were pervasive in New England. But the settlers brought with them and incorporated as much of the common law as they were able, and looked on its precepts very much as did Coke and Hale. Though in America, they were Englishmen, and believed themselves entitled to the protections that English law afforded.

The traditionalism of our Founders is of great importance in understanding the American Revolution, though many relevant data from a teeming record must be omitted from this chapter. On the common law, however, some brief comment may prove useful, in view of the widespread notion that these were English-speaking *philosophes*, embarked on a radical revolution like that in France. So far as the American leadership was concerned, the truth was exactly the reverse—largely because they were common lawyers.

Many of the older spokesmen for American rights had studied law at the English Inns of Court—people such as Andrew Hamilton of New York, John Rutledge and William Henry Drayton of South Carolina, Daniel Dulany of Maryland, John Dickinson of Pennsylvania. Those who hadn't studied there were often taught by those who had. And what they were taught, without exception, was Sir Edward Coke and the common law, Coke's doctrines of limited power in the state, and the relevance of these to the rights of Englishmen.

The extent of this teaching is everywhere apparent in the history of the era. Jefferson speaks of his studies of Coke's *Institutes* (commentaries on the common law) and says that "a sounder Whig never wrote." (Jefferson was, in fact, an expert on the common law.) Patrick Henry said his legal education consisted entirely of reading Coke. The course of study of young John Adams included all the authorities we have cited: Glanville, Bracton, Fortescue—and Coke. Adams recounts his interview with Jeremiah Gridley, in which his mentor told him that "in the study of law, the common law, be sure, deserves your first and last attention, and he has conquered all the difficulties of this law who is master of [Coke's] *Institutes* . . ."[9]

Against this backdrop, the defense that the Americans mounted against the arbitrary policy of North and Grenville is not surprising. It was a common law defense, repeatedly citing Coke and Magna Carta, drawing on the precedents and guarantees of English law. Dickinson's *Letters from a Pennsylvania Farmer*, to pick a prominent example, is a classic common law performance, quoting and citing Coke throughout, and adducing a string of precedents from British history to oppose the taxing powers of Westminster.

The story was much the same when James Otis led the charge against the writs of assistance (open-ended search warrants), invoking Magna Carta, the common law, and Coke's decisions, asserting that the common law could control and override unconstitutional acts of legislation. "The judges of England," Otis said, "have decided in favor of these sentiments when they expressly declare that acts against the fundamental principles of the British constitution are void."[10]

There is much more available in this vein, but a final reference must suffice—John Adams on the Stamp Act. In the resolves he drafted for the town of Braintree, Adams wrote: "We take it clearly . . . to be inconsistent with the spirit of the common law and the essential fundamental principles of the British constitution that we should be subjected to any tax imposed by the British Parliament . . . the most grievous innovation of all is the alarming extension of the power of courts of admiralty . . . no juries have any concern there . . . [this] is directly repugnant to the Great Charter itself; for by that charter . . . 'no freeman shall be . . . condemned, but by lawful judgment of his peers' . . ."[11]

As noted, these common law ideas embraced a higher law component, and this moved to the forefront as the legal tie to England became increasingly frayed and at last was severed. Even so, it is noteworthy that the common law approach continued until the very eve of revolution (in the resolves of the Continental Congress), that American jurists were still attentive to Coke's teachings, and that the appeal to English precedent was manifest even in the move toward independence (see Chapter XIII).

What is most striking about all this is not the radicalism of the revolutionary leaders, but the reverse. As devotees of the common law, the American spokesmen were *traditionalists*, defending the ancient doctrine against the innovations of the British king and Parliament. "The patriots of this province," as John Adams put it, "desire nothing new; they wish only to keep their old privileges."[12] Dickinson gave an even more eloquent statement of this outlook, which in its antiquarianism is a full match for Coke or Hale:

"A dependence on the crown and Parliament of Great Britain is a novelty—a dreadful novelty . . . This word 'dependence,' as applied to the states connected with England, seems to me a new one. It appears to have been introduced into the language of the law by the commonwealth act of 1650. A 'dependence on Parliament' is still more modern. A people cannot be too cautious in guarding against such innovations."[13]

That Dickinson considered an act of Parliament *in 1650* to be an "innovation" is suggestive of the mindset; it was also quite accurate as a matter of historical fact. The assertion of parliamentary power over the colonies indeed had its beginnings at that era—beginnings that grew into a sharp divergence between the British and American views about the subject. From that divergence, as we shall see, there developed the constitutional conflict that became a revolution.

As the American leaders viewed it, *they* were the conservatives in this situation, and to a large extent they were. The struggle that grew into the war for independence, in their analysis, was an extension of the battle led by Coke and others in the courts and Parliaments of the Stuart era, and of the long travail of centuries against the arbitrary reign of power, dating back to Magna Carta. They were spokesmen for a tradition that had said repeatedly that the law was above the king, or any other earthly ruler, and not the other way around.

Viewed in this light, American ideas and institutions may be considered not merely as traditionalist, but as unique *survivals of medieval attitudes* into the modern epoch. The old tradition of limited government under law endured in England at the era of the Renaissance, when it began to be submerged elsewhere in Europe; in America it endured again when it began to lapse in England. The American cause was thus conservative twice over—drawing on the common law tradition for its beginnings, then reaffirming that tradition when the mother country itself moved on to something new and different.

Beyond these considerations, there is another sense in which the common law experience was integral to ideas and practices of freedom. This involves the very *nature of tradition*—as conceived and transmitted to us by the common lawyers. Com-

prehension of this point is central to understanding the workings of a free society, and the radical difference between its
methods and those prevailing in authoritarian systems. To see
this difference is to see a good deal of what really matters.

As noted, the common law cannot be made over by the
decree of any given individual, group, or even generation. It
consists instead of the accretion, over time, of ways of thinking
and acting that many generations have accepted. When you
think about it—and the common lawyers did—this is a *species
of consent*. It means that people are *voluntarily choosing to do
things in a certain way, without any central direction or design*. Another common lawyer of the Stuart era, John Davies,
put it as follows:

"The common law of England is nothing else but the common law and custom of the realm . . . A custom taketh beginning and groweth to perfection in this manner; when a
reasonable act once done is found to be good and beneficial to
the people, and agreeable to their nature and disposition, then
they do use and practice it again and again, and so by often
iteration and multiplication of the act it becometh a custom . . .
customary law is the most perfect and most excellent, and
without comparison the best, to make and preserve a commonwealth. For the written laws that are made by either the edict of
princes, or by council of estates [i.e., Parliament] are imposed
on the subject before any trial or probation made, whether the
same be fit and agreeable to the nature and disposition of the
people, or whether they will breed any inconvenience or no.
But a custom doth never become a law to bind the people, until
it had been tried time out of mind . . ."[14]

Again, the conservatism is obvious, as is the skepticism concerning enactments handed down by either kings or parliaments; there is, however, the further, positive point about the
common law: that it consists of the *spontaneous development*
of practices and institutions, based on the assent of many
people down through the ages, and that this acceptance shows

its social value. Davies thus reversed the usual argument about long-established custom: rather than being good because it is old, it has become old precisely because it is good.

The consensual nature of traditional law and its congruence with the cause of freedom were likewise extolled by the American James Wilson, the foremost legal scholar of the founding generation. Sounding very much like Davies, and also like Coke and Hale (both of whom he cites extensively), Wilson delivered this encomium to the common law: "This law is founded on long and general custom. A custom that has been long and generally observed, necessarily carries with it intrinsic evidence of consent ... Can a law be made in a manner more eligible? Experience, the faithful guide of life and business, attends it in its every step ... The regions of custom offer us a most secure asylum from the operations of absolute, despotic power ..."

So deposing, Wilson attacked the doctrine of unchecked legislative power claimed by Parliament, and supported in the writings of Sir William Blackstone. Such notions, Wilson argued, were contrary to the common law tradition, and to ideas of liberty. They would, he said, "permit the seeds of despotism ... to lurk at the roots of our municipal law." Should they be accepted, "we may bid a last adieu to the maxim which I have always deemed of prime importance ... a free people are governed by the law ... *Thus I will, thus I command, let my will stand as the reason*, is the motto of edicts, proclaimed in thunder, by the voice of a human superior. Far dissimilar are the sentiments expressed in calm and placid accents by a customary law. ..."[15]

This notion of *custom as consent*, in contrast to top-down command, is among the key ideas of the free society. With the statements of Davies and Wilson, in fact, we approach the modern exposition of this point by Hayek, who devotes a series of penetrating essays to the subject. The distinctive feature of a libertarian regime, Hayek argues, is that it permits the organization of society by free decision, and that this results in an ordered system that no single person or even group of people has designed, and that could not have been created by top-down methods. An obvious example is the development of language—a structure that has grown up over a considerable course of time, invented by nobody in particular, but used conveniently by many.

As Hayek demonstrates, the concept of order arising through "grown institutions" is always present in societies that are free, and generally absent from those that aren't. It is a concept difficult for the authoritarian mind to grasp—the assumption being that if commands and blueprints aren't provided from a single center, there will be chaos in society. The basic idea is, *if the government doesn't do it, it won't get done.* This way of viewing things unites all the authoritarian theories known to history, from ancient Rome to James I to modern regimes of statist planning.

We see this contrast clearly in the realm of politics, where the idea of a spontaneous order takes the form of elective, popular self-government. The basic concept of this system is that society can organize itself according to the voluntary actions of many people, coordinating their decisions through a continuing process of agreement and consent. This is of course a central precept of American statecraft, which assumes that such arrangements are compatible with order; a familiar notion to us, but radically different from the Roman doctrine, from the ideas of Hobbes, Rousseau, or Saint-Simon, and from all the modern species of collectivism.

As these last examples suggest, this mindset also generates hostility to the market—the concept of spontaneous order *par excellence.* Supporters of top-down planning assume that, if economic matters are left to free decision, there will be chaos, exploitation, and other social evils. From this it follows that government planners must assert control, imposing order by command. Viewed in this context, the ideas of *tradition, self-*

government, and *free markets* are closely linked; all are aspects of a free society, bearing witness to spontaneous order, and resistant to the planning impulse.

In this conceptual linkage we see once more the unity rather than opposition of conservative and libertarian values, again contrary to the usual teaching. And the linkage is more than theoretical; it was, *e.g.*, largely through the growth of the common law tradition, with its legal defense of property rights and limits on the authority of the state, that a market system was able to develop; conversely, when Roman law conceptions of royal power displace the common law tradition, as in Stuart England, property rights and economic freedoms (as well as others) have been imperiled (see Chapter XVI).

From the foregoing, the many connections between tradition and the practices of freedom should be evident, as should the antilibertarian implications of rationalist assaults on custom. Yet despite all this, there are problems with the idea of reliance on tradition, as in a strictly common law approach. These have to do with issues mentioned earlier: that there are and have been many different traditions in the world, that these can vary widely in terms of fundamental value, and that this raises the question of how one is supposed to decide between them if they come in conflict.

Such questions obviously can't be resolved in terms of "tradition" by itself, since different traditions will each provide a different answer. America became a free society not because we have "a" tradition, but because we have a particular *kind* of tradition that is congenial to freedom. If we were products of a different tradition—that of ancient Egypt, Confucian China, or the Ottoman Empire—then tradition as such would not have produced a regime of freedom.

This brings us back, inevitably, to the *substantive content* of the tradition, and the question of how this is arrived at. Obviously, we need to consider where we get such ideas as the freedom and dignity of the individual, protecting the individual from oppression, the consequent need to limit the compulsions of the state, and related concepts. Such ideas are *transmitted* by our tradition, and *defended* in practices enshrined by custom; but they could not have been, and were not, *created* purely by the operations of tradition, just as they were not invented by unaided human reason.

A second problem with the idea of tradition as such—the sheer accretion of accepted practice—also relates to substance. One aspect of a purely traditional approach is that, while it has stability and changes slowly, it *does* in fact change, as precedents are absorbed into the flow of custom. This is frequently cited as a strength of the common law regime, and no doubt is. Yet there are difficulties with it, since a strictly customary approach affords no principles of fixity, no stoppage to the process. Over time, this glacial movement can transform the very nature of the system.

Again, the example of language is instructive, as anyone can discover who tries to read *Beowulf*, *Piers Plowman*, or even Chaucer. The purely evolutionary change of the English language across the centuries has made these writings almost inaccessible to us, since English by slow but steady alterations has in the interval turned into something different from what it was. (One reason that later writings are more accessible, on the other hand, is that the language became standardized with the advent of printing in the West, and dissemination of the King James Bible.)

Problems of this type were at the root of British-American constitutional conflicts in the eighteenth century. In England, the rise of Parliament at the era of the commonwealth, and its triumph in the Glorious Revolution, established the idea of legislative supremacy, which became the ruling doctrine of the English state. Such ideas were very different from those espoused by Coke, but in a system based on precedent alone the verdict of events gave them all the constitutional warrant that was needed.

In America, on the other hand, these precedents were not received—as witness the comments we have quoted from Dickinson and Wilson. The colonists did not accept the doctrine of parliamentary supremacy, indeed denounced it in the strongest terms imaginable, resisted it by every stratagem they could devise, and fought a war of independence to escape it. In essence, the Americans of 1776–1787 were still at the stage of constitutional doctrine espoused by Coke 150 years before; the English in the intervening time had evolved to something altogether different; the Americans were basically where they had been in the preceding century.

Why the Americans exhibited such great tenacity on this and other matters of government doctrine is a question deserving further study. The point about the British, however, should be clear enough; in a system that is strictly based on precedent, the changes occurring in the English outlook were inevitable, given sufficient time and the usual vicissitudes of politics. A *purely* customary or traditional approach can't in the long run supply a sure defense of freedom. It becomes, indeed, a type of evolutionary, "dominant power" statecraft, *a la* Justice Holmes (also a specialist in the common law).

In this sense, at least, the rationalist critics of pure tradition are correct, although their imagined solution is the wrong one. Unaided reason can't solve the problem, and as the previous discussion indicates, will all too often make it worse. On the evidence before us, reason by itself is even less capable of mounting a consistent defense of freedom than is tradition, providing as it does a ready path for methods of coercion. Nor can we find the fixity we need in tradition and reason taken together, though both are necessary to a free society.

The answer to this dilemma lies, once more, in the *substantive principles* from which the tradition is derived, and in whose service it has developed. To prevent eventual slippage into something entirely different, as America's Founders repeatedly stated, a legal system must have an element of fixity, reference points that are anterior to, and controlling upon, the development of pure tradition. These reference points are ultimately religious and axiomatic in nature, and it is in the teachings of religion that we shall find the sources of our freedom.

6

If Men Were Angels

NEXT TO A BELIEF in religious absolutes, the quality most usually said to lead conservatives to authoritarian practice is their "pessimistic" view of human nature. In biblical terms, this means acceptance of the doctrine of Original Sin, the idea that man is deeply flawed in mind and will, inclined to evil, and imperfect in his knowledge.

That this is an attribute of conservative thought may readily be granted, as is the fact that our ideas about such matters come to us from religious teaching. It is not the whole of that teaching, to be sure, since biblical doctrine also has other things to say about man's status as a child of God and rational being, and these have important bearing on our subject (see Chapter VIII). But in Christian orthodox belief, these higher qualities are corrupted by sin, so that man devoid of grace will be enmeshed in evil.

From such concepts, it is supposed, conservatives and Christians necessarily reach an authoritarian theory of the state. In the usual version, the pessimistic part of the analysis translates to a view that common men cannot be trusted, are unruly, and must be lorded over by their betters. To forestall this unpleasant outcome, theorists of the Enlightenment and their descendants have urged an "optimistic" view of man, embracing exalted notions of unaided reason, natural goodness, perfectibility of the species, and variants of these.

A like analysis is pursued, to different outcomes, by Tory paternalists and big government conservatives who think the state should inculcate virtue in its people. Yes, they say, the ideas of Original Sin and human frailty *do* imply the need for some kind of strong regime to keep these tendencies in check, and that is exactly what we favor. The prototype of this is Hobbes. A more respectable spokesman is Maistre, who defended monarchy and revealed religion against the theorists of the Enlightenment. There are also some devotees of this general idea around today.

Again, agreement between opposing sides on what is thought to be the obvious deduction creates an air of plausibility. But for those concerned to defend the cause of freedom, this is grasping the wrong end of the stick. Ideas about Original Sin will lead to such conclusions only if we focus exclusively on the frailties of the people *being ruled*; the instant we think about the people who are *doing the ruling*, the implications are quite different. In the Christian conception of the matter, after all, these people are *also* flawed and sinful, and since they are the ones who will be wielding power, *their* imperfect nature becomes a salient point of interest.

This skeptical view of men with power is the premise of every theory of the state that stands coherently for freedom and, even more important, of every governing system that has afforded such freedom on a practical basis. We need only recall the counsels of Burke and Adam Smith, Tocqueville and Acton, to see the logic of this connection. Precisely because they had a pessimistic view of human nature and/or the efficacy of unaided reason, all of them wanted limits on the scope of power. Those emphases made them, in our terminology, both libertarians and conservatives.

With Burke, this took the form of opposition to arbitrary

force, deployed by any element in the state, and consequent emphasis on the safeguards of religion, custom, and morality: "Law and arbitrary power are at eternal hostility . . . He who would substitute will in the place of law is a public enemy to the world . . . Power to be legitimate must be according to that eternal, immutable law, in which will and reason are the same . . . If I were to describe slavery, I would say with those who hate it, it is living under will, not under law." No "optimism" in these comments, but also no belief in unchecked power.[1]

It is true that in Burkean theory—and in conservative opinion generally—government ought to be conducted by people who are as wise as possible, experienced and virtuous, so that they they can rightly discharge the duties of public office. But this by no means suggests that they will always or even usually *be* either wise or virtuous. On the evidence of history, as Acton famously noted, the case is all too often the reverse: "If there is any presumption it is . . . against holders of power, increasing as the power increases . . . Power tends to corrupt and absolute power corrupts absolutely. Great men are almost always bad men . . . There is no worse heresy than that the office sanctifies the holder of it."[2]

Here is pessimism indeed about human nature equipped with power, and it comes from the writer who by consensus was the most learned student of such matters in the preceding century. Similar statements could be adduced from his only true competitor for that title, Tocqueville. In these matters, however, we Americans don't have to go to strangers. All the ideas conveyed by Burke or Acton were expressed as well by the people who conducted the American Revolution and drafted our federal Constitution. On few topics were they more vocal, or have we been more copiously informed.

Skepticism about human nature armed with power was, indeed, the motif of American political theory from the outset—beginning with the settlers of New England. That the Puritans were strong believers in Original Sin is of course well known; less frequently noted is that they translated this into ideas of constitutionalism, the rule of law, and careful safeguards against arbitrary power. We have noted the opinions on this subject of theologian John Cotton. Compare the views of yet another early Puritan divine, Thomas Hooker—sounding very much like Burke, or Coke:

"[If] the matter which is referred to the judge . . . be left to his own discretion . . . I am afraid it is a course which lacks both safety and warrant: I must confess I ever looked at it as a way which leads directly to tyranny . . . I should choose neither to live nor leave my posterity under such a government . . . We know in other countries, had not the law overruled the lust of men, and the crooked ends of judges many times, both places and people had been in reason past all relief . . . The law is not subject to passion, nor to be taken aside with self-seeking ends, and therefore ought to have chief rule over rulers themselves."[3]

Mistrust of human nature armed with power was the leading theme of American protest before (and after) the War of Independence, as has been well documented by Bernard Bailyn, Cecilia Kenyon, and other authorities on the topic. Americans of the revolutionary generation were indefatigable on this subject, warning repeatedly of plans to enslave the colonies, the aggressive nature of English policy, the need to defend the cause of liberty against tyrannical abuses. Statements to this effect are pervasive in the pamphlet literature, political sermons, and official declarations of the era.

Typical notions appearing in these manifestos are the "plan of power," "temporal and spiritual tyranny," "a deep laid and desperate plan of imperial despotism," and the like. The colonists, as Thomas Hutchinson reported to England, perceived that "a design is formed to enslave them by degrees." Indeed they did, as witness the repeated protests of Washington, Jefferson, the Adamses, Patrick Henry, and James Otis, who denounced the Stamp Act, *e.g.*, as "a project for enslaving the British colonies."[4]

Moreover, the colonists didn't confine their thoughts about such matters simply to *British* power; they generalized the lesson in terms of human nature and politics at large. Samuel Adams put it that "ambition and lust for power . . . are predominant passions in the breasts of most men." Jonathan Mayhew's version was that "power is of a grasping, encroaching nature . . . [it] aims at extending itself and operating according to mere will, whenever it meets with no balance, check, constraint, or opposition of any kind." (In these assertions, the theological content is fairly plain, since Adams was an old-fashioned Puritan and Mayhew a leading clergyman of Massachusetts.)[5]

The identical views were stressed, in different legal context, at the era of the Constitution. Here the Founders faced the task of establishing a new political order of their own, rather than escaping one controlled by Whitehall; yet the concerns expressed about human frailty, and political power, continued exactly as before. Virtually everyone in our politics, it appears, was a believer in Original Sin, wherever he stood on the specific issues of the day. Simply reading statements on this topic, without other means of identification, one would have no idea at all as to what party or interest was being promoted.

To take the obvious case in point, most supporters of the Constitution were great skeptics about human nature. Concerned about the fiscal weaknesses of the Confederation, Shays' rebellion, and paper currencies, Washington, Hamilton, and Jay deplored the behavior of state assemblies that controlled the system. Hamilton phrased it this way in the *Federalist*: "Why has government been instituted at all? Because the passions of men will not conform to the dictates of reason and justice without constraint . . . there is, in the nature of sovereign power, an impatience of control, that disposes those who are invested with the exercise of it, to look with an evil eye

upon all external attempts to restrain or direct its operations. . . . [Conflict in the Confederation] has its origin in the
love of power."6 *

This was an ingenious argument, considering that Hamilton
was proposing to concentrate power more securely than had
been the case with the Confederation—but we may for the
moment let that pass. The point is that he chose to base his
appeal on the *mistrust of power*, rather than the other way
around. Such pessimism might be considered natural for a
conservative like Hamilton, who was about as close as an
American could be to the opinions of Maistre, and tended to
dwell on the problems and imperfections of humanity.† Similar
reasoning was also used, however, on the other side of the
dispute.

The Anti-Federalists, if anything, were even more insistent
about the evils of human nature—they just turned the cannons
in the opposite direction. Viewing the proposed new governing
system, the critics saw a scheme to efface the liberty of the
states and consolidate all power in one center. Typical broad-
sides against the Constitution warned that "every man has a
propensity to power," that "it is natural for men to aspire to
power—it is the nature of man to be tyrannical," and that
"power was never given . . . but it was finally abused." According to its opponents, the Constitution resulted from "diabolical
plots and secret machinations" to reduce Americans "to slavery
and dependence."7

Anti-Federalists such as George Mason, Richard Henry Lee,

---

* Hamilton had made the same point at the Constitutional Convention: The ills
of the Confederation, he said, stemmed from "the love of power. Men love power
. . . the ambition of [state] demagogues is known to hate the control of the
general government." (McClellan and Bradford, eds., *Elliot's Debates*, James
River Press, 1989, p. 117)

† Though John Jay and Gouverneur Morris were equally mordant on the
subject. Hamilton's method of expression, of course, would also have been
affected by the known attitudes of his audience, a fact that further suggests the
universality of such thinking.

and Patrick Henry were tireless in depicting the evils that would result from a new consolidated system. The Constitution, said Lee, was "dangerously oligarchic," the work of a "silent, powerful and ever active conspiracy of those who govern." In the Virginia ratifying convention, Henry conjured images of an armed and dangerous central government, subjugating states and people. "The ropes and chains of consolidation," he said, were "about to convert this country into a powerful and mighty empire"—in which a standing army would "execute the execrable commands of tyranny."[8]

As these exchanges suggest, political leaders of all factions were as concerned about such matters during the constitutional era as they had been before the revolution. There was no question that human nature was flawed and inclined to evil; it was simply a matter of *whose* human nature was being inspected—that of turbulent people like Daniel Shays and state governments inclined to paper money, or that of asserted would-be aristocrats, trying to take away the liberties of the people. Mistrust of power was thus applied to everything and everybody. There was little hint among the Founders of the selective skepticism then prevalent in France—which assumed the problem was merely certain *kinds* of power, in the hands of decadent kings and nobles, and that all would be well if total authority were conferred upon the representatives of "the people."*

On the contrary, the Founders believed that pure majoritarianism and/or unchecked supremacy in legislative bodies were as bad as any other form of power. At the Constitutional Convention, Edmund Randolph deplored the "turbulence and follies of democracy," while Pierce Butler of South Carolina likewise

---

* The closest approach that I can find is a statement by Roger Sherman at the convention, July 11, 1787: "We ought to choose wise & good men and then confide in them." (*Elliot's Debates*, op. cit., p. 257) Sherman, however, was an old-fashioned Puritan who thought the federal government should have strictly limited powers.

asserted that "in tracing these evils to their origin every man had found it in the turbulence and follies of democracy." Mason also expressed misgivings on the topic, while Elbridge Gerry put it that "the evils we experience flow from the excess of democracy." (Despite these concerns about the Confederation, it should be noted, Randolph, Mason, and Gerry all refused to sign the Constitution.)*⁹

All of this is so far from the optimism of the Enlightenment— and the runaway majoritarianism of the French Revolution— that we are virtually in a different mental universe. On this subject, Jefferson provides an intriguing study, since he is often cited as the leading optimist among the Founders—the closest in outlook to French ideas of pure democracy. As ambassador to Paris in the years preceding the French Revolution, it is true, Jefferson sympathized with the revolutionary cause, though he of course repudiated the ensuing terror. He also took a more complacent view of Shays' Rebellion than did the framers at the convention. Yet Jefferson said a number of other things as well, often of countervailing import.

Most conspicuously, he focused his democratic theories on the rural sector, rather than the cities, whose inhabitants he

---

* John Adams was equally vehement on this theme, and also returned to it repeatedly. He belabored Rousseau and the other *philosophes*, pouring scorn on the idea that the French Assembly, since it concentrated all the power of "the nation," was a safe repository of freedom. "The fundamental article of my political creed," he wrote, "is the despotism, or the unlimited sovereignty, or absolute power is the same in a majority of a popular assembly, an aristocratical council, an oligarchical junto and a single emperor: Equally arbitrary, cruel, bloody, and in every respect diabolical." (Lester J. Cappon, ed., *The Adams-Jefferson Letters*, North Carolina, 1959, Vol II, p. 456)

On this topic, also, the *Federalist* rings the changes: "Of those men who have overturned the liberties of the republics, the greatest number have begun their career by paying an obsequious court to the people; commencing demagogues, and ending tyrants . . . the turbulent democracies of ancient Greece and modern Italy . . . The legislative power is everywhere extending the sphere of its activity, and drawing all power into its impetuous vortex . . ." (*The Federalist*, Modern Library, 1937, pp. 5–6, 80, 322)

described as "mobs" and "rabble." He was also no fan of legislative majorities, as was made clear in his famous assertion in *Notes on the State of Virginia*: "One hundred and seventy-three despots would surely be as oppressive as one . . . An elective despotism was not the government we fought for; but one which should not only be founded on free principles, . . . in which the powers of government should be so divided and balanced among several bodies of magistracy, that no one could transcend their legal limits, without being effectively checked and restrained by the others."[10]

Equally conservative on the question of human nature wielding power was Jefferson's draft of the Kentucky Resolutions, the most emphatic statement of the Anti-Federalist, states' rights interest: ". . . it would be a dangerous delusion were a confidence in the men of our choice to silence our fear for the safety of our rights; that confidence is everywhere the parent of despotism—free government is founded in jealousy, and not in confidence . . . In questions of power, then, let no more be heard of confidence in man, but bind him down from mischief with the chains of the Constitution."[11]

Such quotations could be multiplied at length; they make good aphoristic reading, and contain much wisdom. Enough has no doubt been said, however, to convey the essence of the matter: Mistrust of human nature armed with power was universal among the Founders, and *the basis of the limited-government system that they established*. Hostility to unchecked power was the leading idea in all debates about the Constitution, expressed in one fashion or another by all the major actors. A fair statement of the composite view is that the impulses and disorders of human nature made government necessary, but also made it dangerous. Hence the need for checks and balances, divided powers, safeguards of all descriptions.

The classic statements on this subject are Madison's comments in *The Federalist* and on the floor of the convention: "It is

vain to say that enlightened statesmen will be able to adjust
... clashing interests and render them all subservient to the
public good. Enlightened statesmen will not always be at the
helm." "The truth was that all men having power ought to be
distrusted to a certain degree." "It may be a reflection on human
nature that such devices should be necessary to control the
abuses of government. But what is government itself, but the
greatest of all reflections on human nature? If men were angels,
no government would be necessary. If angels were to govern
men, neither external nor internal controls on government
would be necessary."[12] *

These opinions, it will be observed, converge with those
discussed in the preceding chapter—the Founders' emphasis
on the common law, and their argument that no species of
political power, in either king or Parliament, should be permitted to surpass its limits. Insistence on the rule of law instead of
arbitrary will, and mistrust of human nature equipped with
power, were two expressions of the same mentality. However
the issue might be phrased, the conclusion drawn was always
that the authority of the state must be subjected to definite
boundaries and restrictions.

To gauge the distance between the Founders' opinions on
this topic and those prevailing in France, we need only consider
the roughly contemporaneous statements of Rousseau. His *Social Contract* is a choice example of abstract speculation, with
almost zero regard for circumstance or context. It seeks to
found the idea of government on a doctrine of unchecked
popular sovereignty, exercising dominion over affairs of state
through untrammeled legislative power. This was the theory,
basically, of which the French Revolution was the practice.

---

* cf. Jefferson's comment in his first Inaugural—drafted no doubt with Madison's assistance: "Sometimes it is said that man cannot be trusted with the
government of himself. Can he, then, be trusted with the government of others? Or
have we found angels in the form of kings to govern men?" (Koch and Peden, eds.,
The Life and Selected Writings of Thomas Jefferson, Modern Library, 1944, p. 323)

Rousseau was as great a believer in the "natural goodness" of man as the American Founders were the reverse,* and translated this into a bland assurance that whatever was done by the "general will" of a nation was *ipso facto* proper. Though his ideas are notoriously confusing (and confused), his willingness to consolidate authority in this way is plain enough, and quite amazing. He tells us the essence of the social contract is "the total alienation of each associate, *together with all his rights*, to the whole community," to be disposed of as the "general will" sees fit. "The social compact," he asserts, "gives the body politic absolute power over all its members."[13]

What does this imply for freedom? Not to worry, says Rousseau, since "the Sovereign, being formed wholly of the individuals who compose it, neither has nor can have any interest contrary to theirs, and consequently the sovereign power *need give no guarantees to its subjects*, because it is impossible for the body to wish to hurt all its members . . . the general will is always right and tends to the public advantage." In other words, once you have concentrated power in the proper hands, everything will be fine, and you don't need any safeguards. (It is from such logic that he concludes, in a celebrated passage, "whoever refuses to obey the general will shall be compelled to do so by the whole body. This means nothing less than that he shall be forced to be free . . .") (Italics added.)[14]

There is much more in this vein, which from an American standpoint seems naive and fatuous, and which also supplied the premise for despotic practice under the French Revolution, the regimes of the totalitarians, and many species of collectivist oppression. Rousseau's ideas on other matters also contributed

---

* As he expressed it in a widely quoted letter, his goal was to demonstrate "that man is naturally good and it is by their institutions alone that men become wicked." (Cranston and Peters, eds., *Hobbes and Rousseau*, Doubleday, 1972, p. 297) And again: ". . . man is naturally good . . . What then can have depraved him if . . . not the . . . progress he has made and the knowledge he has acquired?" (*A Discourse on Inequality*, Penguin, 1984, p. 44)

to these outcomes, most notably his worship of emotion and cult of romantic naturalism; but the relevant point for now is that his *optimistic* view of human nature converted into a type of *arbitrary power*—the exact antithesis of the American view about the subject.*

Rousseau's idea of submerging the individual completely in the state would become the leading political precept of all the modern authoritarian movements. It reached its most explicit form in Hegel ("the state is the divine idea as it exists on earth"), and thence migrated into the theories of Marx, and into the totalitarian movements we have examined. This attitude makes the central political question, not how the state is organized (which becomes extremely simple), but *who* is in control of it. Again, this is the reverse of the Founders' theory, which stressed that political power should be so limited and balanced that it would function in the least harmful manner, irrespective of the individuals or factions who might get into office.[15]

The difference between these two conceptions—as events would show—is like night and day. In the approach suggested by Rousseau, a contest for political control is an apocalyptic struggle in which every value is at hazard, the prize of victory is total power, and the penalty of defeat will most probably be extinction. In such a view, the idea of peaceful transitions from one party to the next becomes impossible, and you get the brand of politics notoriously practiced in the modern era. Conversely, in the American system, peaceful transitions from

---

* The contrast in French and American opinion on such topics may likewise be seen in the comments of Turgot about our constitutional system, which eventually made their way to the attention of John Adams. Turgot criticized the American penchant for distributing and subdividing powers, "*instead of collecting all authority into one center, that of the nation.*" (Italics added.) To Adams, this was an incomprehensible—and highly irritating—statement. "What does he mean," Adams demanded, "collecting all authority into one center? What does he mean by the center of a nation? Where would he have the legislation placed? Where the execution? Where the decision of controversies? Emptier piece of declamation, I have never read; it is impossible to give greater proof of ignorance." (Zoltan Haraszti, *John Adams and the Prophets of Progress*, Harvard, 1952, p. 144)

the outset were routine, in part because the power of government was circumscribed and limited. In this respect and others, the Founders' mistrust of human nature led to a libertarian brand of statecraft; Enlightenment "optimism" did the reverse.

If the Founders' ideas about human nature and political power were drastically different from Rousseau and his authoritarian descendants, they were equally distant from what passes today for "liberalism" in our politics. As we have seen in our discussion of Holmesian metaphysics, that liberalism has become, precisely, *an ideology of dominant power*, meaning specifically power in the federal government, and has adopted practices to suit. Piling up ever more authority in the central government, touching every zone of our domestic life, has been the very essence of American liberalism in the modern era, and continues to be its leading feature now.

In pursuit of this agenda, as has been noted, American liberals have adopted an elastic reading of the Constitution that further reverses the mindset of the Founders. They tell us, in essence, that we don't need to worry about concentrated power so long as it is being used for worthy causes, wielded by well-meaning experts, and exercised in behalf of "the people." This is reasonably good Rousseau, or maybe Robespierre, but it is the opposite of Madison, Hamilton, Adams, or even Jefferson. Of course, the liberals also tell us the ideas of the Founders are irrelevant anyway, since our evolving standards have carried us beyond their antiquated notions.

Some twenty years ago, I had a personal encounter on this subject in debate with Sen. George McGovern, a leading exponent of modern liberal doctrine. Senator McGovern, who proved to be an amiable enough opponent, basically argued that the proper response to problems of big government was to get "better people" to run it. My answer, then as now, was that the original premise of our Founders was exactly the reverse: To construct a system that could withstand the problems created by bad rulers, rather than aggregating power in the hope of finding good ones.

In strictly operational terms, this seems to be the chief distinction between the liberal and conservative views of statecraft. The liberal looks at the actual and potential power of government, and imagines all the good things that might be accomplished if only wise and benevolent people were in command. The conservative looks at the same array of power, and envisions all the calamities that might happen if evil people were to gain control. Defined this way, nearly all American leaders of the revolutionary/constitutional era were conservative, and then some.

While the contrast between the Founders and modern liberalism is obvious enough, something also needs saying about the views of the Tory paternalists, referred to at the beginning of this chapter. These are theorists who believe that, since the common people can't be trusted, the American government should be an instrument for imparting virtue to the public. Enough has been said already, perhaps, to suggest the trouble with this notion, most obviously the problem so often mentioned by the Founders—that rulers are apt to be as imperfect as their subjects, and appreciably more dangerous.

A helpful way to approach this topic might be to employ a little common-sense conservatism. When someone talks about using government for some noble purpose, such as promoting "virtue," it may aid analysis to consider the government that we *actually have*. At the risk of seeming partisan, I note that the existing federal government is headed by President Bill Clinton, while the best-known member of the majority party in Congress is Sen. Edward Kennedy. Whatever else may be said about these officials, they are not widely known as exemplars of "virtue." We may add to this some other things that have happened in the federal city down through the years—from Watergate to midnight pay hikes to the curious "cultural" grants made by the National Endowment for the Arts.

Looking at all this—and there is a great deal of it—what reason is there to think the people running the federal government are qualified to *impart virtue* to the nation? The answer, I should think, is not much. The odds are that the average family going peacefully about its business, trying to raise its children, earn a living, and pay its taxes, is closer to what most conservatives consider "virtue" than are politicians suborning votes with pork-barrel spending, contriving secret pay hikes for themselves, or disbursing money to pornographers.

But, it may be objected, we aren't talking about *this* government, which is concededly nonvirtuous; we are talking about a government in which we, and the values we profess, will be in charge. Again, a dose of common-sense conservatism would seem to be the indicated therapy. For the foreseeable future, the likelihood of a Tory-paternalist government's coming to power in the United States is vanishingly remote. If we didn't get such a government under Ronald Reagan, which we didn't, it is improbable that we shall see one in the experience of anyone now living.

Even if we could get such a government, however, the whole idea goes counter to some basic precepts of conservatism. For what this suggests is that we should have *a government of men, and not of laws*; that we want power to be vested in the federal government when we are in control, but not when our opponents are in the saddle. Again, this is the reverse of what constitutional government is supposed to be about—a denial of conservative precept, and also of libertarian doctrine.

These cautionary attitudes, I think, are fully in keeping with the notions of the Founders, and their modest expectations of the state. One can comb through their writings at some length, including popular sermons of the era, and find little to support ideas of redemption by way of politics (which in fact went counter to orthodox theology) or any suggestion that government can accomplish much beyond the tasks of keeping order.* This was true even of such as Hamilton, whose highest aspiration for the central government was that it should maintain the peace, fund the debt, and encourage manufactures.

The Founders generally speaking did believe that government had a secondary role to play in this regard—that, as a bad government could make its citizens worse, one set up on a proper basis should be *supportive* of religion and morality. In our constitutional scheme, however, this role was chiefly to be played by state and local governments. Because of the great religious diversity of the country, the drafters thought it best to keep the central regime as far as possible from sectarian questions. Of all levels of authority in America, therefore, the federal government was the one most plainly set up on an order-keeping basis—hence the furthest from any theory of imposed belief. (See Chapter XV.)

But if this is so, what happens to virtue? To collectivists and Tory paternalists alike, these conclusions seem to mean that people will be allowed to run around being "selfish," doing whatever they like, devoid of proper guidance or instruction. Again, this sort of analysis misses the point, confusing America with a Greek city-state as envisioned by an Aristotle or a Plato. Or conversely, supposing that, if America's Founders neglected to provide for virtue advanced by federal power, they must have been irreligious *philosophes* or Deists. This Greek way of looking at the subject misconstrues the whole endeavor. Two points especially are relevant in this regard.

First, from the Founders' perspective, establishing a regime of liberty under law was not a morally neutral undertaking. Their version of the state was modest, but the ethical con-

---

* The *Federalist*, for example, assumes throughout that government is an order-keeping agency, properly confined to providing defense, keeping the peace, administering justice, and performing certain other practical assignments. The idea of imposing virtue is nowhere to be found, nor is there any grandiose conception of government's abilities in general. "No government of human device and human administration can be perfect," as Madison expressed it. "That which is the least imperfect is the best government." (Op. cit., p. 345)

quences as they saw it were tremendous: It protected human freedom, prevented despotism, and provided an arena of order in which people could go peacefully about their business. This was not a trifling matter to Americans of the founding generation, who had conducted a heroic struggle to protect their liberties; it should be even less so to our own.

None of the Founders, as we have seen, believed that people free of coercion would necessarily make moral decisions; their view of human nature told them quite the opposite. A regime of liberty under law, as they conceived it, could by no means guarantee morality. But it could prevent some of the grossest *im*morality—the suffering and coercion that despotism imposes on its victims; again, a consideration that is hardly irrelevant to our era. A system of limited government cannot ensure that men will act in ethical fashion; it can, however, prevent unethical men from wielding boundless power over others.*

The second point is even more fundamental. Contrary to charges of secularism and irreligion, the Founders not only believed that virtue was essential to the survival of the republic, but also that such virtue was religious in its origin. The materials that go to show this are extensive. Misconceptions about the point are a further example of the notion that, *if the government doesn't do it, it won't get done.* As in the case of Platonic guardians, divine right monarchs, or collectivist planners, it assumes that government must impart the principles of belief and value, or else these qualities will be lacking in the social order.

Once more, the oft-repeated position of the Founders was entirely different. They believed the people must be virtuous to sustain a system of free government, rather than that the government would inculcate virtue in the people. We have already

---

* In this also they were agreed with Burke, who observed that, in economic matters, "to provide for us in our necessities is not in the power of government." He added that "it is in the power of government to prevent much evil; it can do very little positive good in this, or perhaps in anything else." (Peter J. Stanlis, *Edmund Burke and the Natural Law*, Ann Arbor, 1965, p. 57)

noted the opinions to this effect expressed by Washington, Adams, and others among the Founders, sentiments that were commonplace for the era. Madison, with his usual exactitude and balance, expressed it this way: "To suppose that any form of government will secure liberty and happiness without virtue in the people, is a chimerical idea . . . we do not depend on [the virtue of] or put confidence in our rulers, but in the people who are to choose them."[16]

The point was that people in a free society would need the interior guidelines of religious virtue to direct their actions, and also to use proper judgment in selecting the men who would exercise authority. It was further assumed that these officials would need in turn to guide their conduct by moral precepts. Free government and its institutions, thus construed, were more likely to be the product of virtue than the source of it.

Our conclusion brings us out at the point from which we started: Mistrust of human nature—as expressed in biblical doctrine and by the people who founded our society—leads to the idea of *limits on political power*, of whatever type, rather than to its extension. These were the law and the prophets for the Founders, and no analysis that ignores this fact can begin to understand our system.

7

The Rise of Neopaganism

THOUGH TECHNICALLY AND OFFICIALLY said to be discredited by
the fall of the Soviet Union, Marxist and quasi-Marxist concepts
remain embedded in Western thought, to the detriment of our
freedoms. This is most obviously true in the case of leftward
academics who promote class struggle/imperialism theories in
the guise of "multiculturalism," radical feminism, Afrocentr-
ism, and the like. This is indeed a serious matter, and one that
has obvious points of contact with our subject.

The degree to which explicit or laundered Marxism of this
type creates an immediate problem for our statecraft is hard to
gauge; concerted efforts are being made, for instance, to translate its teachings into the curricula of the public schools and
colleges, and the radicals obviously have some allies in the
ranks of government and the media. The long-term effects of
this campaign could be significant. On the other hand, when
such teachings run up against electoral opinion, the radical
agenda is usually defeated. Judged by the general standards of
our discourse, these concepts are far outside the mainstream.
Only in the veriest enclaves of academic leftism could hard-line
notions of class struggle, exploitation, and so on gain any
credence.

More problematic in an immediate sense are aspects of the
Marxist worldview, generally not recognized as such, that have

already penetrated liberal thought and are considered perfectly routine and normal. These conceptions, indeed, might most accurately be described as political axioms that our liberals hold in common with the Marxists, inherited from their common ancestors at the period of the Enlightenment. As suggested by our previous discussion, such shared beliefs are far more numerous than imagined.

Among the most important of these is economic determinism—which is at the base of Marxist theories of society, the state, and just about everything else that has to do with politics and culture. In simplest terms, Marx and Engels taught that material forces and economic struggles generally determine all the rest, so that if you know the economic status of some group of people, you will also know where they come down concerning other matters.* Most notably, Marxists hammer on the idea that religion and morality are merely expressions of dominant economic interests, and need to be attacked and overthrown precisely for this reason.

Such a view emerges readily from any vision of the world that denies the existence of a spiritual power beyond the natural order. In the case of the totalitarian movements, a denial of religious absolutes leads human thought inexorably "back to nature"—to the notion that, since the natural order is all there is, it is from this order that we must take our points of reference.

---

* Thus Marx: "The mode of production in material life determines the general character of the social, political, and spiritual processes of life. It is not the consciousness of men that determines their existence, but, on the contrary, their social existence determines their consciousness." And Engels: ". . . men, consciously or unconsciously, derive their moral ideas in the last resort from the practical relations on which their class position is based—from the economic relations in which they carry on production and exchange." Engels later tried to back off slightly from this view, but only slightly: "According to the materialist conception of history, the *ultimately* determining element in history is the production and reproduction of real life. More than this neither Marx nor I has ever asserted. Hence if somebody twists this into saying that the economic element is the *only* determining one he transforms that proposition into a meaningless, abstract, senseless phrase." (Feuer, op. cit., pp. 43, 271, 397–98)

Thus stated, the idea is virtually a tautology, and Marx's "materialist concept of history" is just one version of its workings. This assimilation of man to nature, as already shown, is a leading feature of all totalitarian systems.

Though less explicitly phrased, this sort of theory is also common in the thought of modern liberalism, for essentially the same reasons. Having denied religious absolutes, liberal thinking gravitates as well to various species of economic determinism. We have noted the views of Holmes, Mill, et al., concerning the naturalist and materialist basis for human existence and human values. In our era, these reductionist notions are translated into practice on a daily basis, from economic planning and social engineering, to the soft behaviorism of the welfare state, to gun control and arms agreements—in which it is quite literally assumed that material objects, rather than the motives of human beings, are the chief causes of social conflict.

Perhaps the most familiar version of this teaching is the idea that crime, illegitimacy, drug abuse, or other types of asocial conduct are traceable to material "conditions" of one sort or another. From this it is thought to follow that the way to deal with such pathologies is to attack the "underlying causes" through housing projects, job training, and other governmental programs, all aimed at changing economic factors. Such behaviorist views have also pervaded our legal system, where it has been argued that economic, biological, or other natural causes are controlling, and that individual offenders accordingly are not responsible for their actions.*

---

* *Cf.* the argument of Clarence Darrow in defending Leopold and Loeb: "Nature is strong and she is pitiless. She works in her own mysterious way, and we are her victims. The mind, or course, is an illusive thing. Whether it exists or not, no one can tell . . . Their parents happened to meet, these boys happened to meet; some sort of chemical alchemy operated so that they cared for each other, and poor Bobby Fischer's dead body was found in the culvert as a result." Darrow's corollary is equally of interest: "I have never in my life been interested so much in fixing blame as I have in relieving people from blame." (Quoted in R. J. Rushdoony, *The Nature of the American System*, Craig Press, 1965, pp. 106–7)

In any common-sense analysis, economic and material factors are important, and any theory of politics that neglects them is destined for confusion. Economics, indeed, is the most essential subject of peacetime statecraft, since it deals with the stuff of everyday existence. If such issues are not properly treated, then people can starve to death, or be deprived of shelter or jobs, fuel supplies or health care—all of which has happened in recent memory. Also, people tend to vote their economic interests and/or advance them through the machinery of the state. All of this deserves attention. It is different, however, from saying that such material factors *determine* everything, including crime or other deviant conduct, cultural attitudes, political creeds and institutions, or ideas about religion.

Likewise, with the policy of nations, questions of economic advantage, or constraint, obviously have a powerful role to play, in matters relating to markets, raw materials, supplies of energy, or tariffs. But to assume that economic or material forces are the only vectors of national conduct is to misread the record disclosed with blazing clarity by the light of Western history. We need merely consider such topics as the emergence of Judaism, Christianity, and Mohammedanism, the founding of the medieval church, the Reformation, the settling of America, religious and ethnic conflicts of the present era. One would be hard pressed to explain these and other world-altering developments strictly or even mainly in terms of economics.

If we examine these matters with any care, we see that the Marxists and other determinists have got the situation topsy-turvy, as they do most other questions that they handle. Rather than beginning with economic status and relations, then working along through ideologies and religions, the process, generally speaking, is the other way around. This emerges clearly from our discussion of the totalitarian movements, and of the liberal theorists who adopted the irreligious premise and have been struggling to avoid the totalitarian outcome.

In such cases, it should be evident that the type of thought adopted at the *level of religion* eventually determines everything else, including questions of economics. Hitler and Lenin didn't develop the views they held because of economic arrangements in Germany or Russia, either before or after their respective revolutions. They held these opinions for axiomatic reasons, beginning with their condign rejection of Western faith. That led to the nihilist theories we have examined, thence to the totalitarian and collectivist systems they inflicted on society. It was the religious attitude, or lack of one, that came first, and the economic consequences that came tagging after.*

Nor can the outlook of such revolutionaries be plausibly traced to economic factors—as, for instance, in the notion that they were driven to rebellion by extremes of poverty. In case after case, iconoclasts of the modern era have emerged from comfortable if not affluent backgrounds. Saint-Simon was a member of the French aristocracy, devoted to high living; Marx was from a middle-class home; Engels was quite wealthy; Nietzsche, Mill, and Holmes all came from most respectable environs. Much the same has been true of revolutionaries in our time—as with the New Left radicals of the 1960s. What is common among such people is not economic hardship, but the *ideas* they have imbibed—ideas that, without exception, disparaged the religious/cultural heritage of the West.

The reason that it works this way should be apparent to anyone not blinkered by materialist assumptions. Our religious beliefs determine our most fundamental attitudes about the world we live in: The nature and meaning of the universe, man's place in the natural order, what it means to be a human being,

---

* It is true, of course, that Hitler and Lenin were aided in their efforts by the chaotic economic conditions existing in Germany and Russia prior to their *coups d'etat*. But those conditions were themselves the result of preceding acts of policy—*e.g.*, the hyperinflation that helped to wreck the Weimar Republic, the terms imposed by the Treaty of Versailles, and so on. And economic problems were hardly the only ones existing in these societies, both of which had long been riven with skeptical, nihilist, and revolutionary doctrine.

the purpose of our lives, how human beings should behave toward one another. These concepts determine the political ethos of society, which will in turn profoundly influence the kind of economic institutions that develop. Likewise, our beliefs about such matters shape the intellectual models by which we construe the data of existence—including those of economics.

In the various religions of the world, different kinds of answers have been provided to such questions—with very different practical outcomes. In Oriental cultures, people have viewed these topics in one fashion, while we in the West have viewed them in another, and these divergent notions have been reflected in markedly different political and economic systems. Eastern societies for many centuries were static in terms of economic, political and scientific endeavors, while Western culture was geared to progress and expansion. Efforts to explain such differences by starting with the economic end of it, and assuming that the religious divergence arose from this, would clearly get the process backwards.

Likewise with Western culture itself. In ancient Greece and Rome, as we shall see, one set of assumptions prevailed concerning religious questions, and a particular kind of politics was developed; in Judeo-Christian culture, a totally different set of axioms appeared, and the political/economic outcomes were changed as well. In the modern era, biblical concepts have been disparaged in their turn, with the results that we have noted. The cycle is constantly being repeated: Assumptions at the level of faith determine the political order of society, which then has its impact on all the other business of living.

This pattern is so persistent, and so plain, that we may formulate it into a kind of law, directly counter to that of Marx and Engels: *Always and everywhere, the governing system that is adopted will reflect the underlying religious presuppositions of the culture,* and as these vary so will the prospects for statecraft, science, economics, and a great deal else. What is truly operative in the world, therefore, might most accurately be described as theological determinism, not economic.

Such a relationship, to be sure, is denied in modern theory— a fact that has great relevance to many controversies of our day. In the secularist or materialist view of life, it is imagined that there is such a thing as a political order that is *not* based on religious axioms, and it is this nonreligious order that is allegedly being defended against the intrusion of Christian zealots. In this approach, what supposedly distinguishes a "religion" is belief in a sovereign, supernatural being. Since secularism either denies such concepts outright, or else forbids them entry to the world of politics, it seems to follow that "religion" is banished from the civil order. This is, however, a delusion.

For one thing, while it is true that religions *generally* presuppose the existence of a Supreme Being, this is not universally the case. We need only consider the Buddhist system in Oriental cultures, and secular humanism in our own; neither of these requires belief in a Supreme Being, yet both have been generally, and officially, acknowledged as religions (and are relevant here in other ways as well).* Equally to the point, while the idea of a Supreme Being is of great importance to the *outcome* in establishing the basic axioms of society, it is not essential to the *process*, which will occur no matter what.

From an earthly standpoint, after all, the significant aspect of religion is the code of beliefs that it supplies concerning ultimate questions, about the nature and meaning of the world, and of our existence in it. All systems of human thought, and all societies, rest on responses to these questions, and have to do so. However agnostic, scientific, or simply indifferent a people may be, they have to live their lives according to *some* such

---

* The Supreme Court has said, for instance: "Among religions in this country which do not teach what would commonly be considered a belief in the existence of God are Buddhism, Taoism, Ethical Culture, Secular Humanism, and others." (*Torcaso v. Watkins*, 1961)

answers, if only by default. It follows that when a given religious outlook is rejected, the effect is not to adopt a worldview devoid of axiomatic concepts, but to replace one set of axioms with another. Functionally considered, these axioms are religions.

That the transition from biblical to secularist belief is in fact a change from one religious system to the next is evident from these considerations. It is made the more so by the fact that these political movements so often wind up presenting themselves, precisely, *as religions.* This is one of the most striking features of the historical record, and it continues down to the present day. Nothing could more clearly illustrate that what goes by the name of secularism is in fact a substitute form of religious faith.

We see this, for example, in Rousseau and his attempt to invent a "civil religion." It was noteworthy as well in the French Revolution, when the Jacobins staged "Festivals of Reason" in the churches and composed their hymns to the "Goddess of Reason." We see it again in Saint-Simon and Comte, who concocted a "new priesthood" and "religion of humanity" to supplant the teachings of the Catholic Church, and in Mill, who likewise propounded a "religion of humanity." Marx stated that "the religion of the workers has no God, because it seeks to restore the divinity of man."[1]*

These developments support our point about "theological

---

* The Nazis, for their part, concocted something called "German Christianity," the cardinal tenet of which was that religious as well as secular loyalties were owed to the Nazi movement and its leader. Rosenberg drafted articles for the "National Reich church," which said, "on the altar there must be nothing but *Mein Kampf . . .*" German officials were required to swear: "We acknowledge that National Socialism is the faith that alone can bring blessedness to our people." (William L. Shirer, *The Rise and Fall of the Third Reich*, Fawcett, 1967, p. 332; Herman Rauschning, *The Revolution of Nihilism*, Alliance, 1939, p. 35) The same phenomenon may be observed in the case of Mussolini's fascism. One part of the catechism that Italian fascists were required to learn was: "Mussolini is always right . . . one thing must be dear to you above all: the life of the Duce . . . Mussolini is always right." (Oakeshott, op. cit., 180–181)

determinism," but also do a good deal more. Most notably, this shift away from transcendent religion shuts off the possibility of spiritual freedom. When religious value is denied in the realm of spirit, but reasserted in the secular order, dominion over every facet of life converges in a single center; the political regime becomes both church and state, and claims authority over faith and conscience. It is this crushing, all-pervasive assertion of power over every aspect of existence, without exception or reserve, that is the truly distinguishing feature of the totalitarian movements. It is what makes totalitarianism "total." And it occurs precisely because what was once considered a domain beyond the power of the state is now assumed to be completely within its purview.

In this result, as in others, the pseudo-religions of modernity bear a striking resemblance to the types of faith that flourished in the pagan era. In the usual case, as shall be discussed, pagan cultures united religious and secular functions in the state, thereby precluding the idea of limits on its power, foreclosing the notion of any higher loyalty, denying refuge to the spirit. Judaism and Christianity opened the door to a different world, in which the ideas and practices of freedom could develop. Modern neopaganism has moved to close that door again, in even more decisive fashion.

That the secular religions of the modern epoch are actually a species of neopaganism appears in many ways. The Renaissance and Enlightenment both made much of their return to pagan ideologies and practices; Rousseau was an ardent neopagan, as was Hegel; Engels and Nietzsche were devotees of pagan doctrines concerning nature; Hitler and Rosenberg made paganism a center of the Nazi cult; and so on. What most obviously united these moderns with the ancients was, precisely, *the immersion of human existence in the cycles and patterns of physical nature*. This was a common theme of the ancient pagan faiths, as well as of many that are still extant. A relevant case in point is Buddhism, which teaches that oneness with the natural order is the highest good, and that the ultimate goal of man's endeavor should be to escape the wheel of recurring existence by absorption in the cosmic process.

Even the most casual observer of our mores can spot the connection between all this and much that is currently going on in American culture. We have seen in recent times a proliferation of neopagan fads and movements, intermingled with mystical, quasi-Buddhist and other Eastern religious notions: "New Age" cults, reincarnation, channeling, yoga, and pop-culture variants of these are evident in great profusion. Add a leavening of astrology, tarot, and other species of superstition, and the signs are pretty hard to miss. The linkage to gnostic-magical conceptions of secret knowledge is interesting and important, but for now the relevant point about these movements is their attitude toward physical nature: All are types of pantheism, stressing in one way or another that human beings should make obeisance to the cosmos.

Against this backdrop, the naturalism, materialism, economic determinism, and other isms of modern political theory come more clearly into focus. The common feature of all these movements is that they view nature itself as ultimate and sovereign. In essence, they make a god of nature. Once this point is grasped, a great deal that is otherwise puzzling in modern life becomes quite comprehensible. Much of it, indeed, is pantheism or other nature-worship, dressed up as secularism or science. Perhaps the most influential case in point is Darwinian evolution, which explicitly replaces (or identifies) God with physical nature, and in some versions even attributes to nature, or some agency within it, ineffable designs. Teilhard de Chardin, for example, speaks of the "consciousness" of matter as the driving force of evolution, a concept in which "the whole physical world contains a psyche but in differing concentrations."[2]

While Teilhard was a mystic and too explicitly religious for many present-day materialists, he differs only formally from more orthodox Darwinians. Consider the remarks of Julian Huxley, a mainstream spokesman for evolutionary doctrine, concerning the improbability of the view that human life came into being through an infinite sequence of mutations. The odds *against* this, he observes, "are given by a number with so many noughts that it would take the average novel to write it out, a number immensely greater than that of all the electrons and protons in the visible universe. This is a measure of our own inherent improbability—*an improbability of the same order of magnitude as that of a monkey with a typewriter producing the works of Shakespeare.*"

This colossal improbability, however, doesn't bother Huxley in the slightest. On the contrary, it merely demonstrates for him "*the immense power of natural selection* operating over the stretches of geological time ... *Just as it took the conscious activity of an outstanding mind* to produce [the works of Shakespeare], so it took two thousand million years of natural selection to generate [human life] ... The most apparently improbable adaptations—providing they can be regarded as conferring biological advantage—*are so many demonstrations of the ... power ... of natural selection.*" (Italics added.)[3] In other words, the more unlikely it seems that things could have have happened in this way, the mightier is the force of "natural selection" in making it occur.

In reading this, one might suppose he is in the presence of Tertullian or Sir Thomas Browne, both famous for the argument that the more impossible something seemed to be, the more devoutly they would believe it. Whatever the merits of Huxley's views about evolution on other grounds, this is a *religious* mind-set; it is the attitude of awestruck faith. The difference is that Tertullian and Sir Thomas put their faith in a God beyond the boundaries of the physical world; Huxley, with the pagans, reposes his in the Ouija board of nature.

Similar worship of physical nature is glaringly evident in the chief political movement of the day—environmentalism. While there are many levels of commitment involved in the environmental program, the overtones of neopagan nature worship are pervasive, and unmistakable. An example ready to hand is provided by Vice President Albert Gore, whose campaign-year book, *Earth in the Balance*, is redolent of pantheism. Gore speaks approvingly of the so-called "Gaia" (earth goddess) theory, which teaches that inorganic nature is "part of life itself." He also writes of "the living world," "the sacredness of the earth," "the sacredness of water," and so on—dragging in references from American Indians, prehistoric European nature worship, and other pagan sources to make his case.[4]

Gore argues that all of this is congruent with Christian faith, denying the historic difference between the pagan metaphysic and that of the Bible—which is, precisely, the view that nature itself is *not* divine, and emphatically not "sacred" in the sense that it is entitled to be worshipped. While this all-important distinction is blandly effaced by the vice president, it is fully appreciated, and stressed, by other environmentalists, who aren't encumbered by the need to run for office in a country still nominally Christian in its outlook.

Thus, in one Sierra Club tome, we encounter activist Gary Snyder, who developed "an interest in Oriental thought, in Buddhism, in American Indians, in tribalism, in communal living." Snyder studied Zen Buddhism in Japan, and having been offended by the "Old Testament's injunction to conquer the landscape," found more wisdom in the Buddhist precept: "Not only men but animals, not only animals but grasses and stones are capable of winning enlightenment." He explained that "ecology demonstrates on the empirical level the myriad interrelationships in nature. Buddhism, on another level, asserts the same interdependence of each of these elements."[5]

An overview of environmentalist thinking in this vein is provided by Alston Chase, himself a long-standing member of the movement but a dispassionate observer rather than supporter of its neopagan, Buddhist notions. As Chase points out, the Buddhist strain in environmental thought dates back at least to John Muir, and has been notable in many of its modern avatars. Justice William O. Douglas, who allowed that he preferred trees to people, did a stint at a Buddhist monastery. David Brower, founder of Friends of the Earth, asserted: "We are in a kind of religion, an ethic with regard to terrain, and the ethic is closest to Buddhist, I suppose." Paul Ehrlich described it as "a movement wrapped up in Zen Buddhism."[6]

The extent of all this, and the consequences of it, are truly astonishing to people who think the environmental movement is simply an effort to clean up the parks and stop pollution. The Buddha was supposedly badly shaken when he saw that farm laborers had disturbed some ants by turning up the earth. This is in keeping with much environmental agitation now, as in the waxing doctrine of the equality of species. One spokesman discourses, for instance, on chicken liberation, arguing that while some people say chickens are docile and dependent, "it is worth remembering that similar charges used to be made about the character of slaves." A second pushes even further, asking: "What, after all, does a rock want?"[7]

All of this may seem quite absurd, but the people speaking are not mere dwellers on the fringes of society; the extreme environmentalists and their pagan view of nature have had great impact on the course of national policy in such matters. They have enormous influence in the major environmental organizations, and these in turn have dictated federal legislation and regulatory action concerning wilderness areas, endangered species, wetlands, industrial development, automobile use, energy exploration, and other topics.

When taken to this level, the movement is in direct and obvious conflict with the religious traditions of the West. The existence of this theological combat is not usually noted in our public discourse, but is acknowledged often enough in intramural "green" discussion. Historian Lynn White put it this way in an influential essay, reprinted by Friends of the Earth in their *Environmental Handbook*:

"Especially in its Western form, Christianity is the most anthropocentric religion the world has ever seen . . . Man shares, in great measure, God's transcendence of nature. Christianity. . . . insisted that it is God's will that man exploit nature for his proper ends . . . *By destroying pagan animism, Christianity made it possible to exploit nature in a mood of indifference to the feelings of natural objects* . . . Man's effective monopoly on spirit in the world was confirmed, and the old inhibitions on the exploitation of nature crumbled."[8]* (Italics added.)

In terms of our larger theme, all of this has great significance—not only in the nature worship of the environmentalists, but in the resulting match-up of concepts on either side of the divide. Note that the side which *denies* the traditional religious notions of the West *also* denies the concepts of industrial progress and economic development of our society, while the side that *affirms* the traditional outlook is that which favors technology, industry, and economic advance. Again, the pairings are exactly the opposite of those suggested by the conventional teaching, which pits our religion against the workings of a free economy (see Chapter XVI).

A further example in this genre may be cited, and it is one that we have already touched on: The issue of abortion. Al-

---

* White thus brought the issues clearly into the open; but for most of the mystical neo-Buddhists, this was too dangerous a step to take. As Chase comments: "Realizing that in rejecting Christianity, they were far ahead of the rest of the country, few announced their apostasy. . . . Thus an open break with traditional religious beliefs was avoided. Instead, leaders of the new awakening conducted their own private searches for substitutes to the mainline faiths. In fear of offending our Judeo-Christian culture, they often confined their heresies to private correspondence or cloaked them in the patina of anthropological interest in primitive religions." (*Playing God in Yellowstone*, Harcourt Brace Jovanovich, 1987, p. 310)

though some prolife activists say it isn't—and pro-abortionists say it shouldn't be—this is very much a religious question, and it sorts out exactly along the lines of biblical vs. neopagan attitudes. Indeed, for the reasons stated, the notion that such an issue can be decided on any *other* than religious grounds is an impossibility, since the questions involved are precisely those to which basic axioms must provide the answers.

This issue, in fact, is a perfect illustration of nearly all the points we have been making. Science, for example, can tell us much about the unborn child; it can tell us when there is a heart beat, when features form, when there is stirring, and so on. It can develop procedures for treating the unborn baby in the womb, through the practice of fetology. It may even tell us that this is a human life as biologists define it. What science cannot tell us, however, is how we should treat this unborn baby; whether we should construe it as a person, and hence a legal life as well as a biological one; or whether we should define it as a mere lump of protoplasm, to be disposed of at the discretion of its mother and her physician.

On this question, as on many others, the division between the biblical and pagan worldviews is quite clear: The Christian tradition from the earliest period says the unborn child is a human life that deserves respect and ought to be protected*; the pagan view tells us it is not a legal person, and thus entitled to no protection. According to the religious axioms we profess, we will supply our answers to these questions. The point was acknowledged, intriguingly enough, by Justice Harry Blackmun, who delivered the pro-abortion decision in *Roe v. Wade.* His opinion notes, for instance, that "abortion was practiced in Greek times as well as in the Roman era, and that 'it was resorted to without scruple.' . . . Greek and Roman law

---

* Thus Tertullian: "We are forbidden to terminate the life of the womb . . . to prevent the child from being born is merely premature murder . . . What is to be born is fully human . . ." (Herbert A. Musurillo, S. J., ed., *The Fathers of the Primitive Church*, Mentor, 1966, p. 159)

afforded little protection to the unborn . . . Ancient religion did not ban abortion."

The chief exception to this in pagan times, Blackmun notes, was the Hippocratic Oath, attributed to the Pythagoreans: "But with the end of antiquity a decided change took place. Resistance against suicide and against abortion became common. The oath became popular. The emerging teachings of Christianity were in agreement with the Pythagorean ethic." There then follows a discussion of protections afforded the unborn under the English common law—focused mainly on the question of "quickening," or first discernible signs of life, given the medical knowledge of the era.[9]

It is not made very plain in this discussion why Blackmun considers the views of ancient heathens relevant to American constitutional law (except, perhaps, as a method of debunking the Hippocratic Oath); he simply presents the pagan and Christian views as if both were entitled to respectful hearing—with the weight of the evidence going to the pagans. He thus tells us, almost in as many words, that permissive abortion is a move away from Christianity to a resurgent pagan ethic.

A further illustration of the theme is the campaign to change societal views of homosexuality—to treat it as an "alternative lifestyle," as valid in its way as heterosexual conduct. Among other things, this is a reversion to pagan ways of thinking. Most obviously, homosexuality was accepted among the ancient Greeks and supplies the premise of Platonic discussions about the nature of love. Similar views prevailed in Babylon, Egypt, and imperial Rome. All of this was unequivocally condemned by the religion of the Bible. As cogently argued by Dennis Prager, the current effort to relegitimize homosexuality is thus an attempt to turn Western culture back to pagan attitudes and behaviors.[10]

If we view other issues through the lenses of this analysis— e.g., "earth goddess" variants of feminism or idolatry of Indians—the true character of the modern political-cultural struggle becomes apparent. On the question of prayer in the schools, for instance, it is clear beyond all peradventure that the First Amendment was not intended to bar such practices from the classroom, or indeed from any other public places (see Chapter XV). Yet from the standpoint of modern theorists, this is nothing to the purpose. Acknowledgement of the God of the Bible is offensive on the face of it, since it directly challenges the naturalist, neopagan precepts of the secular religion.

On the other hand, it is considered perfectly proper for children from religious homes to be taught the precepts of Darwinian-Huxleyan evolution, extreme environmentalism, the value-free "alternative lifestyle" view of homosexuality and sexual conduct generally, and other neopaganism in their school work. It is asserted that such teaching is nonreligious, but, as we have seen, this is an impossibility. By such instruction, axioms about the origin of the world and the meaning of human existence are imparted, even as the competing axioms of traditional faith are banished.* Children may be taught the precepts of neopagan nature worship; they may not be taught the precepts of the Bible.

All of which explains much of the hostility visited on the Christian right and anyone else who presumes to speak up for the biblical axioms. These axioms are denied by neopagan secularism, and are to be supplanted by the naturalist credo of the modern era. Any attempt to propagate biblical religion within the civil order, to make it the premise of our politics, amounts to an attempt at theological counter-revolution.

---

* In certain cases, the discrimination is explicit—as in the Oregon school that supplanted Christmas with a "winter solstice program," in which children "partake of the sun and moon cake," "seat themselves according to their astrological signs," and are entertained by "New Age dancing and pagan drumming." (Cited by state Rep. Ron Gamble, D-PA., June 12, 1992) Two headlines from news stories on a single day sum up the problem in a nutshell: "School Board to Consider Condom Distribution," and "Justices Bar Bible Handouts at School." (*Washington Times*, May 18, 1993)

Should such attempts succeed, neopaganism itself must be displaced. Using the term as it is employed in popular discourse, there always is, and must be, an "establishment of religion" in our society, or any other. The question being fought out today is, quite simply, which religion shall be established.

8

The Birth of Liberty

THE RESURGENT PAGANISM of our era is neither unconscious nor accidental. The modern intellect has had a lengthy love affair with pagan culture, in which the achievements and mindset of the ancients are held up as models for our thought and forerunners of our institutions.

This outlook is of course the reciprocal of a distaste for Christianity, although some of it at this point may be put down to sheer confusion. It was the religion and metaphysics of the Bible that overthrew the pagan state, then was subjected to a neopagan onslaught at the era of the Renaissance, redoubled by the French Enlightenment and its offspring. While the larger history is nowadays neglected, the religious-secular quarrels that we experience are in direct descent from this enduring conflict, dating from the remotest ages of society.

Not, to be sure, that the issues are exactly the same as they were back then, given a culture suffused for two millennia with the beliefs and habits of our religion. Since much of what we take for granted in our politics has been shaped by this experience, a neopaganism following in its wake is different in many ways from the original. Yet despite this evident distinction, the crucial points of controversy remain essentially what they always have been.

By far the major *political* issue between these competing worldviews is the question of human freedom. Obviously, the principal conflict is theological, but this leads for reasons noted to countless disagreements in the realm of statecraft. Contention about nature and society, the significance of the individual, and the power of political officials marked the pagan-biblical confrontation from the outset, and it continues to do so now. For those who care anything about human freedom, these are important matters to get straight.

Unfortunately, most of what we are taught about this subject is false—is, indeed, entirely backwards—and error committed at this level leads to mistaken conclusions at many others. In the conventional history lesson, paganism is identified with the cause of liberty, Christianity with oppression. We are used to hearing much about Periclean Athens or Republican Rome, the thought of Plato and Aristotle, and so on, as if these were the ancestors of our freedom. Concerning all the major points at issue, such teachings are woefully mistaken.

This is not the place nor am I the person to enter into the subtleties of Greek philosophy or Christian apologetics, the philosophical battles between them, the degree to which Western culture absorbed some classical components, and the like. These are tasks that have been undertaken by some of the profoundest scholars of our era, and the reader interested in this aspect of the topic is referred to the excellent studies they have published.[1*] Our purpose here, as elsewhere, is more limited—to examine the impact of the competing doctrines in the realm of politics, with special attention to the question of human freedom.

Within this context—which is certainly broad enough—the critical proposition is as follows: *The ancients knew nothing of our ideas of limited government and personal liberty, and*

* See the bibliographical discussion beginning at page 325.

given their peculiar conception of the world could not have done so. Whatever our views about the classical contribution otherwise, in this regard there is little disagreement—though you would scarcely know it from the way that we are taught our history.

The point may be conveniently made by reference to Aristotle, in many ways the most agreeable of the pagans, often cited as a precursor of our institutions. Granted that there are many things in Aristotle that have been received into our culture, most notably in the writings of St. Thomas and the other medieval schoolmen (who also, it should be added, gave the philosopher a gloss that was less Greek than Christian).[2] But so far as human freedom is concerned, Aristotle is about as far from our beliefs as it is possible to get. Consider these excerpts from the *Politics*:

"... that some should rule and others be ruled is not only necessary, but expedient; from the hour of their birth, some are marked out for subjection, others for rule ... It is clear ... that some men are by nature free, and others slaves, and that for these latter slavery is both expedient and right ... against men who though intended by nature to be governed, will not submit ... war is naturally just ... we cannot consider all those to be citizens who are necessary to the existence of the state ... no man can practice virtue who is living the life of a mechanic or laborer ... the good of the state and not the individual is the proper subject of political thought and speculation ... The citizen should be moulded to suit the form of government under which he lives ... Neither must we suppose that any of the citizens belongs to himself, for they all belong to the state."[3]

It is apparent that, however much we may learn from Aristotle on other matters, he is hardly a spokesman for personal freedom or limited government, and could not conceivably be the source of our ideas about these subjects. Had we quoted

instead the works of Plato—well known for their authoritarianism—the point would be even more explicit.* In this
respect, if not in others, both philosophers were typical of
pagan culture, which routinely subjected the individual to the
state.

Where, then, do the ideas and practices of freedom come
from? We can begin to answer that question by turning from the
philosophy of the ancients to the pages of the Bible, where we
encounter a different mindset altogether. There is, for instance,
the famous passage from the Book of Samuel, recounting the
episode (once cited frequently by writers on such matters) in
which the children of Israel demand a king like all the other
nations. Samuel confers with the Lord and tells the Israelites
what will happen if they get their wish:

"This will be the manner of the king that shall reign over you.
He will take your sons and appoint them for himself, for his
chariots, and to be his horsemen, and some shall run before his
chariots;

"And he will appoint him captains over thousands and captains over fifties; and will set them to ear his ground; and to
reap his harvest, and to make his instruments of war, and
instruments of his chariots;

"And he will take your daughters to be confectionaries, and
to be cooks, and to be bakers;

"And he will take your fields, and your vineyards, and your
oliveyards, even the best of them to give to his officers and give
them to his servants;

"And he will take the tenth of your seed, and of your vineyards, and give them to his officers, and to his servants;

"And he will take your menservants, and your maidservants,

---

* Among other things, Plato recommended rule by philosopher-kings and
"guardians," sharing of women and children among these, eugenic breeding,
marriages controlled by the state, infanticide, abortion, and strictest censorship,
all aimed at moulding citizens to the design of his ideal republic.

and your goodliest young men, and your asses, and put them to his work;

"He will take the tenth of your sheep; and ye shall be his servants;

"And ye shall cry out in that day because of your king which ye shall have chosen you; and the Lord will not hear you in that day."—Samuel I, 8.

All too obviously, where skepticism of political power is concerned, it is the biblical viewpoint, not Aristotle's, that is our own. Here is no assumption that the state should mould the individual, that some people are by nature slaves, that the citizens "all belong to the state," or other such authoritarian dogma. Rather we find a mistrust of kings, concern about the burdens they impose, fear of those who wield the sword of secular power. Similar attitudes would be expressed, at considerable length and on many occasions, in the ensuing Christian era.

The point is not merely that the biblical view of kings contrasts so sharply with the opinion of the ancients; it is instead that the underlying theologies of the two cultures were such as to lead to these divergent outcomes. The classical way of thinking led inexorably to untrammeled power in the state, and to subjugation of the individual. The biblical model leads to limitations on that power, and hence to freedom.

Of the many religious differences that contribute to these effects, the starting point, as observed in Chapter VII, is a total contrast in views of nature. In the pagan world, nature and its components were seen as aspects of divinity—mysterious, ultimate, and eternal. The normative view was pantheistic—another concept we have already met with. The forms of this were many, but the underlying ideas were pretty much the same. There was a god of the sun, of the moon, of the sea, the forest, the wind, and countless others, including those related to specific households and other particular locations.

In this way of thinking, the individual was everywhere subject to compulsions—first by nature itself, thereafter by the state. A world presumably ruled by powerful and capricious deities was a hazardous and baffling place. It was beset by forces that could dictate events, prosper or ruin a harvest, flood the river or dry it up, lead to success or failure in battle, produce calamity or safe conduct in a voyage, and so on. These and many other aspects of life were thought to be governed by spirits and demons inhabiting nature.

The psychological subjection entailed by such an outlook is difficult for us to grasp. "The whole of nature," T. R. Glover notes, "teemed with beings whom we find it hard to name. . . . These nature spirits . . . were far from being the only superhuman beings that encompassed man . . . The whole world believed in divination . . . The flight of birds, the entrails of beasts, rain, thunder, lightning, everything was a means of divination . . . That superstition so gross was accompanied by a paralyzing belief in magic, enchantment, miracle, astrology and witchcraft generally is not surprising."[4]

In as clear a case of "theological determinism" as history affords, pagan societies had political systems that reflected these ideas, including elaborate public ceremonials, sacrifices, and priestly offices. They also had a distinctive view of state authority, in whatever form or under whatever name it functioned. In this approach, the foremost job of the political ruler was to communicate with and appease the deities in the natural order—"to integrate society and nature," in Henri Frankfort's terminology. The king or magistrate was thus the leader in a religious cult, which made the state the vital linkage between humanity and the gods. The political effect of this arrangement was immense.

Most obviously, it meant the state and its rulers were assumed to have a magical, sacred character. This was notoriously true of semi-Oriental regimes in ancient Egypt and Sumeria, or the Roman Empire, where the monarch himself was thought to be divine, or nearly so, but it was also evident in ancient Greece, including the Athenian democracy. We are so accustomed to hearing the Athenians or Romans of the Republic described as people like ourselves that this enormously important fact, and its political meaning, are frequently neglected. In these societies, according to Fustel de Coulanges:

"Man felt himself at every moment dependent upon his gods, and consequently upon the priest king, who was placed between them and himself . . . He it was who knew the formula and the prayers which the gods could not resist. . . A king was a sacred being . . . the man without whose aid no prayer was heard, no sacrifice accepted . . . [A Roman consul] has in his hands the auspices, the rites, prayer, protection of the gods. A consul is something more than a man; he is a mediator between man and the divinity; to his fortune is attached the public fortune; he is, as it were, the tutelary genius of the city."[5]

From such a view of the state and its officials there arose an authoritarian brand of politics. Self-evidently, this way of thinking united secular and religious powers in one—precluding many notions that we associate with freedom. The king or emperor was also a *magus*, if not in fact a deity. The physical forces of compulsion were fused with spiritual authority, giving the state a total lien on the affections and energies of its people. Nor could there be any effective appeal to a higher law above this power, *since the state itself was the arbiter of what that law intended.* (The affinity of this concept to modern notions of top-down command should be fairly plain, and will be examined further.)

Given this combination of beliefs, such ideas as personal freedom and limited government could scarcely be imagined. In the pagan system, the individual was thoroughly surrounded by and subjected to the state; it encompassed every aspect of his being, and routinely sacrificed his interests to its own. This helps explain the fact that Plato and Aristotle simply assumed, no questions asked, that all the ends of life should be enveloped by the state, or *polis.* ("By persuasion or constraint," as Plato put it, the law "will unite the citizens in harmony, making them share whatever benefits each class can contribute to the common good; and its purpose in forming men of that spirit was not that each should be left to go his own way, but that they should be instruments in binding the community into one.")[6]

Indifference to the well-being of the individual was universal in the social practices of the ancients. We have discussed the opinion of Justice Blackmun concerning pagan views about abortion; he notes with manifest approval that ancient societies thought there was nothing much the matter with abortion, and uses this as a partial sanction for his ruling that we should practice it ourselves. He fails to add, however, that the ancient Greeks and Romans also believed in outright infanticide and the wholesale "exposure" (abandonment) of children. It would be interesting to learn if we should adopt these pagan customs also:

"Most of the new born infants [born to slaves] were killed or exposed. Even in philanthropic Athens, the father had the right to expose his children, and new born infants were hardly ever picked up on roads and public places except to be made into slaves" . . . "The state was under no obligation to suffer any of its citizens to be deformed. It therefore commanded a father to whom such a son was born to have him put to death. This law was found in the ancient codes of Sparta and Rome. We do not know that it existed at Athens; we know only that Aristotle and Plato included it in their ideal codes . . ."[7] *

Equally indicative was the pagan view of slavery. As seen in our passages from Aristotle, pagan thought at what was arguably its most congenial found nothing offensive in the practice, considering it instead to be quite normal. Servitude was so common in the ancient world, indeed, that hardly anybody

---

* Thus Plato: ". . . only the offspring of the better unions should be kept . . . those of the inferior parents and any of the children of the rest that are born defective will be hidden away, in some appropriate manner that must be kept secret . . . [Of certain unions] no child, if any be conceived, shall be brought to light, or, if they cannot prevent its birth, to dispose of it on the understanding that no such child should be reared." (F.M. Cornford, ed., *The Republic of Plato*, Oxford, 1957, pp. 159–161)

thought to question it—although there were some doubts expressed at a late period by the Stoics. This was notoriously true of Sparta, but was true as well of "democratic" Athens.

While we don't know the exact number of slaves in Attica at the time of Pericles, there is no question that it was large—and that the workaday economy depended on it. Tocqueville cites an estimate of 20,000 free men vs. upwards of 300,000 slaves, though this seems excessive. Zimmern, a great fan of the Greeks, believed there were fewer Athenians in servitude, perhaps 75,000 to 150,000. A comprehensive estimate by Ehrenburg suggests that anywhere from one-third to one-half of the total population were slaves.

Whatever the figures may have been, the prevalence of slavery in Athenian society is obvious—a fact complacently accepted (or else ignored entirely) in panegyrics to its "democracy" and "freedom." One enthusiast for the Greeks argues that the Athenian assembly was not an urban rabble (and is thus to be admired) precisely *because* "there was not a single major job, domestic, industrial, or agricultural, now performed by hired men which was not almost exclusively performed by slaves."[8] (An argument also casually tossed off by Rousseau.)

The slavery prevalent in Greece was even more so in ancient Rome. Gibbon tells us that, at the time of Claudius, fully half the population of the empire consisted of slaves—a number he puts at 120 million human beings. Other estimates provided by his editor suggest the proportion of slaves to free men might have been as high as two or three to one. A modern authority gives lower figures, calculating that, at the time of Trajan, slaves in the city of Rome itself amounted to a third of the population.[9] As to the condition of these wretched people, Uhlhorn observes:

"A slave was not regarded by the ancients as a man; he had neither a free will nor any claim whatever to justice, nor any capacity for virtue ... Flores characterizes the slaves as another race of men ... The slave was not a person, but only a thing whose owner had in it all the rights of property, to use it or misuse it. The slave himself had no rights . . . His testimony was inadmissible in a court of justice. If his deposition was needed, he was subjected to torture. Only in this way could his evidence have weight."[10]

There is much more like this available in the record, but the point no doubt has been sufficiently made. The pagan societies of Greece and Rome practiced slavery on a systematic basis, and thought it was the most natural thing in the world. It is true, as we well know, that slavery continued into the Christian epoch, and in particular continued into the history of the United States.* The constant tendency in the Christian world, however, was toward the condemnation and amelioration of this evil, which we see occurring wherever the records are sufficient to assess the outcome.† The whole approach, and ultimate result, were totally different from that prevailing in antiquity—when the best minds of the era approved the practice and came up with sophisticated reasons for its existence.

These matters are not much discussed in the conventional treatment, as indeed they cannot be if the pretense is going to be sustained that the pagans gave us our ideas of liberty, or that our political culture is descended from these sources. A system that endorses slavery and infanticide, which denies any importance to the individual, and which exalts the power of the state beyond all limits, bears no resemblance to our concept of freedom. What it closely resembles, instead, is the totalitarian systems of the modern era—a resemblance that is more than coincidental.

---

* Where its intellectual defenders drew heavily on the example of the pagans. See the comment of George Fitzhugh (1850): "Liberty and equality are new things under the sun. The free states of antiquity abounded with slaves." (Eric McKitrick, ed., *Slavery Defended*, Prentice-Hall. 1963)

† For example, Maitland's calculations of the reduction in English slavery and steady increase in the number of free men in medieval England, as reflected in Domesday Book. (*Domesday Book and Beyond*, Norton, 1966, pp. 35–36) The persistent efforts of the church to mitigate and do away with slavery are recounted, *e.g.*, by Harold Berman, *Law and Revolution* (Harvard, 1983), pp. 65, 320, 617)

In this respect, another passage from Aristotle may prove instructive: ". . . when a whole family, or some individual happens to be so pre-eminent in virtues as to surpass all others, then it is just that they should be the royal family and supreme over all, or that this one citizen should be the king of the whole nation . . . *the only alternative is that he should have the supreme power, and that mankind should obey him, not in turn, but always.*"[11] (Italics added.) This also was a common view among the pagans, applied to kings, lawgivers, and other heroic figures. Aristotle called them "great-souled men." Plato wrote of "divine men" and "golden" men ordained to rule above "the herd." One Pythagorean writer expressed it: "The monarch has an irrepressible authority (and is therefore not limited by consent); he is a living law; he is like a god among men."[12] *

From this background, it becomes much easier to understand not only the *lex regia* of the Romans but also the "superman" concepts vaunted by classicists such as Nietzsche, Hegel, and other neopagan devotees of power. It is not so much that the modern absolutists derived their views from pagan forebears, though such influences obviously existed, but that like assumptions in questions of religion led to similar outcomes in the state. In both cases, a humanity pulled down into the vortex of mysterious nature, deprived of reference points beyond its workings, required a more-than-human leader to solve the riddles of existence.

Clearly, the ideas and institutions of human liberty would have had a difficult time emerging from this cluster of assump-

---

* Even Cicero—the ancient most admired and emulated in the Christian West—spoke of the brave and good who are "intrinsically divine." As Cochrane comments: "In these conclusions, the Latin version of classicism proclaims its inability to rise above the cult of power. In so doing it paved the way for the recognition of Augustus Caesar as a political god. We are now in a position to see the point to which the pursuit of 'strictly human excellence' . . . has brought us; we have crossed the frontier of mere humanity and entered into the reign of supermen . . . Henceforth, the hopes and expectations of mankind are fixed upon the 'august' being to whom they have placed themselves in tutelage." (*Christianity and Classical Culture*, Oxford, 1957, pp. 112–113)

tions, and they didn't. Instead, they came from the worldview of the Bible, which counters pagan doctrine at every point along the road to freedom. With the advent of biblical revelation, virtually everything relating to our subject is transformed, beginning with the idea of Divinity itself, then spreading to all aspects of thought and practice. The view of physical nature, in particular, is radically altered. Monotheism replaces the pantheism of the ancients, and the idea of creation *ex nihilo* supplants the notion of an eternal cosmos. The physical world is God's creation, bears the imprint of its maker, is harmonious and intelligible, but is not divine; nor is any other object or being in the created order.

The total difference in approach—and its implications for the psychology of the West—may be seen in the challenge to the Greeks laid down by Clement of Alexandria: "Why, pray you, do you infect life with idols, imagining winds, air, fire, earth, sticks, stones, iron, this world itself to be gods? . . . Let none of you worship the sun; rather let him yearn for the maker of the sun. Let no one deify the universe; rather let him seek after the creator of the universe . . . He is always uniformly and unchangeably impartial, measures and weighs all things, encircling and sustaining the nature of the universe by His justice as by a balance."[13] Similar statements might be cited from Irenaeus, Tertullian, Augustine, and other fathers of the early church.*

In metaphysical terms, this altered view of nature is the bedrock of our civilization, turning upside-down the paradigms of the ancients, and laying the foundation for virtually every-

---

* Augustine says, for instance: "No pious person worships the world for the true God"; "Let us Christians, therefore, give thanks to the Lord our God—not to heaven and earth . . . but to Him who has made heaven and earth," and many words to similar effect. He attacks astrology as "a delusion," and denounces the idea that "the souls of the world and its parts are the true gods." (*The City of God*, Modern Library, 1950, pp. 236, 138, 154, 213) This is, among other things, a direct rebuttal of Plato, who taught that the world itself "is a blessed god." (*Timaeus and Critias*, Penguin, 1977, p. 34)

thing that we regard as being distinctly Western. From the outset, defenders of the orthodox religion steadfastly maintained the doctrine that God had created both form and matter out of nothing. This meant that physical nature was neither autonomous nor eternal—these being attributes of divinity—and also that the world had a beginning, had existed for a definite period, and would eventually have an end. From these and related conceptions in the biblical teaching, as shall be seen, we get the most characteristic features of our culture.

Nowhere was the transformation more dramatic than in Western attitudes about the state. In the scriptural view, the king, or emperor, or *polis*, no longer plays the magical-religious role assigned by pagan doctrine, and cannot do so. Since there *are* no deities in nature, the job of the political leader in appeasing them, in integrating their caprices with the workings of society, is abolished. From this development we derive the notion of kings as order-keeping, secular officials—rather than sorcerers micromanaging a "low crowd of gods," as St. Augustine caustically phrased it. Frankfort explains it this way:

"The transcendentalism of Hebrew religion prevented kingship from assuming the profound significance which it possessed in Egypt and Mesopotamia. It excluded, in particular, the king's being instrumental in the integration of society and nature. It denied the possibility of such integration. The Hebrew king normally functioned in the profane sphere, not the sacred sphere . . . The king played little part in the cult . . . He did not interpret the divine will; that . . . was the task of the priests . . . [thus biblical religion] bereft kingship of a function which it exercised all over the near East, where its principal task lay in the maintenance of harmony with the gods of nature . . ."14

The distinction between the Creator and His creation profoundly affected the powers of rulers in other ways as well. In the biblical view, if nature itself was not divine, neither was any human being. All were creatures of God, and bore the image of their maker; but none was *himself* divine, or even nearly so. Whatever their earthly talents or inequalities, men were men, and therefore sinners; there were no "supermen," "human gods," or "great souled men" who could do whatever they wished and rule at pleasure over others. All were equally subject to the law of God. Nor could there be any question of worshipping kings and emperors, as Jews and Christians steadfastly refused to do.

This matter of the sovereignty of God, and the refusal to worship any creature or any aspect of creation, is at the root of the nonstop prophetic war against idolatry, the defiance of Shadrach, Meshach, and Abednego, and much else that we read in the biblical story. Christians such as Polycarp and Justin Martyr, and many others whose names are less well known, were perfectly willing to obey the emperor in secular matters; but they were not willing to bow down and worship him. The earliest Christian martyrs were put to the sword precisely for this offense—refusing to swear "by the genius of our Lord the emperor."[15] The first half of *The City of God* is a dissertation on the theme that nothing in the created order is entitled to be worshipped.

We see the identical issue in the early councils of the church, chiefly called to assert the absolute transcendence of God against heretical notions that would lead to any form of creature-worship. These councils seem almost incomprehensible to the modern intellect—as in the debate over whether Christ was of "like substance" or "same substance" with the Father, whether the Son was "created" or "begotten." But these questions went to the very heart of Christian doctrine—that nothing human or created *as such* could be worshipped as divinity ("same substance" and "begotten" were thus the orthodox responses). Understanding this point about the Trinity is crucial in addressing not only matters of idolatry or emperor worship, but all subsequent efforts to "divinize" anything but God Himself. *No believer in biblical religion can grant divin-*

*ity to the state, or any ruler, or any being or object in the created order.**

From this drastic scaling back of earthly power, we get still other distinctive features of our culture. In essence, the conceptual space vacated by the state was occupied by other forces in society, appropriate to the realm of grace rather than the methods of coercion. Because the king or emperor was no longer the mediator of divine intent, there arose a separate source of spiritual awareness and instruction: the prophets of the Old Testament, the Christian churches under the dispensation of the New. *Not only was there a law above the king, there was a spiritual force that could construe it, independent of the power that he wielded.* This is a departure of such immense significance in the growth of Western freedom that it would be impossible to overstate it.

From this background, we can more readily understand the skeptical approach to kingship expressed in Samuel—and its jarring contrast to the view of Aristotle. Samuel could speak out against the power of kings precisely because they were *not* the sole or even chief interpreters of divine intent, because they too were under the law of God, because God's message could be imparted independent of their will. The prophets and the church address the issues of the spirit, without the intervention of the state, while political rulers perform the secular tasks of keeping order.

The biblical focus on religious virtue as a matter of will and conscience likewise constricted the authority of the state. We have noted the emphasis placed by Aquinas on the inner, voluntary nature of right decision. The point is stressed repeatedly by Augustine, who tells us, *e.g.*, that "what is here required is not a bodily action, but an inward disposition. The sacred seat of virtue is the heart . . ."; that "these precepts pertain rather to the

---

* An excellent discussion of these early councils and their import is provided by R. J. Rushdoony in *The Foundations of Social Order* (Craig Press, 1968).

inward disposition of the heart than to the actions which are done in the sight of men"; that any who supposes that secular rulers can exercise power over faith "falls into an even greater error"; and many other statements to like effect. The spiritual realm is inward, while secular politics deals only with externals.[16]

It is from these interconnected notions that we derive our ideas about the division of church and civil government, or "separation of church and state," as we now call it. Augustine and Aquinas are generally viewed as the principal fathers of medieval Christendom; as the foregoing suggests, they may also be looked upon as the fathers of libertarian statecraft, whose basic function is to provide a framework of external order, but which has no competence in questions of belief and conscience. This view of the matter, as we have noticed, was also professed by America's Founding Fathers; far from being the work of secular neopagan theory, it was a product of biblical revelation, totally contrary to the practice of the ancients.

Finally, as the scriptural model scaled down the power of the state, it simultaneously raised up the individual. Given the usual emphasis on the "individualism" of the pagan era or the Renaissance, versus the long slumber of the Christian Middle Ages, this too is a point that is much neglected. Yet it is central to our understanding of the cause of freedom. We have discussed the "pessimism" in the biblical concept of human nature, as expressed in the idea of Original Sin; but there is also a "Christian optimism," as Gilson calls it, rooted in the idea that human beings are God's children, rational beings in His intelligible creation.

This way of looking at the person gives rise to a form of individualism unknowable to the ancients. It begins with affirming the inherent worth of every human being—created in the image of God, possessed of an immortal soul, embarked on a dramatic journey in quest of its salvation. Such a conception poses a relationship of the human species to divinity completely different from that obtaining in the pagan era: one in which each individual has a personal link to the Creator of all existence, independent of earthly power. This tremendous concept and its transforming influence in terms of human personality is stressed repeatedly in Judaic and Christian doctrine.*

Hence the radically different view of slavery pronounced so often in Christian teaching. Compare to the normative pagan attitude on the subject, for instance, the comments of Augustine, denouncing "the inconceivable horror of slavery": "[God] did not intend that His rational creature, who was made in His image, should have dominion over anything but the irrational creation—not man over man, but man over the beasts ... It is a name ... introduced by sin and not by nature."¹⁷ This is the view of human liberty and equality in the sight of God that in time would leaven the whole of Western culture.

This biblical individualism has been well known, and heartily disliked, by the opponents of Western faith. Its resistant character was fully recognized by the Roman emperors. It was understood as well by modern foes of biblical religion such as Nietzsche, Comte, and Russell—all of whom attacked

---

* In Hebraic religion, as Will Herberg notes, "man's personality is taken as the inexpugnable reality of his being; it is because man is a person that he can hear God's word and respond to it." ". . . Greco-Oriental religion affirms an impersonal immanent reality; Hebraism proclaims its allegiance to the Lord of life and history, the Creator of the Universe, a transcendent Person with whom man can establish genuinely personal relations." (*Judaism and Modern Man*, Meridian, 1953, pp. 50, 53–54)

Gilson puts it as follows: "Created of God as a distinct individuality . . . man is henceforth the protagonist of a drama, which is none other than that of his own destiny . . . We have now but one choice, between a misery and a beatitude, both equally eternal. Nothing could be more resistant than an individuality of this kind, foreseen, willed, elected of God, indestructible as the divine decree that gave it birth; but nothing also could be more alien to the philosophy of Plato, or to that of Aristotle . . . From the opening of the Christian era it is no more of man that we speak but of the human person . . . The whole interior life of the Christian man ... consists in gradually building up, constantly rectifying, unceasingly perfecting a personality which will only attain its full stature in a future life." (*The Spirit of Medieval Philosophy*, Scribners, 1940, pp. 193, 206, 203)

Christianity for its "individualism." Comte saw Christian belief as the great stumbling block to his collectivist ambitions, since it "sanctified personality with an existence which, by linking each man directly with an infinite power, profoundly isolated him from humanity." We may dissent from Comte's conclusions while acknowledging that he was shrewd enough to know his enemy.[18]

Our passages from Aristotle and Samuel thus stand duty for two radically different notions of the political order—differences that would recur, with amazing regularity, throughout the course of Western history. From the pagan view of pervasive power in the state, and its magical or god-like rulers confronting a mass of men perceived as lesser beings, there arose a highly repressive form of government, and a theory to back it up. In essence, this theory said the state and its rulers were the source of all authority, because they were its linkage to the deities in nature. It is this view that provides us with the *lex regia* of the Romans, and all its many variations. "The king is the law speaking" because he is in communion with divinity, as ordinary men are not; his rule is the price that men must pay for harmony with the gods, and for order in the state.

From a biblical standpoint, conferring such total power on a ruler or body of men, and the reasons given for it, are equally repugnant. No human being can be treated as divine, or above the law, or entitled to make his will the rule of society's existence. Nor can the people over whom the rulers wield their power be treated as a herd of atomistic beings, animals, or objects; they are persons created in God's image, possessed of dignity and reason, and capable of living out their earthly lives in a regime of liberty. Such was the foundation of our political culture, and the provenance of our freedom.

9

The Making of Magna Carta

In POPULAR SPEECH, "medieval" and "feudal" are routinely used as epithets—sometimes thoughtless, sometimes not. Casually uttered, the words convey a sense of the decrepit or outmoded. In self-conscious usage, they have a more particular meaning. To say that something is medieval is to suggest an outlook that is not only old and probably boring, but also imbued with the beliefs and values of Christianity. And these, according to the standard teaching, are specifically out of fashion.

Indeed, the terms "medieval" and "Middle Ages" are condescending by their nature—suggesting an entire millennium of Christian piety and custom was merely an intermission in the progress of the species.* This was, supposedly, a kind of dead time between the collapse of the Roman Empire and the rise of modern civilization—a span of one thousand years or so when nothing very interesting happened, and what did occur was generally distasteful: The reign of superstition and autocracy, mental stagnation, a long slumber of the human spirit.

As ever, the point of such discussion is to establish an inverse ratio between the reign of faith and the ideas of Western liberty.

---

* As "Renaissance" and "Enlightenment" are the reverse; if something is "reborn" (in this case, pagan culture and its attitudes), then whatever had killed it is now rejected and condemned by history; the "enlightenment," for its part, allegedly overcame the preceding centuries of Christian darkness.

When Christianity held sway, the Catholic Church was the most powerful institution in the world, and Europe known as "Christendom," the cause of freedom allegedly languished. Only when Christian precepts were rejected at the Renaissance did we get the good things of the modern era: scientific exploration and "humanist" inquiry, the consolidation of the nation-state, the rise of democratic practice.

In the liberal version of our history, this is perhaps the central teaching. It is from this view of the Middle Ages, beyond all other sources, that we derive the notion of an impassable gulf between our faith and our free institutions. If this enormous span of Christian civilization really was a period of repression, then we have empirical proof that our religious beliefs and political freedoms are in conflict—the "facts" that undergird the irreligious theory. The accuracy of this treatment is thus a matter of the first importance.

We have earlier noted some matters of record suggesting that this view of the medieval period is mistaken. This is, if anything, an understatement. We can come a good deal nearer the truth, in fact, by standing the familiar thesis on its head: as an abundant record demonstrates, *it was the era of the Middle Ages that nourished the institutions of free government, in contrast to the ideas and customs of the ancients.* Conversely, it was the rejection of medieval doctrine at the Renaissance that put all Western liberties at hazard, leading to autocracy in Europe and despotic practice in the modern era.

To grasp the fallacy of the usual view, we need only reflect a moment on Magna Carta, the primary document in the history of our freedoms. Magna Carta is a lengthy catalogue of safeguards against the abuse of power, guarantees of religious liberties, legal rights, taxation by consent, and so on. These form the basis of much that was embodied in the common law, as discussed in Chapter V, by which the liberties of Englishmen (and Americans) were tenaciously defended. No historian can ignore the central role of Magna Carta in the development of libertarian practice.

But Magna Carta is, of course, a *medieval* document; it was agreed to at the zenith of the Middle Ages, and represented all the leading tendencies of the era. It expressed the medieval concept of the state, employed the political methods common to the age, and was achieved through the combined exertions of two supremely medieval institutions—the Catholic clergy and the feudal barons. That this landmark in the growth of Western freedom was based on medieval sources suggests, to put it mildly, something erroneous in the standard treatment.

Confusion on this point is an extension of that considered in the preceding chapter. Contrary to the standard history, as we have seen, the pagan world was not even close to understanding our approach to freedom. Only with the advent of biblical religion and its distinctive views of Deity, nature, man, and government, did people begin to grasp the idea of limited power in the state. The era in which these notions were assembled into the edifice of freedom was, precisely, the Middle Ages. It was in this period that biblical attitudes toward secular power, and many other things, suffused the whole of European culture, and thereby created the institutions of the free society.

As might be expected from biblical ideas of kingship, the foremost political concept of the Middle Ages was *constitutionalism*—establishing limits on the power of kings, and on the scope of government in general. In the doctrines and practices of the era, as concerned the state, there was no place for the *lex regia* of the ancients. "Medieval theory," as von Gierke comments, "was unanimous that the power of the state stood below the rules of Natural and above the rules of positive law . . . During the Middle Ages we can scarcely detect the beginning of that opinion which would free the sovereign . . . from the bonds of the Natural Law . . ."[1]

Of the several sources that embodied this idea of limits, the foremost, by a tremendous margin, was the church. The point is as significant as it is ironic. Nowhere is the conventional history more misleading than in its portrayal of medieval clerics as agents of repression. On net balance, it is fair to say, *the Catholic Church of the Middle Ages was the institution in Western history that did the most to advance the cause of constitutional statecraft.* This resulted from its constant readiness, in the spirit of the Hebrew prophets, to challenge the might of kings and emperors if they transgressed the teachings of religion.

The alacrity with which the church spoke out about this subject is the salient feature of the medieval record. We see it very early when St. Ambrose states that "the emperor is within the church, not above it . . . things that are divine are not subject to imperial power"; when St. Augustine says, "it is not for judges to judge of the law but according to the law"; or when St. Isidore asserts that "the title of kings is held by proper administration, by wrongdoing it is lost."[2] Even more emphatic was the famous missive of Pope Gelasius to the Emperor Anastasius:

"There are two powers, august emperor, by which the world is chiefly ruled, namely, the sacred authority of the priests and the royal power. Of these, that of the priests is the more weighty, since they have to render an account for even the kings of men in the divine judgment . . . While you are permitted honorably to rule over human kind, yet in things divine you bow your head humbly before the leaders of the clergy and await from their hands the means of your salvation. In the reception and proper disposition of the heavenly mysteries, you recognize that you should be subordinate rather than superior to the religious order . . ."[3]

These sentiments, obviously, are light years from the ideas of Plato and Aristotle, and also from the words of humble deference to princes that would become the norm in absolutist kingdoms. Their impact in proclaiming limits on the scope of secular power, in posing a check to royal pride, and in advancing the

Western concept of separate spheres allotted to church and state, is manifest. The implications were apparent all over Europe, but the developments of special interest to our story are those occurring in medieval England.

In questions pertaining to the higher law and secular authority, the maxims of an Ambrose or Gelasius were often brought to bear by English priests and jurists. An Anglo-Norman law book of the twelfth century declares: "Against the command of God and the Catholic faith no order is valid." In the thirteenth century, Robert Grosseteste, bishop of Lincoln, argued that "princes and secular judges cannot establish laws contrary to the law of God." Thomas à Becket believed the same, as did his secretary, John of Salisbury: ". . . it is said that the prince is absolved from the obligation of the law, but this is not true in the sense that it is lawful for him to do unjust acts . . . Inferiors should cleave to and cohere to their superiors . . . but always and only on condition that religion be kept inviolate. . . ."4 *

Not content with stating such ideas, English religious leaders were often engaged in political battles that put them to the test of practice. The contests between Becket and Henry II, Henry VIII and Sir Thomas More, are the cases usually cited, but there were a great many others. Among the more important were the endeavors of Archbishop Stephen Langton, involved in repeated conflict with King John and widely accounted the intellectual force behind the drafting of Magna Carta. In Langton's view, "whatever service is rendered to the temporal king to the prejudice of the eternal king is undoubtedly an act of treachery." He was on hand to make the point at Runnymede (as was Grosseteste) and also helped obtain a reaffirmation of the charter in 1225. His successor, Edmund of Abingdon, did the same a decade later.5

---

* Becket's view, in a letter to Henry II, echoed Gelasius: "Kings receive their power from the church, while the church receives hers not from kings but from Christ." (C. H. McIlwain, *The Growth of Political Thought in the West*, Macmillan, 1950, p. 228)

The church lent its prestige to Magna Carta in other ways as well. Since the charter guaranteed the liberties of religion (the first article of the sixty-three that are listed), clerical interests were bound up closely with its precepts, and the clergy sought to strengthen its authority among the faithful. One archbishop ordered that it be posted in every cathedral, while another had it read out to the people both in Latin and in English. This considerable record of church involvement with the charter, again, is directly contrary to the standard treatment. (Such clerical methods of instruction would also play a role in the later history of English freedoms.)

While the church was the principal influence in restraining monarchy in the medieval epoch, it was not alone in taking this position. Power in the Middle Ages was fragmented, not only as between church and state, but among competing secular interests, so that the monarchs of Europe were hedged about with many countervailing forces. It was this wide diffusion of authority that led to the rise of representative institutions, as well as to other distinctive features of the medieval order.

The long retreat of Roman power and the repeated migrations of the era had created a patchwork of tribes and races, engaged in frequent wars and depredations, with no central government to control things. In these straits, people did what they could to organize some method of protection. This became the feudal system, in which individual barons, each with a band of armed retainers, established centers of defense across the map of Europe. Granted the many terrible things that may be said about this system, it led to political outcomes of the highest value: It meant that *power was de-centralized*, and the resulting diffusion of military forces contributed decisively to the cause of freedom.

Because of this arrangement, the barons were often capable of enforcing in practical terms the limits that the church pronounced in theory—Magna Carta supplying the premiere example. While we rightly honor this document and its provisos, we need to recall the conditions that made it possible. The only reason John agreed to it, after all, was that he confronted armed, determined, and angry people he couldn't defeat on the field of battle (the argument he would use in trying later to get it annulled). The charter was thus not only medieval, but also quite specifically a *feudal* product.

Most of the pledges and concessions made by the Plantagenet kings would be extracted through such military pressure. In 1233, we are informed, the obstreperous magnates of Henry III told the king he and his foreign minions might be driven from the country, and "came to parliament . . . so well attended that they seemed in condition to prescribe laws to the king and ministry."[6] During his long but shaky reign, John's successor endured a regency, rule by a baronial council, and defeat at Lewes by Simon de Montfort. (It was because of the military power de Montfort and other barons brought to bear that we get the first vestiges of a supposedly representative, if temporary, House of Commons.)

Even with Edward I, the most revered of the Plantagenets, the barons were apt to behave in truculent fashion.* Edward II, as weak as his father had been strong, was embroiled in constant conflict, ultimately deposed and murdered. By the close of the fourteenth century, the nobles "were trying ministers and favorites of the king [Edward III] in opposition to his wishes, as in 1376. In the next reign [Richard II] this claim was carried to the point where the lay lords . . . passed sentences of death on the king's confidants, as in 1388." A decade later, in a precedent that would echo down the centuries, Richard would be deposed as well—a result presaged in the contemporaneous

---

* Hume recounts an episode in which Edward informed two of his magnates they would have to fight in Gascony, which they refused to do. Edward angrily told the Earl of Hereford, "Sir Earl, by God, you will either go or hang." To which the earl responded, "By God, Sir King, I will neither go nor hang." And he didn't. (David Hume, *The History of England*, the American News Company, n.d., Vol. II, p.114)

comment that "at least two-thirds of the English Knights and squires [had previously been] hostile to the king."[7]

That background should make it plain that English kings of the Middle Ages were hardly absolute, inasmuch as they confronted tough and warlike people who had ideas and interests of their own, and the means of doing something definite about them. This situation did much to discourage claims of royal greatness, and to suggest to Englishmen that kings were not entitled to do whatever they wanted.

If the decentralization of military force was a restraint, the diffusion of wealth was scarcely less so. The barons and clergy, knights and burgesses, all had property and income, herds and crops, which under laws of feudal tenure and/or conditions of the time could not summarily be taken from them. Kings who wanted further revenue—and they always did—were obliged to truck and barter with their subjects. It is from this requirement, above all others, that representative government as we know it is descended. Because the king could not "live of his own," he had to call people together to ask for more resources. The people, thus assembled, were the Parliament.

The pattern of these transactions is remarkably uniform. A typical account shows the king in need of funding, asking his subjects for assistance, and being told he can receive it if he offers something in return—safeguards of economic and legal liberty, relief of burdens, restoration of former privilege. The tone of these proposals is usually polite (sometimes not, as in the cases cited), but the bargain struck is always "grievance" for "supply." Hence the linkage, in our ideas of statecraft, between ideas of liberty and limits on taxation.

The connection between finance and freedom is clear in the earliest going—most conspicuously, once more, in Magna Carta. As recorded in Article 12, the king agreed "no scutage or aid is to be levied in our realm except by the common counsel of our realm . . . Aids from the city of London are to be treated likewise." Throughout the thirteenth century, grants of revenue to the crown were conditioned on reissues of the charter.* Other provisos were also made a condition of financial help, many of a familiar nature. In 1244, for instance, the barons turned up complaining to the king about violations of past agreements, "the waste of former subsidies, and the maladministration of his servants."† [8]

By the dawn of the fourteenth century, the fiscal requirements of the crown had prompted a wider effort to come up with money, and thus a broadening of the franchise. Having reached the limits of his usual sources among the lords and clergy, Edward I began to cast about for new ones, and found them in the prosperous tradesmen of the towns and cities. We thus arrive at the famous "burgesses," who were to join the lesser barons and county gentry in the commons. We also arrive at Edward's oft-quoted maxim: "A most just law, established by the careful providence of sacred princes, exhorts and decrees that what touches all should be approved by all."[9]

Thereafter the commons and/or the burgesses would be expressly cited in the roster of those consulted by the king, and in the guarantees involving taxes. Edward promised, for example, that "no tallage or aid" should be levied without "the good will

---

* In 1224, we are informed, "a new confirmation of Magna Carta was demanded and granted . . . and an aid, amounting to a fifteenth of all movables, was granted for the indulgence." (*Hume,* op. cit., p. 10) Between 1225 and 1237, Magna Carta was confirmed twice more in return for taxes. In 1253, Henry III received a grant of further aid, but only after a solemn reaffirmation of the Charter. Further confirmations were provided by Edward I in 1297, and 1301.

† The full passage in Hallam from which this is taken reads as follows: "In 1241, a subsidy having been demanded for the war in Poitou, the barons drew up a remonstrance, enumerating all the grants they had made on former occasions, but always on condition that the imposition not be turned into a precedent . . . On a similar demand in 1244, the king was answered by complaints against violations of the charter, the waste of former subsidies, and the maladministration of his servants. Finally the barons positively refused any money." In 1258, also, "no aid was granted for the assembly demanded reforms as a condition of the grant being made." (Henry Hallam, *The Middle Ages,* A.C. Armstrong and Son, 1882, Vol. I, p. 121; George Haskins, *The Growth of English Representative Government,* A. S. Barnes & Co., 1960, p. 62)

and assent of the archbishops, bishops and other prelates, earls, barons, knights, burgesses and other free men of our realm."* This became a notable precedent in the battle against arbitrary taxes—which was in turn the principal issue in British constitutional history.[10]

From this brief account, we can see the medieval genealogy of English freedoms, including the growth of Parliament, taxation by consent, safeguards for property and legal privilege— concessions and guarantees that became leading features of the common law tradition. The net effect was a practical analogue to the notion of a higher law—an achievement of immense importance. It is one thing, after all, to *say* the power of kings should be limited by law, quite another to make it stick. This translation of theory into practice was exactly what the Middle Ages, with their wide diffusion of authority, were able to accomplish.

The melding of these concepts appears repeatedly in legal statements of the era, as the jurists say *the king is bound by the law, and this means he must govern by consent.* At the time of Henry II, for example, Glanville asserted that "right and justice ought to rule in the realm rather than the perversities of will"; wherefore, "the king was to do all things rightly in his realm by the judgment of the magnates of the realm, that he was to fear God and protect the church, that he was to maintain good laws and customs, and destroy evil practices, and that he was to perform just judgments by the advice of the magnates . . ."[11]

---

* From the standpoint of many called to these assemblies, attendance was not a privilege but an onerous duty. This way of looking at the matter reinforced the impulse to seek redress of grievance, so that the taxpayers could get something out of the transaction. We accordingly see the humbler commons of the period, as well as the imperious nobles, addressing petitions to the crown. One such, in 1340, finds the commons voting aid, on the proviso that the king "considering the great charge and subsidies" under which his subjects were laboring, and a recent grant "which seemed to them very heavy," "should grant the petitions which they have put before him and his council . ." (A. R. Myers, ed., *English Historical Documents*, Vol. IV, Oxford, 1969, p. 440)

A century later, in the days of Grosseteste and de Montfort, Bracton gave the concept even more definite expression. "These laws," he said, "since they have been approved by the consent of those using them and confirmed by the oath of kings, can neither be changed nor destroyed without the common consent of those with whose counsel and consent they have been promulgated. For the king has no power in his lands, since he is the minister and vicar of God, save that alone which he has of right ... [The law] is not anything rashly to be presumed by the will of the king, but what has been rightly defined with the king's authorization on the advice of his magnates after deliberation and conference concerning it."[12]

This was the thesis Fortescue would espouse, in statements we have already noted. "A king of England," he observed, "cannot of his pleasure make any alteration in the laws of the land, for the nature of his government is not only regal, but political [constitutional]. Had it merely been regal, he would have a power to make whatever innovations and alterations he pleased in the laws of the kingdom, impose tallages and other hardships upon the people whether they will or not, without their consent, which sort of government the civil [Roman] laws point out when they declare *Quod princip placuit, legis habit vigorem* [what pleases the king has the force of law]."

The situation is quite different, Fortescue added, "with a king whose government is political, because he can neither make any alteration or change the laws of the realm without the consent of his subjects, nor burthen them against their will with strange impositions, so that a people governed by such laws as are made by their own consent and approbations enjoy their liberties securely, and without the hazard of being deprived of them, by the king or any other."[13]

This is so good a *precis* of the common law position that we may let it do service as our summary of the matter. As may readily be seen, it is a clarion statement of constitutionalism, taxation by consent, defense of the liberties of the subject—all attributes of free government as we know it. As may be seen as well, it is also an exposition of the *medieval* notions that had grown up in England—crystallized in Magna Carta, the role of Parliament, the belief that law instead of will should be the guiding precept of the state. All very different from the conventional picture of a sleepwalking, benighted, or repressive era.

Even as Fortescue was offering this synthesis, however, innovations were afoot that would severely test the medieval system. Foremost among these was the explicit revival of the *lex regia* of the Romans—the very maxim of unbridled power that Bracton, Fortescue, and the common law tradition had so energetically combatted. In conceptual terms, as Maitland has authoritatively described it, this was the doing of the Renaissance and its enthusiasm for pagan doctrine. An important aspect of its teaching was, precisely, the "reception" of Roman legal theory concerning royal power; this had self-evident appeal to European monarchs, including those of England.

Such theoretical currents might not have had much impact on the untheoretical English, but they were matched by seismic changes in the feudal order—including a weakening of the nobility through fratricidal conflict, development of a court party in the Parliament, and other mutations in the system. By far the most important of these was the defection of Henry VIII from the see of Rome—a fertile source of conflict in church and civil government and a powerful blow against the medieval balance. This schism vastly increased the power of the crown, both by the riches taken from the monasteries and by the conversion of English clerics from a stance of countervailing power to one of backing and apology.* As all this coincided

---

* On the other hand, the half-way Reformation achieved by Henry, and pursued by his successors, would prove to be a source of further religious opposition. The Henrician church became "reformed" chiefly if not entirely because Henry rather than the Pope was now in charge of it; in many aspects of belief and ceremony, it continued to be Roman Catholic. This was offensive to those of zealous Protestant opinions, who would become the Puritans of our histories.

with the progress of the Roman doctrine, nothing was apparently lacking to break down the limits established in the Middle Ages.

What is most remarkable is that the medieval constitution did, somehow, survive. Why this happened is an absorbing question, but the crucial thing from our perspective is that the tradition soldiered on—and thus remained available, in the succeeding era, for export to the Western Empire. The absolutist view of kingship, while advanced repeatedly in England, was as many times rejected. One instructive case involved the clerical statesman Stephen Gardiner, who spent a long career maneuvering among the religious/political forces buffeting Tudor England. He recounts a touchy interview in which the Roman doctrine was directly mooted before King Henry (a Renaissance monarch if ever there was one) by Thomas Cromwell: "Is not that that pleaseth the king a law?"

Gardiner's answer suggests his subtlety in dealing with this dangerous king, and his own adherence to the rule-of-law tradition. He replied, he says, that "I had read indeed of kings that had their will always received for a law, but I told him the form of his reign, to make the laws his will, was more sure and quiet . . . If you begin a new matter of policy, how it will frame, no man can tell; and how this frameth, you can tell; and I would never advise your grace to leave a certain for an uncertain." (Gardiner would give the same astute advice to Mary Tudor when she ascended to the throne.)[14]

Further evidence that the rule of law persisted in the Tudor era was provided by John Aylmer, bishop of London, at the accession of Elizabeth. Answering the protests of John Knox, who objected to having a woman on the throne of England (or Scotland), Aylmer offered a rationale for kingship echoing the views of Gardiner, Fortescue, and Bracton. In essence, he argued in favor of Elizabeth precisely *because* the power of the monarchy was limited, and the government of England controlled by checks and balances—meaning any harm she might inflict would be contained.* This unflattering defense of the queen did nothing to sway the intransigent Knox, but it was an excellent summary of the common law position.

Further such comment would appear at intervals during Elizabeth's reign. Richard Onslow, solicitor general and speaker in the Parliament of 1566, restated the medieval thesis, for instance, in terms identical to Fortescue's or Bracton's: "By our common law, although there be for the prince provided many princely prerogatives and royalties, yet it is not such as the prince can take money or other things, or do as he will at his own pleasure without order, but quietly suffer his subjects to enjoy their own, without wrongful oppression; wherein other princes by their liberty do take as pleaseth them."[15]

Two other Elizabethan cases in this vein may be briefly cited for their predictive value. The first involved the Puritan Peter Wentworth, who demanded liberty of parliamentary speech (1576), quoted Bracton on the law, criticized the queen, and wound up in the Tower—the prototype of a stubborn breed that would change the course of Western history. The second was the ruling of the Court of Common Pleas in *Cavendish* (1587), holding an edict issued by the queen "against the law of the land . . . in which case it was said, no one is bound to obey such an order." These episodes prefigured much that was waiting to be born in British politics. They also suggested that the medieval idea of limited kingship was still alive, if not entirely well, in Shakespeare's England.[16]

In the age of the Stuarts, the challenge would be more overt, less skillful, and calamitous for the royal interest. These mon-

---

* "The regiment of England," Aylmer wrote, "is not a mere monarchy . . . nor a mere oligarchy nor democracy, but a rule mixed of all these, wherein each one of these have or should have like authority . . . Those that in King Henry VIII's days would not grant him that his proclamations should have the force of a statute were good fathers of the country and worthy of commendation in defending their liberty . . . If . . . the regiment were such as all hanged upon the king's or queen's will . . . you might peradventure make me fear the matter more . . ." (McIlwain, op. cit., p. 104)

archs had an inveterate longing for Roman views of kingship, which they were seldom bashful in expressing. The ideas of James I had been spelled out while he was king of Scotland, in a book entitled *The Trew Law of Free Monarchies* (1598). This was an unflinching statement of the Renaissance conception, a flat denial of the common law approach, and a defiance to the band of rising pamphleteers who preached an even less respectful view of kingship (see Chapter X).*[17] It was a doctrine that Englishmen had not been used to hearing since Richard II had been deposed, two centuries before, for saying "the laws were in his mouth" (a precedent that, for the Stuarts, would prove to be an evil omen).

Once ascended to the throne of England, James set out to do what he had written, and to expound his absolutist views to Parliament. Its privileges, he said, "were derived from the grace and permission of his ancestors and himself," "that which concerns the mystery of the king's power is not lawful to be disputed," and "it is presumption and high contempt in a subject to dispute what a king can do"—the full-blown Continental doctrine. He tried to enforce these precepts by governing through proclamations, raising duties without consent of Parliament, and otherwise behaving, when he could, like a sacred monarch on the Roman model.[18]

From the history we have recited, the response of Parliament, now chock-full of Peter Wentworths, will not appear surprising. The Commons had a different theory of their rights, telling James his view tended "directly and apparently to the

---

* The following excerpts suggest the flavor: "The king is the overlord of the whole land; so is he master over every person that inhabiteth the same, having power of life or death over every one of them . . . The power flows always from himself . . . which makes the king to be a speaking law . . . The king is above the law, as both the author and giver of strength thereto . . . He is not bound thereto but of his own good will, and for good example-giving to his subjects . . . A good king, although he be above the law, will subject and frame his actions thereto, for examples sake to his subjects, and of his own free will, but not as subject or bound thereto . . ."

destruction of the very fundamental privileges of our House, and therein of the rights and privileges of the whole Commons of your realm of England." As to what they could discuss, they added, "the liberties, franchises, privileges and jurisdiction of Parliament are the ancient and undoubted birthright and inheritance of the subjects . . . the commons in Parliament have the like liberty and freedom to treat of these matters in such order as in their judgments shall seem fittest." The courts, also, were showing signs of further independence, with Coke as chief justice in the forefront.* [19]

This was the constitutional whirlwind reaped by Charles I. Again, the proximate causes were economic, though with a considerable portion of religious acrimony thrown in for good measure.† Among other policies that inflamed the Parliament, Charles attempted to raise a revenue on his own, locked up opponents in the Tower, and quartered soldiers in private homes, while pursuing a rigorous policy through Archbishop Laud aimed at suppressing Puritan tendencies in the church. The reaction that had been building for a generation exploded in the Parliament of 1628, noteworthy not only for its Puritan

---

* In a monopoly case deriving from Elizabeth but decided under James, Coke found a company chartered by the queen was "a monopoly and against the common law . . . The Queen was deceived in her grant . . . it is a dangerous innovation, as well as without any precedent, or example, as without authority of law or reason . . ." Addressing James, Coke decided that "the king cannot change any part of the common law, nor create any offense by his proclamation, which was not an offense before, without Parliament." Moreover: "The common law has so admeasured the prerogatives of the king, that they should not take away, nor prejudice, the inheritance of any; and the best inheritance that a subject hath is the law of the realm." (Roscoe Pound, *The Development of Constitutional Guarantees of Liberty*, Yale, 1967, pp. 146–147, 163: Hallam, *Constitutional History of England*, A.C. Armstrong and Son, 1882, Vol. I, p. 331)

† On all the matters in dispute, Charles and his agents came down squarely for the Roman doctrine. At his second Parliament, Charles had Archbishop Laud preach the duty of obedience, and himself asserted that "Parliaments were altogether in his power for their calling, sitting, and dissolution; therefore, as he found the fruits of them good or evil, they were to continue to be, or not to be." (Hallam, op. cit., p. 370)

members such as Eliot and Pym but also for the fact that Coke, now banished from the court, was a conspicuous member.

It was this Parliament that adopted the Petition of Right, reaffirmed the common law tradition concerning taxes, and voted resolves demanding Puritan orthodoxy among the clergy. The principal elements of the Petition, destined to take their place with Magna Carta as cherished safeguards of British freedom, laid down a series of challenges to the crown: "That no man hereafter be compelled to make or yield any gift, loan, benevolence, tax or such like charge without common consent by Act of Parliament . . . That no free man . . . be imprisoned or detained . . . That your majesty would be pleased to remove the . . . soldiers and marines [quartered in homes] . . . and that . . . commissions for proceeding by martial law may be revoked and annulled."[20]

When friends of Charles tried to insert a saving clause concerning the "sovereign power" of the king, this was rejected, and Coke delivered a ringing answer: "This is *magnum in parvo*. It is a matter of great weight, and to speak plainly, will overthrow all our Petition . . . I know that prerogative is part of the law, but 'sovereign power' is no parliamentary word. In my opinion it weakens Magna Carta and all our statutes, for they are absolute, without any saving of 'sovereign power' . . . Take heed what we yield unto; Magna Carta is such a fellow that he will have no sovereign."[21]*

Magnum in parvo, indeed. Virtually every element of the English constitution, from control of taxes, to the guarantees of the common law, to the independent power of religion, was here arrayed in battle against the throne. We see, in starkest terms, the collision of medieval and Renaissance conceptions of the matter. Coke and Pym speak for the old tradition, the

---

* Pym's version was: "All our petition is for the laws of England . . . We cannot leave to him a sovereign power; also we were never possessed of it." (Quoted in Andrew McLaughlin, *Foundations of American Constitutionalism*, Fawcett, 1961, p. 111)

notion of a law above the state, constitutional limits on the king. The Stuarts and their party talk of "sovereign power," grace and permission, and absolute authority. Something had to give, and that something, for the moment, turned out to be the Roman view of statecraft.

I apologize for offering this headlong sketch of so many decisive events in British history. Some such *precis* is required, however, to correct the usual misreading of the medieval record, and also to form an understanding of our American institutions. For it was precisely the medieval concept of limited power in the state that the settlers brought with them when they landed, and precisely at this juncture that the bulk of them made the decision to set sail from England. Both the background and the timing are crucial to any study of our beginnings.

For the English emigrants of the early 1600s, the struggle between the Stuarts and Parliament, between "new monarchy" conceptions and Coke's redaction of the common law, were defining events of a political lifetime, whose lessons would be lastingly imprinted on our society. Equally to the point, it was to this constitutional history that the Founders of the following century would repair when they came up against claims of unchecked power made by the British ministries and Parliaments. The heritage of our country was that of liberty under law, and it was emphatically medieval in its origins.

10

The Social Contract

IN AMERICAN THEORIES of free government, a special place of honor is reserved for "social contract." That this should be the case is not mysterious. Contractual notions of the state, whatever their asserted problems,* contain within them many features of libertarian doctrine.

For one thing, the concept assumes a mutual arrangement, in which people of whatever rank are in some basic sense on equal footing. One party to a contract cannot dictate to another; both have rights as well as duties; neither may ignore the things agreed to. Applied to affairs of state, such thinking leads to theories of consent. If all begin from equal status, the political order they arrive at must be based on their agreement. Officials wielding power get it from the resulting bargain, and are bound by its provisions.

This leads to a further precept—at least in the free government version: If the contract is violated by either party, then the arrangement is no longer valid. When a ruler fails to provide the services agreed to, or otherwise breaks the compact with his

---

* Two obvious problems that suggest themselves: If the people are to be freed of their obligations under conditions of violated contract, who decides when this has happened? And if the people themselves make this decision, isn't this a formula for unceasing revolution? These questions are considered in Chapter XIV.

subjects, their obligations are thereby canceled. They can resist such violations, demand redress, or—*in extremis*—replace the ruler with another. In these ideas we recognize not only the rationale of the Glorious Revolution and Declaration of Independence, but other principles that undergird the free society: The sovereignty of the people, the rule of law, limits on official conduct.

Unfortunately, the way this idea is usually treated once more conspires to darken counsel. As typically explained, it is yet another product of rational speculation, with principal credit going to John Locke. In his *Second Treatise of Civil Government*, we are informed, Locke spelled out a theory for the Glorious Revolution; the Americans imbibed the notion from his book, then used it in their conflict with the British. Since Locke's rendering is utilitarian (though Locke himself was a professing Christian), this seems to confirm the rationalist basis of our politics. A nation that received its thought from Locke (at least the Locke of 1690) is perforce a creature of secular invention.

Again, however, what has been taught as standard history turns out to be mistaken. As may readily be shown, social contract theory was not the work of secular theoreticians, or a rejection of the medieval heritage; nor was it a fanciful doctrine floating loose from known arrangements; nor did the settlers of North America derive the concept from John Locke. So many statements contrary to the usual teaching may seem strange, and perhaps hard to demonstrate. The difficulty, however, is the other way around. The materials to support these comments are so extensive that the challenge is to compress them into manageable form—which raises the interesting question of how the usual histories contrive to miss them.

In discussing the medieval period, we have noted the prevalence of beliefs and practices that limited the power of kings. That record by itself should be enough to cast some doubt on the conventional treatment; if a king could legislate and tax only with the concurrence of Parliament, and if one chamber of that Parliament in turn was chosen by election, even with a limited franchise, we have obviously gone a considerable way toward consensual notions of the state. Likewise, as has been shown, the common law was understood by its supporters to be a species of consent, albeit extending over many generations.

To all of this, however, there must be added one other aspect of the medieval background: The fact that the feudal order was, in legal terms, an intricate *network of contracts*—and that political thinking of the era was saturated with its precepts. It is remarkable, indeed, that any discussion of social contract can possibly omit this, since it was the very essence of the system. The relation of lord and vassal was that of protection in exchange for service, arranged on a contractual basis. This point is made by all authorities on the era, who note that feudal agreements were reciprocal in nature, and had to be respected on both sides.

The concept was stressed in a famous missive from Bishop Fulbert of Chartres to the duke of Aquitaine, in the year 1020: "The lord also ought to act toward his faithful vassal in the same manner in all these things. And if he fails to do this, he will be rightfully regarded as guilty of bad faith, just as the former, if he should be found shirking, or willing to shirk, his obligations would be perfidious and perjured."[1] From which it followed that, if the lord defaulted his side of the bargain, the vassal's allegiance would be dissolved as well. Marc Bloch explains it this way:

"Whatever the inequalities between the obligations of the respective parties, those obligations were nonetheless mutual; the obedience of the vassal was conditioned upon the scrupulous fulfillment of his engagement by the lord. This reciprocity in unequal obligations . . . was the really distinctive feature of European vassalage . . . [the homage of the vassal] made the lord no mere master . . . but a partner in a genuine contract. 'As much,' writes Beaumanoir,* 'as the vassal owes his lord of fealty and loyalty by reason of his homage, so much the lord owes his vassal.' "[2]

The consequences of such an outlook in curtailing power were many. One such was that, as the agreement created obligations, it also defined their limits. The lord could require so much from his vassal, but no more, and he had to refrain from injuring his vassal's interests.[†] Since the political order of Europe was organized on feudal principles, the implications for the conduct of kings should be apparent. Rulers at the apex of the pyramid were likewise bound, could exact no more than specified, and had to deliver what they promised. Otherwise, the allegiance of their vassals was dissolved; they had the right, according to *The Mirror of Saxon Law* (ca. 1220), "to resist a lawless decision by [the] king." Consider these specifics from the political-legal records of the era:

"In his statute of 1188 Alphonse of Leon agreed that he would not make war or peace except by the advice of bishops and nobles of the realm. In Aragon in 1283 Peter III agreed that he would only make war by the advice of nobles, knights and townfolk, and that the nobles were not bound by the conditions of their feudal tenure to serve overseas.

"In the kingdom of Jerusalem it was recognized that the king's vassals might resort to the renunciation of fealty and rebellion in certain specified circumstances, as, for example, when the king imprisoned or deprived a vassal without judgment or persistently denied justice to his men.

---

* French canon lawyer Philippe de Beaumanoir, a contemporary of St. Thomas.

† Thus "the Frankish capitularies, which refer only indirectly to the vassal's obligation of keeping faith, carefully specify the ways in which he may be wronged by his lord. According to an edict of Charlemagne, a vassal is justified in deserting his lord for any one of the following reasons: if the lord seeks to reduce him to servitude, if the lord plots against his life, if the lord commits adultery with his wife, if the lord attacks him with drawn sword, if the lord fails to protect him when able to do so." (Carl Stephenson, *Medieval Feudalism*, Cornell, 1961, p. 20)

"In Hungary, King Andrew II agreed in the Bull of 1222 that 'if we or any of our successors ever wish to revoke this concession in any way, bishops, lords and nobles, each and every one both now and in the future have our authority to resist and contradict us and our successors without taint of any infidelity.'

"In Aragon, in the *Privilegio de la Union* of 1287, King Alphonso III pledged the good behavior of the crown by the surrender of 16 castles and by the acknowledgement that his vassals could choose another king if he contravened their privileges."[3]

As with the more general melding of clerical and baronial concerns, church doctrine tended to reinforce these notions. When it came to keeping contracts, the church had a double interest: As guarantor of agreements made under a religious oath, it had a strong incentive for insisting that they not be violated (a stricture likewise urged against the barons). It also had more immediate reasons for proclaiming the conditional nature of royal power, since that power was often in conflict with the church itself.

Accordingly, contractual doctrines appear from an early date in statements of the clerics. We have noted assertions of religious spokesmen that there was a higher law above the power of kings, and that decrees contrary to divine intent were null and void. The step from these opinions to actual resistance is not a very long one. We encounter just such a statement in the eleventh century, in the historic controversy between the emperor and pope, beginning with a dispute over lay investiture of bishops, and culminating with the submission of the emperor at Canossa. In this conflict, a spokesman for the church provided a clarion statement of contract theory, and of resistance to earthly rulers:

". . . when he who is chosen to defend the good and hold the evil in check himself begins to cherish wickedness . . . is it not clear that he justly forfeits the dignity conceded to him and the people stand free of his rule and subjection, since it is evident that he was the first to violate the compact on account of which he was made ruler? . . . It is one thing to rule, another to act the tyrant in a realm. For as faith and reverence ought to be rendered to emperors and kings for the sake of safeguarding . . . the realm . . . if these rulers break out into tyranny, it is no breach of faith or piety that no fealty or reverence is paid to them."[1]

The thought and practice of the Middle Ages thus produced two related concepts limiting the rule of princes: the idea of their implied or explicit contract with their subjects; and the idea of the higher law above the state, represented in the prerogatives of the church. Kings who violated either could be resisted.* In the medieval era, to be sure, such notions generally weren't assembled, according to the modern practice, into an abstract theory of republics. In an age when custom and religious veneration were the dominant forces in European thought, the construction of secular theories on a systematic basis was not a frequent pastime. What crystallized these elements into the patterns that we recognize was the division of Christian Europe at the Reformation.

The main political point about the Reformation was not the usual thesis of Whig history—that the Protestant cause was one of freedom and self-government, while that of Rome was superstition and autocracy. Though the Protestants of Europe and America certainly believed such things (and thereby helped to spawn "the liberal history lesson"), the political meaning of this religious crisis was rather different: By splitting Christianity into warring factions, it established a source of

---

* "Laws may be unjust in two different ways," according to St. Thomas. "First, by being contrary to human good . . . as when an authority imposes on his subjects burdensome laws, conducive, not to the common good, but rather to his own cupidity or vainglory . . . Secondly, laws may be unjust through being opposed to the divine good: such are the laws of tyrants conducing to idolatry or anything else contrary to the divine law; and laws of this kind must nowise be observed because, as stated in Acts V. 29, 'we ought to obey God rather than man.' " (Curtis, op. cit., p. 196)

bitter conflict between the princes and their people, involving, sadly, the most powerful motives for repression—but also for resistance.

The Reformation created a confessional landscape in which a ruler of one faith confronted a sizeable number of his subjects who espoused another. At a time when toleration was seldom thought of and almost never practiced, such monarchs would typically try to impose a uniformity of belief, giving nonconformists a painful choice between their king and their convictions. This sent them back to medieval sources to discover precedents for rebellion. So widespread were these attempts that it would be possible to show the movement from medieval to modern doctrine by citing only Roman Catholic spokesmen.* Since we are dealing with American ideas and institutions, we shall pursue the Protestant side of the development. The settlers of America, after all, were chiefly Protestants, and came here to practice Reformation teachings.

In this respect, the preeminent source of American thinking was the experience of the Puritans in England and Scotland, in almost continuous struggle with British monarchs for upwards of a century. These events, however, were international, and this had bearing on their outcome. Calvin and Henry VIII were contemporaries, as were Richelieu and John Winthrop, Louis XIV and John Locke, William of Orange and Increase Mather. All these people were engaged in a wide-ranging struggle in which the stakes were of the highest—religious supremacy in Christendom, and territorial control of Europe. The resulting upheaval sent missionaries, diplomats, and armies moving in all directions; it also created groups of exiles, both Protestant

* A series of essays by J. N. Figgis, in point of fact, has done the job before us. Beginning with the Conciliar movement within the church, and moving thereafter through the writings of the Catholic League and the Jesuits, Figgis rehearses virtually every doctrine associated with modern libertarian government: the higher law, limited kingship, the sovereignty of the people, government by contract, the right of resistance, and a good deal more. (*Political Thought from Gerson to Grotius*, Harper, 1965)

and Catholic, seeking refuge from persecution and preaching theories of rebellion.

In England and Scotland, France and the Netherlands, the Protestant interest early on assumed a posture of disobedience. In all these cases, the lead position was taken by the followers of Calvin, and these became the organizational vanguard of the Reformation. Whether this resulted from the accidents of the case or was inherent in the Calvinist system is an issue of dispute. Part of it no doubt was that Calvin had his own "republic" at Geneva, to which English Puritans such as Thomas Cartwright looked for inspiration;* for our purposes, enough to note that the Calvinists were at the forefront, and that from this sector emerged the most emphatic statements of contract and resistance.

Calvin was French, and it was in France against the Catholic monarchy that the Protestants waged their earliest and most celebrated battles. The effort of the Huguenot nobility and merchant class to conduct a Protestant worship veered between a policy of relative toleration and periods of warfare and repression, most notably the slaughter of Protestants on St. Bartholomew's Day in 1572. These episodes sent refugees streaming into Holland and England, and later to America, bearing tales of horror that inflamed the Protestant sensibility. They also spurred the Huguenots and their supporters to proclaim explicit theories of opposition to faithless kings.

Among these were the writings of Francois Hotman, who produced a series of tracts opposing the expansive view of royal power revived with the "reception." (One of his essays is called *The Anti-Tribonian*—Tribonian having been the jurist

---

* It was Cartwright's exposition and defense of Calvin's system, for example, that occasioned Richard Hooker's response in behalf of the Anglican settlement—which became *The Laws of Ecclesiastical Polity*. This defended ideas of tradition in the church, while acknowledging that human authority was ultimately founded on consent. The latter comments were quoted extensively by Locke—as admissions against the royalist interest.

who assembled the Roman pandects for Justinian.) Hotman argued that the subject's "duty of obedience is conditional," and that "when a king becomes a tyrant and treacherously massacres his subjects" he may be resisted. Similar views were expressed by Theodore de Beza, Calvin's second-in-command, who had attempted to negotiate a *modus vivendi* for the Huguenot nobility at the court of Charles IX. After St. Bartholomew's, Beza wrote a treatise declaring that "it is God alone whom we are bound to obey in all cases without exception" and that "magistrates were created for the people and not the people for the magistrates." These statements clearly indicate the continuity of the Protestant doctrine—like the Catholic—with the precepts of the medieval era.[5]

Nowhere is such continuity more evident than in the most famous of the Huguenot manifestos, the *Vindiciae Contra Tyrannos*, first published in 1579 and widely reprinted in the ensuing century. It is at once intensely feudal and strongly modern—building on the precedents of biblical teaching and the principles of vassalage to a contractual theory of the state. The feudal character of the *Vindiciae* is sometimes cited as an oddity, but this is typical of modern history that begins with secularist conclusions rather than the evidence of the record. Feudal practice, as we have seen, was very much the essence of the matter. Among other things, the *Vindiciae* offers a medieval view of kingship, government by contract, the right of resistance, and even a species of federal doctrine. Here are some excerpts:

". . . the Holy Scripture doth teach, that God reigns by his own proper authority, and kings by derivation . . . That God hath a jurisdiction proper, kings are his delegates. It follows then, that the jurisdiction of God hath no limits, that of kings [is] bounded . . . kings should acknowledge that, after God, they hold their sovereignty and power from the people . . . let them remember and know that they are of the same mould and condition as others, raised from the earth by voice and acclamation . . . it is

from God, but by the people's sake that they do reign. . . *There is
ever, and in all places, a mutual and reciprocal obligation
between the people and the prince . . . If the prince fail in his
promise, the people are exempt from obedience, the contract is
made void, the rights of obligation of no force.*"[6] (Italics added.)

All in all, as clear a statement of government by contract as
may be found—and the date, as noted, is 1579. The resemblance to and derivation from the medieval sources are plain
enough, as is the transmutation of these into modern doctrine
on the anvil of religious conflict. As may be shown in some
detail, this is only one of many such examples. One other,
almost exactly contemporaneous with the *Vindiciae*, is the Act
of Abjuration of the Dutch Republic.

Calvinists under the rule of Catholic Spain, the Nether-
landers struggled for upwards of a century, first to gain their
independence, then to defend it against the designs of Louis
XIV. In justifying their resistance to the Spanish Crown, the
Dutch went back, like everyone else, to feudal precedent. The
process of reasoning is identical to that employed in the *Vindiciae*. Insisting on the rule of law above the king, spokesmen
for the infant republic sounded the usual medieval themes. As
their foreign minister St. Aldegonde observed, "God has given
absolute power to no mortal man, to do his will against all laws
and all reasons."[7]*

To this precept we see joined again the clerical-feudal notion
of a contract between the monarch and his subjects. When the
monarch violated the higher law, the Dutch asserted, and
abridged the contract by which he ruled, resistance was i
order. The Act of Abjuration (1581) puts it this way: "All ma·
kind know that a prince is appointed by God to cherish hi·
subjects, even as a shepherd to guard his sheep. When, therefore, the prince does not fulfill his duty as protector, when he
oppresses his subjects, destroys their ancient liberties and

* St. Aldegonde had been a student at Calvin's academy in Geneva.

treats them as slaves, he is to be considered not a prince, but a tyrant. As such, the estates of the land may lawfully and reasonably depose him, and elect another in his room."[8]

There is no doubt that these French and Dutch examples had a contributory influence on events in England. Protestants throughout Europe of course knew about the massacre of St. Bartholomew's; there were many Huguenot refugees in England, and English Puritans were vehement supporters of the French resistance; Hotman's work was translated and circulated by the Whigs; the *Vindiciae* was reprinted in English, in whole or in part, at least eight times between 1581 and 1689—at junctures when the Puritan or parliamentary interest was seeking to justify resistance to the crown.

The influence of the Dutch, if anything, was even more direct. Holland at the time of the Tudors and Stuarts served as a frequent haven for British dissenters such as Cartwright and—in the final stages of the struggle—Whig leaders suspected of plotting against the later Stuarts. These included the earl of Shaftesbury and his secretary, who happened to be none other than John Locke. And Holland was of course the country that provided England with the rulers who came across the water at the Glorious Revolution (with Locke a passenger aboard the ship that carried Princess Mary to her throne).

It is not necessary, however, to insist on the influence of these sources, however great the degree of contact and affinity. For the identical developments were occurring in the British Isles themselves. From the remotest periods we see the formula of contractual obligation in the English records, leading to the concept of resistance. As in so many other respects, Magna Carta provides an obvious example. It included in its provisions a council of twenty-five barons who were to serve as "conservators of the compact" (Hallam's phrase), entitled to seek redress against the king in case of violation. The doctrine is the same as in the Golden Bull of Hungary or the *Privilegio de la Union* of Aragon. John agreed that, were he to violate the charter, the barons had the right to "distrain and annoy us by every means in their power . . . till the wrong shall be repaired to their satisfaction."9 *

Formal and at least semi-official statements of contractual/ resistance doctrine, on feudal grounds, occurred under Edward II and Richard II, both deposed by rebellious barons. When Edward fled to Wales, a Parliament dominated by his foes adopted a formula that read in part as follows: "The king having left his kingdom without government and gone away with notorious enemies of the . . . realm, diverse prelates, earls, barons, and knights . . . by the assent of the whole commonality of the realm . . . unanimously elected the said duke [Edward III] to be guardian of the kingdom . . ."10

The deposition of Richard was even more notably feudal. He was charged with policies contrary to the statutes and his coronation oath, imposing onerous taxes, seizure of lands, violating Magna Carta—as well as saying "the laws were in his mouth." It was accordingly declared that "the realm of England with its appurtenances was vacant," that the estates of the realm "renounce liege homage and fealty" to Richard, and that "none or all of these . . . from this time forward shall bear you faith, nor do you obedience as to their king."† These feudal precedents would be explicitly recalled, three centuries later,

* In the succeeding reign, when the nobles battled Henry III, feudal notions of resistance came inevitably to the fore. We read, for instance, of the Earl of Pembroke, who said "the king had denied him justice . . . on which account he had thought himself absolved from his homage . . . Even Henry fully admitted the right of taking arms against himself if he had meditated his vassal's destruction, and disputed only the application of this maxim to the Earl of Pembroke." (Hallam, *The Middle Ages, Vol. II*, pp. 364–365).

† According to one contemporaneous account, the Duke of Gloucester and Bishop of Ely confronted Richard with this statement: ". . . that if a king, by bad counsel, or his own folly and obstinacy, alienated himself from his people, and would not govern according to the laws of the land and the advice of his peers, but madly and wantonly followed his own single will, it should be lawful for them, with the common assent of the people, to expel him from his throne, and elevate to it some near kinsman of the royal blood." (Op. cit., p. 275) The "near kinsman" was Henry IV.

at the decisive moment of British constitutional history.[11]

In Britain as on the continent, the crucible in which such feudal notions were transmuted into modern theory was the Reformation. What had been implicit and occasional now became a systematic doctrine, fusing the medieval concept of the higher law with feudal principles of contract. Again, the examples are profuse. The earliest cited by the authorities in such matters—so early that it is still arguably medieval—occurs in the writings of John Major at St. Andrew's. A scholastic who was the teacher of Knox and George Buchanan, Major put it this way, ca. 1525:

". . . all civil authority is derived from the will of the community as a whole . . . A king is merely a delegate and an agent. . . . If a king go out of bounds or misuse his power and prove incorrigible, he may rightfully be deposed, and even put to death. The deposition of a king should, indeed, be brought about only by lawful authority and not by mere violence. But it may always be rightfully effected by the estates of the realm."[12]

Buchanan, tutor to James I, friend of Beza, and widely accounted the most learned man in Europe, expressed the almost identical doctrine: "The king is a delegate and an agent and is responsible to the community . . . Whatever powers have been given to the king may rightfully, for good cause, be taken from him and resumed by the people . . . The rights of the people are inalienable . . . A king who disregards the understanding on which he was created may be said to break an implied contract, becomes a tyrant, and forfeits all his rights." Further: "It is clear that kings exist only for public purposes. They must, originally, have been established by an act of the people. Under the law of nature, no man may rightfully assume any authority over his fellows; but the people by giving authority to one of its own members could create a king."[13] *

---

* As Major was the first and Buchanan the most learned of the Scottish divines to advance this thesis, Knox was the most famous. In his sermons rousing the

The defiance trumpeted from press and pulpit by Scottish Calvinists did not fail to find an echo with their English cousins. One such was Christopher Goodman, a Calvinist teacher of divinity at Oxford, who fled to Geneva during the reign of Mary. There he became a friend of Knox (and also Calvin and Beza). In 1558, he published a book called *How Superior Powers ought to be obeyed of their subjects; and wherein they may lawfully by God's word be disobeyed and resisted.* The title sums up the now-familiar theme, expounded in these passages:

"When kings or rulers become blasphemers of God, oppressors and murderers of their subjects, they ought no more to be accounted kings or lawful magistrates, but as private men to be examined, accused, condemned and punished by the law of God, and being condemned and punished by that law, it is not man's but God's doing . . . When magistrates cease to do their duty, the people are as it were without magistrates . . . If princes do right and keep promise with you, then do you owe them all humble obedience. If not, ye are discharged and your study ought to be in this case how ye may depose and punish according to the law such rebels against God and oppressors of their country."[14]

In the epoch of the Tudors, such statements were generally made in exile, from the comparative safety of Strasbourg or Geneva. In the reign of James I, however, as Puritan forces gained in power, assertions of resistance became more audible in England proper. We have noted the generally fractious atti-

---

Kirk against Mary Tudor, fierce opposition to rule by Anglican bishops and face-to-face encounter with the Queen of Scots, Knox put in fiery rhetoric the doctrines that his colleagues expounded: ". . . it is no less blasphemy to say that God hath commanded kings to be obeyed when they command iniquity . . . If princes exceed their bounds, madam, and do against that wherefore they should be obeyed, it is no doubt they may be resisted, even by power . . . He hath not created the earth to satisfy the ambition of two or three tyrants, but for the universal seed of Adam . . . If rashly [the people] have promoted any manifestly wicked person . . . most justly may the same men depose and punish him . . ." (Harry Emerson Fosdick, ed., *Great Voices of the Reformation*, Modern Library, 1952, pp. 109–114)

tude of Parliaments at this era. Of particular interest in this context were the statements of Sir Edwin Sandys, in the Commons of 1614: ". . . the origin of every monarchy, he declared, lay in election. The people, he asserted, gave their consent to the king's authority only with the clear understanding that there were 'certain reciprocal conditions,' which 'neither king nor people could violate with impunity' . . . a monarch who pretends to rule by any other title might be forced to relinquish his throne whenever there was sufficient force to compel his abdication."[15]

Though the historians who provide us this consider it unprecedented, the matter we have reviewed shows it to be standard fare in Calvinist statements of the era. The novelty was not in what was said, but where—a House of Commons that under the Tudors had been accustomed to speak with some degree of deference to the crown, on pain of winding up like Peter Wentworth in the Tower. There would be more statements like that of Sandys in Parliament from this point forward.

Our survey has brought us back to the period that produced the settlement of America. Before leaving the English scene, however, it may be useful to note two further examples in this genre. One is Milton's *Tenure of Kings and Magistrates*, a fiery, eclectic compilation of every kind of opinion that could justify the overthrow of kings, combining classical examples, common law, and contract theory. The importance of this document, beyond the distinction of the author, was its grim service to the Puritan cause—justifying the execution of Charles I.*

---

* "It is affirmed from diligent search made in our ancient books of law that the peers and barons of England had a legal right to judge the king, which was the cause most likely . . . that they were called his peers or equals . . . If our law judge all men to the lowest by their peers, it should in all equity ascend also and judge the highest. . . . If I make a voluntary covenant with a man to do him good, and he prove afterward a monster to me, I should conceive a disobligement. If I covenant not to harm an enemy . . . and he after that should do me tenfold injury and mischief . . . I question not that his afteractions release me . . . How . . . justly then may they fling off tyranny, or tyrants, who being once deposed can be no more

The second example is equally momentous—and even more significant in our constitutional history: the formula used to explain the Glorious Revolution. Given the background we have reviewed, the emergence of social contract theory at this juncture is hardly an astonishment; since medieval theory, common law tradition, and feudal precedent all converged in this direction, it would have been more astonishing if it had not. This threefold influence—indeed the very language we have quoted—was fully apparent when James II was declared no longer king of England.

In the convention Parliament of 1688–89, the terms to justify deposition of the king were debated at some length. As the example of Edward II had been invoked against his great-grandson, so Richard's deposition was cited in the wrangle over James—most notably to prove the throne could be considered "vacant" once the king had decided to flee the country.† On this point as on most others, the proponents of feudal-contractual doctrine carried the day, clearing the path for William and Mary to be installed as his successors.[16]

By an overwhelming vote in the Commons, and by a closer one in the Lords, Parliament adopted a resolution that is usually considered the cornerstone of modern Whig philosophy, which it was, but which was also the capstone of the medieval fabric: "That King James II, having endeavored to subvert the constitution of this realm by breaking the original contract between king and people; and by the advice of Jesuits and other wicked persons having violated the fundamental laws; and

---

than private men, as subject to the reach of justice and arraignment as any other transgressors?. . . ." (*Complete Prose of Milton*, Odyssey, 1948, pp. 295–312)

† The Tory position was that the throne was never "vacant," but was filled by hereditary right as soon as it was, for whatever cause, relinquished. The object of the opposing view, with James as well as Richard, was to clear the way for parliamentary action in naming a successor. The "vacant" throne idea, to us abstruse, was thus a sideways approximation to the concept of elective kingship, with Parliament doing the electing. (See Macaulay, *The History of England*, Donohoe Bros., n.d., Vol. II, pp. 558–593)

having withdrawn himself out of the kingdom; has abdicated the government, and that the throne is thereby vacant."[17]

As may readily be seen by comparison of these many statements, we are dealing with an unbroken chain of belief and practice. From the medieval clerics to the *Vindiciae* and the Act of Abjuration, from feudal precedent to the cashiering of the Stuarts, it is all one body of doctrine—stretching backwards to the Middle Ages, forward to modern notions of social contract. In the language of Americans a century later, we shall find it all repeated—concept for concept, and word for word.

What does this tell us about the supposed invention of contract theory by John Locke? All too obviously, Locke could not have been the source of this development, since almost all of it predated him, in some cases by upwards of a century. Having been born in 1632, and not having published his *Civil Government* until 1690, even the ingenious Locke would have had a difficult time inventing notions that were espoused in 1614, or 1579. The chronology suggests it was the other way around. Locke was the scion of a Puritan family, an active partisan of the parliamentary cause, close to the leading lights of the Whig party. He had before him the history of conflict and advocacy we have reviewed, and a good deal more, and doubtless knew it much better than do we; he had the doctrines of Buchanan; he had the examples of the Huguenots and the Dutch; he had the declamations of Milton and other spokesmen for the Puritan interest.

Looking at this in terms of our previous discussion, indeed, we can see that the debate is fundamentally of a religious nature—is in fact the same dispute that first arose in the conflict between pagan and biblical views of statecraft. Partisans of absolutism such as the Stuarts and their spokesman, Filmer, argue for the Roman notion of *top-down power*, in which the king pronounces edicts, makes his will the law, and is the source of order in society. Locke contends, along with the Puritans of 1628 and their descendants, for the medieval concept of a *law that is exterior to the king*, binds him as it does his subjects, and is grounded in the consent of the people being governed. These are also essentially the positions that were adopted by opponents of the common law and those who saw it as a needed check on power.[18]

The point of these reflections is not to disparage Locke, or even to explain him, a task that has baffled the most learned. It is rather to correct the larger, tendentious purpose to which his writings have been put. All too clearly, the ideas of contract and resistance were not derived from secular invention, but from doctrines of the higher law and feudal notions of allegiance, fused in the crisis of the Reformation. The origins of the concept were medieval and religious, thereafter being put in secular language—like so much else considered in this essay—and devoted to chiefly secular uses (not all of which were beneficial).

But, it may be objected, even if Locke didn't really invent such notions, he did harvest and formulate them in compelling terms, mostly shorn of their religious content. And since the American settlers got their contractual views from him, it follows that the colonial version reflects his secular emphasis. Hence the Enlightenment provenance of our thinking remains intact. Unfortunately for the conventional treatment, this saving formula runs into the identical problems encountered in the European history. Even in the American context—one might say, especially in the American context—all the ideas and institutions of free government, including contract theory, far predated Locke, and did so in the most explicit terms imaginable.

11

The Dissidence of Dissent

THE DEBACLE OF BRITISH colonial policy in the eighteenth century, to which we owe our existence as a nation, resulted from a difference of constitutional theory, but also from a failure of comprehension. Most English statesmen of the period didn't understand America, and so pursued a course that guaranteed rebellion. An exception to this rule was Burke, who knew a lot about the colonies and had a keen awareness of their temper.

In his speeches on our behalf, Burke discussed the English origins of our system, the resulting emphasis on personal freedom, representative government, and the issue of taxation. He also noted that distance from the ministries in Whitehall had encouraged habits of self-reliance. Most to the present point, he stressed the unique religious character of the colonies. In this regard he said the following:

"Religion, always a principle of energy, in this new people is in no way worn out or impaired; and their mode of professing it is also one main cause of this free spirit. . . . The religion most prevalent in our northern colonies is a refinement on the principle of resistance; it is the dissidence of dissent, and the Protestantism of the Protestant religion. This religion, under a variety of denominations agreeing in nothing but in the communion of the spirit of liberty, is predominant in most of the northern provinces. The colonists left England when this spirit was high, and in the emigrants was the highest of all . . ."[1]

On this topic, as on others, Burke knew whereof he spoke. The "dissidence of dissent" was an apt description of these people. They were supporters of the Puritan and parliamentary cause, which implied belief in a law above the state and opposition to the unchecked power of kings, especially in questions of religion. From such axioms, as we have seen, the Calvinists of Europe had derived a spirit of resistance to rulers accused of transgressing the laws of God. All of this, one might suppose, would have been enough to give an independent aspect to New England. As it happens, however, there was a great deal more. The people who settled North America were not only Calvinists and Puritans, but advocates of a religious view that was the most fiercely independent of them all.

In discussing these settlers and their handiwork, it is well to remember that they were English, and that their attitudes on countless matters of politics, law, and social custom revealed this. They brought with them ideas about the common law, the rights of Englishmen, and forms of civic organization reflecting the history we have examined. Yet if 90 percent of Puritan ideas and customs were of traditional English origin, the 10 per cent that set them apart was obviously of great importance; the differences, after all, led them to make their journey. And these points of divergence, above all else, concerned the nature of Christian doctrine about consent, resistance, and limits on the reach of earthly power.

From the standpoint of the conventional history, the fact that America was founded by believing Christians, for specifically religious reasons, is an intense embarrassment. That zealous Puritans should have created a society that somehow became the world's premiere exemplar of personal freedom in no wise fits the usual teaching—would *prima facie* seem, indeed, to show the opposite. This difficulty must be disposed of.

The means of doing this are two, and are frequently used,

singly or in combination, to expunge the Puritan contribution from the record. The first is to glide over or ignore the fact of these religious origins, starting serious treatment of American history at some later point, usually a little before the War of Independence. In discussions of this type, the Puritans are dour and distant characters in funny hats, remote from the really important phases of our beginnings.

The second approach, when the Puritans are not ignored entirely, is to attack them. In this rendition, they are depicted as mean, reactionary people who tried to impose their views on everyone else, and created a dictatorial regime to do so. Seen this way, the job of establishing liberty in America began with overthrowing all things Puritan, replacing them with techniques of rational speculation. In either version, the conflict between religious piety and libertarian government is maintained.

On any fair appraisal of the American Puritans, this portrayal is off the mark. It is certainly true that they didn't believe in religious toleration as we know it (nor, for that matter, did virtually anyone else in the seventeenth century, up to and including Milton, Locke, and Roger Williams). On the other hand, they also didn't believe in imposing their religious views on others. They had a different theory about this subject altogether. In the teaching of New England, religious faith was entirely voluntary. While the settlers thought the state should support and cooperate with the church, they did not suppose the state could force belief. They viewed church and state alike as associations of the willing faithful. This was, indeed, the essence of their doctrine.

As diligent scholarship has shown, the people who first came over to New England professed this concept in a way uniquely favorable to the practice of self-government. This was the so-called "covenantal theology," preached in all the churches of the region. This resembled the usual Calvinist outlook, but it went a good deal further. As argued by founders of the movement, the correct approach in church polity was to consult the Scriptures, rather than the habitual practice of the English clergy. Such inquiry convinced the Puritans the proper form of organization was not a matter of king and bishops dictating forms of worship, but of believers joined together in voluntary fashion.

Drawing on the covenantal doctrines of the Old Testament and the small apostolic churches created under the dispensation of the New, these theorists specifically stressed the authority of the congregation in choice of ministers. Among those who advanced this notion were Protestant pastors Robert Browne, William Ames, and Henry Jacob. While such teachings varied, in the essentials they were agreed. And though they are little known to history (except for Browne, whose name initially was given to the movement), they were largely responsible for the doctrines that shaped our country.

In 1580, Browne had founded a congregational church in Norwich, attracting hostile notice from the authorities. Two years later, he fled to the Netherlands, where he published his *Treatise of Reformation without tarrying for any*. His conception of the matter was that "the kingdom of God was not to be begun by whole parishes but by the worthiest, be they never so few . . ." He added that "the church . . . is a company or number of Christians or believers, which by a willing covenant made with their God, are under the government of God and Christ . . ."[2]

The idea was further expounded by Jacob. A church, he said in 1605, is "a particular congregation being a spiritual corporation of believers, & having power in itself immediately from Christ to administer all religious means of faith to the members thereof." He added that the church thus formed was "an entire and independent body politic," which could be created only by "a free mutual consent of believers joining & covenanting to live as members of a holy society together in all religious & virtuous duties as Christ and his apostles did institute and practice in the gospel."[3]

As may be imagined, such teaching was offensive to the monarchs and episcopacy of England. Congregationalism denied the power of the king to rule the church as he saw fit, a power that Henry VIII had been at pains to take from Rome and had brutally defended against Reformers and the papacy alike. Moreover, the logic thus applied to ecclesiastical affairs could readily be translated to the realm of politics. James I had said a Presbyterian system agreed with kingship as did "God with the devil," and that "no bishop" meant "no king"—and congregationalism in this regard went well beyond the Presbyterians.[4]

From the outset, the Brownists had been subject to intensive persecution. In 1583, two men were executed merely for having copies of Browne's writings in their possession. In 1593, nonconformist leaders John Greenwood and Henry Barrow were hanged at Tyburn, and Congregationalist John Penry was drawn and quartered. Under James and later under Charles I, ministers who preached the doctrine were haled before ecclesiastical tribunals, and many were driven into exile.

Among those who felt the pressure of such persecution were members of a tiny church at Scrooby, in Nottinghamshire. The minister of this congregation was John Robinson, who had been an associate of Browne at Norwich. The leading elder was William Brewster, then bailiff to the Calvinist-leaning Archbishop Sandys of York (himself an exile in Geneva at the time of Mary). The views of the Scrooby congregation, as Robinson explained them, were identical to those of Browne and Jacob: ". . . a company consisting of but two or three, separated from the world, and gathered into the name of Christ by a covenant . . . is a church, and so hath the whole power of Christ . . . A company of faithful people thus covenanting together [is] a church, though they be without any officer among them . . ."[5]

In 1607, five members of this church were summoned before the ecclesiastical commission in York for being "disobedient in matters of religion." The congregation sought refuge in Holland, settling first in Amsterdam, then in Leyden. A decade later

they decided to move again, to the English colony of Virginia—
where they could own land, live as farmers, and manage their
own institutions. The exiles this time were fortunate in their
connections: the son of the archbishop of York was none other
than Sir Edwin Sandys, whose contractual view of government
we have already noted, and who happened to be a leading
member of the Virginia Company. This company was a redoubt
of Puritan and covenantal sentiment under James (a fact which
later caused him to put it out of business).

Sandys and his allies managed to get the exiles a patent for
settling in Virginia. They accordingly set sail in September 1620,
arriving off the coast of Massachusetts (even then a bit beyond
the northern reaches of Virginia) in November, and proceeded
to organize themselves according to the covenantal teaching.
Such was the provenance of the people known to history as the
Pilgrims.

Of similar but slightly different background were other believers in the congregational theory, not yet ready to give up on
England's established worship. The Pilgrims were explicit sep-
aratists and made no secret of their desire to sever ties with the
official church. The position of other Congregationalists was
more complex; though professing covenantal principles, they
thought these could best be defended by reforming Anglican
practice from within. So believing, such divines as John Cotton,
Thomas Hooker, and Thomas Shepard continued preaching as
long as they were able. This went on for a decade after the
Plymouth Pilgrims had departed, until Charles shut down the
Parliament of 1628–29. If this Parliament was a watershed in
English constitutional history, it was even more decisive for
America—since it triggered the events that led directly to our
founding.

For the next eleven years, Charles proceeded to rule without
a legislature, raising money on his own, jailing opponents, and
seeking through Archbishop Laud to suppress dissent among
the clergy. As a result, many who had sought to new-model the

establishment at last despaired, and decided they too should leave the country. Between 1629 and 1640, no fewer than twenty thousand Puritans fled from England, to America. This was an astonishing number, considering the distances and hazards of the journey. Though there had been small settlements before, it was this hegira that made the American colonies both permanent and substantial.

As important as the numbers were the character and opinions of the people who made the trip. The exodus was chiefly led by ministers, some of whom brought whole congregations with them. These were highly educated men, graduates of Cambridge and Oxford. Preeminent were Cotton, forced to resign his pulpit in 1633, and Hooker, cited before the high commission in 1630. They sailed together for America, soon to be followed by Shepard, Nathaniel Ward, and Roger Williams. Also leaving at this juncture was John Winthrop, a lay attorney, country squire, and devout believer in covenantal precepts. After Charles prorogued the Parliament in March of 1629, Winthrop met with other members of the Massachusetts Bay Company and devised a plan to remove their operations—and their charter—entirely to New England.

Though technically nonseparating, these Puritans held views remarkably similar to those of Plymouth Colony: the higher law, the covenantal nature of authority, the autonomy of local congregations. These resembled the contractual themes examined in Chapter X, but with this difference: The former were chiefly assertions about resistance to unlawful power; the New England spokesmen, required to create a government of their own, offered constructive statements about the proper basis of the state.

We have noted the ideas of Cotton in this respect, stressing that all human power should be subject to strict limitation. On matters pertaining to consent and covenant, he was equally explicit, endorsing the views expressed by Browne and Jacob. The theory of the congregational dissenters, as Cotton put it,

was that ". . . the ministers of Christ and the keys of the government in his church are given to each particular congregational
church respectively. And therefore neither ministers nor congregations are subject to the ecclesiastical jurisdiction of cathedral churches . . . but by voluntary consociation"[6]

Cotton was also quite definite on the origins of state authority, and the need for such arrangements to be founded in consent. "It is evident by the light of nature," he wrote, "that all civil
relations are founded on covenant. For, to pass by natural
relations between parent and children, and violent relations
between conqueror and captives, there is no other way given
whereby a people . . . free from natural and compulsory engage-
ments, can be united or combined together in one visible
body."[7] The echoes of the medieval doctrine, of the *Vindiciae*,
of Buchanan and Goodman are clear enough—as are the pre-
figurings, at the distance of roughly half-a-century, of Locke.
These elements are present as well in Hooker, as the following
passages clearly show:

"Mutual covenanting and confederation of the saints in the
fellowship of the faith according to the order of the Gospel is
that which gives constitution and being to a visible church . . . It
is free for any man to offer to join with another who is fit for
fellowship or to refuse . . . Therefore, they that do join, it is by
their own free consent and mutual engagement on both sides
. . . there is no man constrained to enter into such a condition,
unless he will; . . . among such who by no impression of nature,
no rule of providence, or appointment of God, or man, have
power each over the other, there must of necessity be a mutual
engagement, each of their own free consent . . ."[8]

We have the further example of Winthrop, who would become the leading political figure of Massachusetts. In his famous "city upon a hill" address aboard the *Arbella*, and in his
statements as governor of the Bay, Winthrop gave similar expressions of covenantal theory. Defending the commonwealth
against those who were *not* members of the covenant, he said,

for instance: "The essential form of a common weal or body politic such as this is . . . the consent of a certain company of people to cohabit together under one government for their mutual safety and welfare . . . for no man hath lawful power over another, but by birth or consent, so likewise . . . no man can have just interest in what belongeth to another without his consent . . . [Hence] no commonweal can be founded but by free consent."[9]

These statements should leave no doubt as to the specific sources of contractual doctrine in American thought, or the fact that these were inspired by religious teaching. The point is made still more conclusively by the policy of the settlers in creating their church and civil institutions. Especially noteworthy, given their nonseparating status, was that all the churches initially established in New England were on the congregational pattern. The first was founded in Salem on July 20, 1629, in the following manner: "About 30 heads of families, having formed a church covenant, elected . . . their teacher and pastor by ballot, the two ministers having admitted that they had no right to officiate without an 'outward calling' from the faithful."[10] The same procedure was invoked when the first church of Boston was formed under the stewardship of Cotton, when Shepard arrived to take up his duties, and in the other early churches.

The pattern was also evident in the political arrangements that were adopted, a development puzzling to some historians. A prime example is the Mayflower Compact, often treated as if it came from nowhere—a strange assertion of modern themes at a supposedly primitive time, like finding a computer printout locked up in a Victorian strongbox. For those familiar with the covenantal teaching, however, the compact is not at all surprising. It also refutes the notion that no community known to history has actually been created by social contract. It reads as follows:

"In the name of God, Amen. We whose names are underwritten, the loyal subjects of our dread Sovereign, Lord King James, by the grace of God, of Great Britain, France, and Ireland, King, Defender of the Faith, & c., having undertaken for the glory of our king and country, a voyage to plant the first colony in the northern parts of Virginia; do by these presents, solemnly and mutually, in the presence of God and one another, *covenant and combine ourselves together into a civil body politick*, for our better ordering and preservation, and furtherance of the ends aforesaid."[11] (Italics added.)

This agreement was executed on November 11, 1620— predating Locke's *Second Treatise* by seven decades. It proved to be an accurate precursor of the Plymouth polity, which thereafter featured annual elections for governor, deputy governor, and legislature. As with the churches of the era, the pattern was repeated often in the experience of New England. Here, for example, are the words of the Fundamental Orders of Connecticut (1639), the colony established and led by Thomas Hooker:

". . . well knowing where a people are gathered together the word of God requires that to maintain the peace and union of such a people there should be an orderly and decent government established according to God, [we] *do therefore associate and conjoin ourselves to be as one public state or commonwealth*; and . . . enter into combination and confederation together, to maintain and pursue the liberty and purity of the gospel of our Lord Jesus which we now profess . . ."[12] (Italics added.)

In keeping with such notions, this first of America's written constitutions ordained that "there shall be yearly two General Assemblies or courts," the first to be an election meeting in which the governor and magistrates of the colony would be chosen: "which choice shall be made by all that are admitted freemen and have taken the oath of fidelity, and do cohabit in this jurisdiction (having been admitted inhabitants by the major part of the town wherein they live), or the major part of such as shall be then present."[13]

A third example is Rhode Island, established because Roger Williams was such a rigid separatist that he abjured the theoretically conforming Massachusetts churches. The Rhode Island charter said its government should be "democraticall, that is a government held by the free and voluntary consent of all, or the greater part of the free inhabitants."[14] Despite the singularities of Rhode Island, the parallels to Plymouth and Connecticut—and adherence to covenantal teaching—are apparent.

These arrangements, especially those of Rhode Island, are sometimes noted in the conventional histories, if only to contrast them with Massachusetts. These smaller "liberal" settlements, it is suggested, were formed in opposition to the Puritan oligarchy and its reactionary doctrine. The Massachusetts theocrats, supposedly, resisted popular government at every step along the road; and since they were the quintessential Puritans, their conduct shows the true hostility of Christian faith to representative institutions.

One problem with this thesis is that Massachusetts, from the outset, *had* an elected, representative government—something that could not be deduced from the standard treatment. When this inconvenient fact must be referred to, it is put down to "demands" of the people that the oligarchs "grudgingly" conceded, and similar formulations. There is, however, scant evidence for this as it pertains to the creation of the colony (though there were plenty of subsequent wrangles about political matters of all sorts, as there were in all the other settlements).

Like the Virginia Company (whose example and fate the New England settlers had plainly studied), Massachusetts Bay was a commercial corporation. By its charter, it was to be run by a governor, a deputy governor, and eighteen "assistants," or directors, who were also "freemen," or shareholders of the corporation. Of those who emigrated, there were only the governor, the deputy, and six assistants. It was this commercial corporation that Winthrop and the others turned into the government of the colony—which seems to us an odd proceeding, but was customary for the time. (As with the Virginia Company and other commercial ventures of the era, the corporation was vested with political powers—to aid in the development of permanent colonization.)

When the Bay Company arrived in Massachusetts, the only people legally entitled to vote in its deliberations were its eight freemen-shareholders, all of whom were also corporate directors. Yet at their meeting of October 19, 1630, it was agreed by "the general vote of the people" that the freemen should elect the assistants, and shortly thereafter no fewer than *116 people* were admitted to exercise this privilege. (According to the calculations of Edmund Morgan, this would have been most of the male inhabitants, excluding indentured servants.)[15]

From the standpoint of the conventional teaching, this is all tremendously mysterious, and could only have come about if somehow the reactionaries had reluctantly yielded to the clamoring masses. If this portrayal were accurate, it would suggest that Winthrop and his cohorts were the most incompetent oligarchs known to history, since they no sooner set foot on American soil, after travelling three thousand miles to set up their theocracy, than they instantly handed over the power they were so anxious to retain.

Especially curious is the fact that Winthrop, though a supposed oligarch, was over a span of eighteen years repeatedly elected governor by the very people who had extorted power from him. Equally peculiar, in the years when he was not elected governor, Winthrop served as deputy governor, or assistant, peacefully stepping aside for others. This behavior is hard to reconcile with the image of a flinty autocrat, trying desperately to retain his post. It looks instead like someone who believed in the process of election, abided by the outcome of the voting, and was in turn respected by the people casting ballots.

Against the backdrop of the covenantal doctrine, of course, this otherwise baffling series of events is completely comprehensible. Given the many statements on this point by Winthrop and the congregational ministers, such measures were totally straightforward. They were an expression of the religious beliefs that led these people to America in the first place.

This obvious construction is borne out by many other actions taken by the authorities of the Bay. In 1632, an election was called, in which the General Court "ordered that two men be chosen from every plantation [i.e., settlement], to confer with the governor and assistants about raising taxes." (Winthrop explained the summons in a paraphrase of Edward I: "So as what they should agree upon should bind all.") In that election year, as well, *all* officials of the colony, including the governor, deputy governor, and assistants, were chosen by the expanded body of the freemen.[16]

Likewise congruent with covenantal doctrine and its stress on local congregations was the order of the General Court concerning towns. To this enactment of 1635 we owe the famous institution of the New England town meeting, and the tradition of localism that became a distinctive feature of our statecraft. The decree of the General Court reads as follows: "Whereas particular towns have many things which concern only themselves, it is therefore ordered that the freemen of every town, or the major part of them, shall only have the power to dispose of their own lands and woods . . . and make such orders as may concern the well ordering of their town . . . to levy and distrain . . . also to choose their own particular officers, as constables, surveyors of highways, and the like."[17] *

---

* Wertenbaker comments: "Under this act the town became to the state what the congregation was to the church. Localism in religion, which had become so vital a feature of Puritanism, was to be matched in New England by localism in government. Scholars, pointing out the town was rooted in English customs and tradition, trace its origin to Anglo-Saxon institutions. Yet it seems obvious that the founders of New England shaped it and gave it unusual powers for the

It is often objected that the founders of the Bay colony were
not "democrats," and this is true enough. Their opinions were
nearer to what would become known as "republican," holding
that members of the community had the power of election, but
that officers once elected should do the governing. They also
believed in, and in large measure achieved, the concept of
checks and balances. In a dispute of 1635, some of Winthrop's
opponents contended for a kind of simple majoritarianism, in
which the deputies could outvote the less numerous assistants,
now also magistrates. Winthrop resisted this, arguing the need
for concurrent powers. The General Court agreed, declaring
that "no law, order, or sentence shall pass as an act of the court
without the consent of the greater part of the magistrates on
the one part, and the greater number of deputies on the other."
In effect, this gave the colony a bicameral legislature.[18]

Still other features of free government were added in the
early going. Also in 1635, obviously a busy year, the General
Court appointed a committee to devise a system of laws "in
resemblance to a Magna Carta." Such a code was adopted in
1641 and did indeed resemble Magna Carta—incorporating
many of its provisions as well as principles of biblical law. As
instructive as the contents were the methods of adoption. The
draft of the Body of Liberties, Winthrop records, was "sent to
every town, to be considered first by the magistrates and el-
ders, and then to be published by the constables to all the
people, that if any man should think fit, that anything therein to
be altered, he might acquaint some of the deputies therewith
against the next court."[19]

Given all this, what was it that made the regime despotic?
The usual answer is restriction of the franchise—since only
church members were allowed to vote. According to James

---

purpose of aiding and buttressing the individual congregation." From the foregoing discussion, it would appear that these two explanations are comple-
mentary. (T.J. Wertenbaker, *The Puritan Oligarchy*, Grosset & Dunlap, 1937,
p. 45)

Truslow Adams, a vehement critic of the Puritans, this requirement disenfranchised "four out of five" inhabitants of the Bay,
negating claims in its behalf to truly representative government. Though frequently repeated, this statement is implausi-
ble on its face.

As discussed, the very idea of Massachusetts was to found a
community of believers, based on the bond of covenant. A
parallel in our era would be a commune, religious order, or
seminary devoted to a particular creed. If one day a group of
strangers showed up on the doorstep, saying they wanted to
live and work there without subscribing to its tenets, they
would quite probably (and properly) be turned away. An influx
of such people, after all, would change the very nature of the
institution.

This was exactly how the Puritans viewed the issue. Their
advice to nonbelievers was, not to stay in Massachusetts and be
lorded over, but to set up shop in some other venue. There was
plenty of wilderness, they noted, to go around. As Nathaniel
Ward expressed it, non-Puritans "shall have free liberty to keep
away from us, and such as will come to be gone as fast as they
can, the sooner the better."[20] Whatever one's opinion of this
policy, it makes it unlikely that Winthrop's Massachusetts was
teeming with non-Puritans. Nor is it probable that many people
could have wandered there not knowing of its religious character, which was, of course, its salient feature. (The equivalent
now would be a settler's moving to Israel, only to find out with
astonishment that it is a Jewish state, or to Saudi Arabia, without knowing it is Moslem.)

All of this means it is improbable, to say the least, that 80
percent of the adult males in Massachusetts were unchurched,
and thus disqualified from voting. Powell's researches on the
village of Sudbury show virtually every adult male inhabitant
to have been both a church member and a voter. Katherine
Brown cites similar data concerning Roxbury, Watertown,
members of the state militia, and the Bay Colony in general.

And, as Morison observes, the number of church members often exceeded the number of voters, since participation in political affairs was not to the taste of everyone back then, as it is not today.[21]

The Puritan approach, indeed, was at the time an extension of the franchise, rather than a restriction, since it made the vote available to believers regardless of property or position (a point of complaint among those of aristocratic outlook). This made it, as of 1632, the most open voting system in the world, excepting only its Plymouth neighbor. As Michael Hall, *et al.*, observe: "It is difficult to determine exactly what proportion of the population was entitled to vote in Massachusetts under this franchise, but without a doubt it was a far larger proportion than was entitled to vote in any European country."[22]

Casting further light on the question are religious data from the period just before the revolution—more than a century after the settlers arrived in Massachusetts. Though even at this later time there is considerable room for speculation, by and large the records are more complete and conclusions more reliable. And what the data show is that the population of Massachusetts, ca. 1750, was overwhelmingly Congregational, by a margin of ten-to-one—if not a great deal higher.

At this period, indeed, Jonathan Mayhew reckoned the Congregational portion of the colony as greater than other denominations by a ratio of fifty-to-one. This seems excessive, and may be put down to Mayhew's zeal in behalf of the Congregational interest. This estimate, however, was later confirmed by Thomas Hutchinson, the leading Tory, who reported to England that virtually all the colonists were of this outlook. In 1760, Ezra Stiles gave a more modest breakdown—about eight-to-one in favor of Congregationalists vs. all the others.[23] There seems no good reason to doubt these statements, coming as they do from such divergent sources. They are the more instructive in that they derive from the middle of the eighteenth century, at the peak of the Enlightenment era, such as it was in North America.

By this time the original charter had been revoked, the religious requirements for voting had been rescinded, the zeal of the early Puritans had abated, and religious diversity was obviously greater than at the outset.

Yet even in these circumstances, according to the estimates, Congregationalists made up between 85 and 98 percent of the Massachusetts population. The level of congregationalism a hundred years before would have been a good deal higher—though 98 percent doesn't leave much margin for expansion. On the record, the religious qualification for the vote, as of the 1630s, excluded hardly any adult male in the colony, indentured servants excepted. By the standards of the day, this proviso afforded Massachusetts something pretty close to universal manhood suffrage.*

Thus, in an amazingly brief interval, the founders of New England had created most of the features of representative, balanced government: a theory of constitutionalism, power wielded by consent, annual elections with an expansive franchise, a bicameral legislature, local autonomies, and a Bill of Rights. Not bad for a bunch of grasping tyrants, working in a trackless wilderness three thousand miles from civilization, in the span of a single decade.

As Tocqueville would note two centuries later, the ideas and practices thus established became the template for American institutions. With remarkably few changes, the forms of government created in New England were repeated in the other colonies and states, and thereafter in the federal Constitution. This great observer of our politics considered the performance to be impressive, and in this respect as in most others

---

* This point is reinforced by Robert Brown's meticulous researches into voting requirements and patterns in the colony after 1691, when the franchise was based on property instead of religion. Even with this change-over, Brown demonstrates, very few adult males in Massachusetts were excluded from the vote, again contrary to the usual image. (See *Middle Class Democracy and the Revolution in Massachusetts, 1691–1780*, Cornell, 1955)

his judgment was grounded in a careful survey of the record.

Though totally contrary to the usual teaching, the achievement of these settlers is not that hard to fathom. They were simply applying in consistent fashion their covenantal notions, along with precepts familiar from the English common law. Such developments seem puzzling only if the religious backdrop is ignored; unfortunately, since many historians have been anxious to condemn or downplay our religious heritage, this is exactly what has happened.

As with the theories considered in the preceding chapter, these notions were obviously not of secular or Enlightenment provenance, and in particular were not derived from Locke. Again, the chronological factor is decisive; the evidence cited here not only predates the *Second Treatise*, most of it predates the existence of Locke himself. The Mayflower Compact was written in 1620; Massachusetts and its elections date from 1630; the statements quoted from Cotton and Hooker from 1635–38; the Fundamental Orders of Connecticut from 1639; and so forth.

Equally mistaken is the left-handed way of stating the connection—that, by uncanny foresight, Thomas Hooker or the authors of the Mayflower Compact "anticipated" Locke, and that by virtue of this feat deserve some kind of honorable footnote in the secular history. This, too, gets the situation backwards; the point is not that Cotton or Hooker (or Buchanan, or the *Vindicae*) "anticipated" Locke, or Jefferson. It is rather that the Puritans, Locke, and the Founding Fathers were all inheritors of the medieval doctrine, the covenantal teachings of the sixteenth century, and the common law of England, and constructed theories of the state in keeping with this background.

These comments have dealt only obliquely with some of the familiar charges against the Puritans—the disputes with Roger Williams and Anne Hutchinson, the persecution of the Quakers, the sumptuary laws, the Salem witch trials of the 1690s. Our effort has been to trace the pedigree of institutions, rather than to attempt a defense or condemnation of the Puritan regime in its entirety. Enough to say that, even if every other critique of the Puritans is granted *arguendo*, their political accomplishments remain. The founders of Massachusetts were not democrats, proponents of toleration, or libertarians—far from it. They were devout believers who based church and civil authority on their reading of the Scriptures. They planted on American soil virtually every institution of free government with which we are familiar—and did so squarely on the basis of religious precept.

12

The American Revolution

THOUGH NO SINGLE dispute could possibly capture the complex events and themes that led to America's War of Independence, the episode that arguably came the closest began on the evening of March 5, 1770.

On that date, Captain Thomas Preston and a squad of British redcoats confronted an angry mob in Boston, protesting the presence in their city of two regiments sent there to uphold the tenuous power of the crown. Chunks of ice were thrown, insults shouted, one of the soldiers was knocked to the ground. In the melee, the redcoats fired their weapons, resulting in the deaths of five Americans. This was the "Boston massacre," forever infamous in revolutionary legend.

This violent clash enraged the citizens of Massachusetts, already embittered by years of wrangling with the British. Opponents of Whitehall's imperial policy, led by James Otis and John Adams, had fiercely contested efforts to tax the colonies, the seizure of goods and vessels, and other coercive measures of the preceding decade. Adams had been in the forefront of the protest, leading resistance to the Stamp Act and providing legal aid to merchants charged with violating trade laws.

Preston and his men were brought to trial before a Massachusetts jury, amid inflammatory calls for vengeance. The plea of the accused was self-defense, against the actions of an unruly mob. Their lead attorney was—John Adams. Thanks to the arguments made by Adams and Josiah Quincy, Jr., another Patriot spokesman, Preston was acquitted, as were most of the other redcoats (two were convicted of manslaughter, but let off with light sentences, six others found not guilty).

That incident tells us much about the American Revolution, the leaders who nursed it into being, and the people who would thereby gain their independence. It is noteworthy that Adams and Quincy would defend the soldiers at the height of an emotional outcry against the British—an outcry to which they were intensely sympathetic. Even more so is that a Massachusetts jury could see its way to an acquittal, however sharp the lawyers. That says something about the average American of the day, and prevailing notions of law and justice. (So does the fact that Adams, weeks after having accepted the soldiers as his clients, was elected to the colonial assembly, receiving almost 80 percent of the ballots cast.)*

These are items to bear in mind when we are asked to bracket the American Revolution with the carnage that would occur in France, replete with guillotines, mass terror, and official mayhem. There were indeed scenes of mob action and civil disobedience in America: tar and feathers, the Boston Tea Party, and other such disorders once open warfare had been started. But there was as well, throughout, a countervailing stress on legal form and opposition to unbridled violence. As Adams would comment almost two decades later:

"I begin to suspect that some gentlemen who had more zeal than knowledge in the year 1770, will soon discover that I had good policy, as well as sound law, on my side, when I ventured

---

* There is a theory that Sam Adams arranged for his cousin to conduct the defense, in order to keep information about the riot from being aired in court. This may well be. It doesn't change the fact that acquittal of the soldiers was contrary to the Patriot desire and interest, or that John Adams was risking a great deal by taking on the case. (See Catherine Drinker Bowen, *John Adams and the American Revolution*, Grosset, 1950, pp. 364–365, 382–383)

to lay open before our people the laws against riots, routs, and unlawful assemblies. Mobs will never do to govern states, or command armies. I was as sensible of it in 1770 as I am in 1787. To talk of liberty in such a state of things! Is not [a popular agitator] as great a tyrant, when he would pluck up law and justice by the roots, as a Bernard or Hutchinson [royal governors of the province], when he would overturn them partially? . . ."[1]

Adams' role in this affair, and his reflections on it, argue that there was something different about the American Revolution—something that set it apart from the vicious insurrections of the modern era, with which we are unhappily familiar. Indeed, this is merely part of a vast array of data that point to such conclusions. On any sober appraisal of our history, the most remarkable things about the revolution were its conservatism, self-restraint, and penchant for the rule of law.

Again, this is a reversal of the accepted teaching. It is quite usual for even the most dispassionate histories of the revolution to describe the Patriots as "radicals," while their pro-British foes are routinely called "conservatives," thereby equating radicalism with the cause of independence. Some ideological theorists, as is well known, have pushed the "radical" theme to even greater lengths, portraying the revolution as a species of class struggle. As a little inquiry will determine, such treatment turns the facts of record inside-out.

To see the point, we need only extend the contrast with events in France. Quite apart from its taste for beheading people, the French upheaval was authentically radical, in every way that can be imagined. Its object was to overthrow existing institutions, sever contact with the past, and invent society *de novo*. The doctrines that it advanced were purely theoretical, having almost no basis in experience or established law. And it sought to reach utopian goals through unchecked, completely arbitrary, power.

If this is the standard for radical revolution, then "radical" is precisely what the American Revolution wasn't. In every major aspect, it was the reverse of what would occur in France, and thereafter in many other modern revolutions. Rather than trying to overturn the existing order, the American War of Independence was an effort to preserve that order; rather than rejecting the counsels of tradition, it was traditionalist to the last degree; and instead of trying to organize society by abstractions, it resorted constantly to the lessons of experience.

Above all else, the American Revolution was hostile to any and all ideas of unfettered power, from whatever source it was derived or in whose interest it was wielded. This was indeed the very essence of the struggle; it was also a direct result of the conservatism of the Founders, and the principal reason that the government they created would be the freest known to history. The point of connection would appear repeatedly throughout the revolutionary/constitutional era.

By far the most conspicuous feature of the Patriots' dispute with Whitehall was that they prided themselves so much on *being English*. The constant theme of the colonials was that they were loyal, true-blue Englishmen, devoted to the British constitution and hence to British freedoms. Thus, to pick a few examples, Rhode Island Gov. Stephen Hopkins described the English system as "this glorious constitution, the best that ever existed among men." Rev. John Tucker of Massachusetts, in a 1771 election sermon, prayed that "this excellent constitution, formed and established by the wisdom of ages, be preserved inviolate, the source of blessings to this and future generations." Virginia's Carter Braxton, in 1776, extolled "the wisdom of that Constitution and government, which raised the people of that island to their late degree of greatness."[2]

These statements were sincere—if hopelessly outdated, by London standards, in their construction of the British system. The colonists had a high regard for England and its traditions, and constantly made their plea for liberty in this spirit. Once more, the atmosphere was completely different from that in France: Where Frenchmen talked about the "rights of man," devoid of historic or legal context, Americans proclaimed the "rights of free-born Englishmen," a phrase they used with metronomic regularity. And even when the argument was pressed back to its axiomatic basis, in terms of natural law or religion, allusions to English legal history would continue.

The focus of this Anglophilia was the body of belief and practice examined in Chapter V: the heritage of the common law, as expounded by Lord Coke, threading back to Magna Carta. The outlook was well suggested again by Adams, who observed that "the liberty, the unalienable, indefeasible rights of men, the honor and dignity of human nature, the grandeur and glory of the public, and the universal happiness of individuals, were never so skillfully and successfully consulted as in that most excellent monument of human art, the common law of England."[3] And the common law approach, as we have seen, was about as far from ideas of radical innovation as it was possible to get.

The attitude also suffuses Jefferson's memoir of events in January 1777, in the early days of revolutionary fighting. At this juncture, Jefferson, George Mason, and other eminent men met in Fredericksburg to draft a set of laws for now-autonomous Virginia. Here, if ever, was a chance for American "radicals" to step forth in good Enlightenment fashion, and devise a legal code embracing all their pet abstractions. What they produced was by and large the opposite: *a painstaking adaptation of existing law*—albeit with changes dictated by their altered status—based on American experience and the British legal background. This legislative goal was stressed by Jefferson and Mason in their separate recollections of the project.*

---

* This was the famous revisal committee whose members also included George Wythe, Edmund Pendleton, and Thomas L. Lee. Most discussions of Jefferson's efforts in this regard focus on the changes he proposed—concerning, e.g., laws respecting primogeniture or religious freedom—and omit this remarkable testament to his conservatism. Mason's summary of the revisal effort reads as follows: "*The common law is not to be meddled with, except where alterations are necessary*, the statutes to be revised and digested, alterations proper for us to be made; the diction where obsolete or redundant, to be reformed; *but otherwise to undergo as few changes as possible* . . . Laws to be made on the spur

Advocates of the "radical" version of our founding might ponder Jefferson's explanation of this effort: *"In the execution of my part,"* he said, *"I thought it material not to vary the diction of the ancient statutes by modernizing it, nor to give rise to new questions by new expressions. The text of these statutes had been so fully explained and defined, by numerous adjudications, as scarcely ever now to produce a question in our courts."* The resulting adaptation, he added, included parts of the common law that needed legislative definition, "all the British statutes from Magna Carta to the present day, and all the laws of Virginia, from the establishment of our legislature to the present time, which we thought should be retained. . . ."[4] (Italics added.)

The point about this episode is not merely what it tells us about the legal-mindedness of Jefferson and his colleagues, although that is certainly apparent. It is also that these alleged "radicals" were concerned to *maintain a system that was already in being*—based on centuries of precedent and settled practice. It was to this body of long-established, well-adjudicated law that the colonists referred when they invoked the "rights of free-born Englishmen." English legal safeguards, the Patriots argued, crossed the Atlantic with the initial settlers, embodied in the patents that approved the journey. The royal charters of Virginia, for example, said that subjects dwelling there "shall have and enjoy all liberties, franchises and immunities . . . as if they had been abiding and born within this our realm of England." The other patents were less explicit, but squinted in the same direction. The Massachusetts charter of 1629 said the laws affecting the settlers there should be "laws not contrary to the laws and statutes of England." Rhode Island's specified "laws not repugnant to the laws of England."[5] And so on.

---

of the present occasion [i.e., the war], *and all innovating laws to be limited in their duration."* (Italics added.) (Gilbert Chinard, *Thomas Jefferson*, Ann Arbor, 1962, p. 91)

To the British, these phrases simply meant Americans should be subject to the laws of England, as expressed in the decrees of Parliament. To the colonists, they meant something rather different: the rights and privileges embedded in the common law—trial by jury, *habeas corpus*, government by consent instead of edict. Most relevant to the dispute with Whitehall, they meant the right of Englishmen to be taxed by their elected representatives—chosen by the people who had to pay the taxes.*

As Jefferson's comments indicate, this wasn't mere nostalgia for the ancient country. It was also an expression of the Patriots' own considerable history in the new. At the epoch of our founding, it should be recalled, English colonists had been living in America for a century and a half, a span of time respectable even by British historical standards and by our own enormous. To get perspective, we need only observe that roughly as many years had passed between the settlement of Plymouth (1620) and the inauguration of George Washington (1789) as thereafter elapsed until the election of John Kennedy (1960).

During all this period, the colonies had enjoyed substantial independence, especially with regard to Parliament, and most especially in matters of taxation. This is much neglected in conventional histories that depict American advocates of resistance as "radicals" or "Whigs" (or, even better, "radical Whigs")—terms suggesting not only a yen for reckless innova-

* Colonial protests to this effect were many, and emphatic. The New Jersey assembly stated, for example: "We look upon all taxes laid upon us without our consent as a fundamental infringement of the rights and privileges secured to us as English subjects." Other assemblies used the identical formulation: ". . . that great badge of English liberty, of being taxed only with our own consent" (New York). ". . . that inherent right of every English subject, not to be taxed but by his own consent or that of his representatives" (South Carolina). "That the colonists may not be taxed but by the consent of their own representatives . . ." (Rhode Island) (Knollenberg, op. cit., pp. 184, 198–199. Jack P. Greene, ed., *The Reinterpretation of the American Revolution*, Harper & Row, 1968, p. 159)

tion but also an affinity to claims of parliamentary power. Such notions are totally inaccurate, misstating the nature of the struggle in almost every way that matters. "Whigs" in America at this period, as may readily be shown, were the polar opposites of "Whigs" in England.

For one thing, there is the fact that the Americans thought themselves more closely connected to *the king* than to the Parliament—a point that is all-important in understanding the revolution. Since the earliest settlements had received their charters from the crown, the colonists argued, they owed no allegiance to the House of Commons. Their own assemblies were their legislatures, which alone could exercise the power of taxation. This thesis was advanced by every leading advocate of the Patriot interest: Dickinson in the *Pennsylvania Farmer*, Richard Bland in his *Inquiry Into the Rights of the British Colonies*, Adams in *Novanglus*, Hamilton in *The Farmer Refuted*, Jefferson in the *Summary View*, Wilson in his *Considerations on the Authority of Parliament*.*

The colonists' view about this matter is often treated as a peculiar "theory of the British Empire," invented for the occasion by wily strategists of independence. Once more, however, this misconceives the whole endeavor, and ignores the facts of colonial history prior to the War of Independence. The reason that the Americans held this opinion—and were so unanimous in doing so—is that it was grounded squarely on the record. Rather than trying to found their practice on an abstract

---

* The views of Wilson, whose knowledge of and attachment to the British common law we have already noted, were entirely typical. ". . . the commons of Great Britain have no dominion over their equals and fellow-subjects in America . . . [the colonists] took possession of the country in the king's name; . . . they established governments under the sanction of his prerogatives, or by virtue of his charters; no application for those purposes was made to parliament; no ratification of the charters or letters patent was solicited from that assembly . . . the only dependency which they ought to acknowledge is a dependency on the crown." (Samuel Eliot Morison, ed., *Sources and Documents Illustrating the American Revolution*, Oxford, 1965, pp. 111–113)

theory, the colonists were doing exactly the reverse. In good conservative fashion, they based their theory on long established usage.

Representative institutions, as we have seen, were part of the colonial experience from the beginning, and not only in New England. Chronological pride of place in this respect goes to Virginia, though the story there was complicated by many factors. In August 1619 the Virginia Company had authorized the Old Dominion to set up an elected House of Burgesses, along with an appointed council, "to make and ordain whatsoever laws should by them be thought good and profitable for our subsistence."[6]* This would make Virginia's elected legislature the oldest such assembly in the world outside the British Isles—and in one view of the matter its achievements exceeded those of England. Such a distinction was not one that Virginians of the eighteenth century (or the twentieth) were likely to forget, or surrender without a struggle.

Even when James in 1624 shut down the parent company and made Virginia a royal colony, the early impetus toward self-government would continue—bringing off the improbable feat of combining elective institutions with allegiance to the Stuarts. Representatives of the colony's infant "boroughs" still met on a regular basis for the next few years, though details of what they did are murky. Beginning in 1630, the General Assembly came together formally in annual meetings, passing laws and tending to other official matters. This was the period, it may be recalled, when Charles was ruling by decree in England. Thus even when Parliament was out of business, for a span of eleven years, Virginia's assembly continued to function.

Its right to do so was confirmed by Charles in 1641, greatly

* A major player in this initiative was Sir Edwin Sandys, who the following year would help the Plymouth Pilgrims in their journey to America. One could make a plausible case that Sandys was the founding father of self-government in our country. (See Alf Mapp, Jr., *The Virginia Experiment*, Open Court, 1974, pp. 13–80; A. L. Rowse, *The Elizabethans and America*, Harper, 1959, pp. 80–82, 105–107)

endearing the king to his Virginia subjects; so much so that the following year, they petitioned him *not* to reinstate the Company, but rather to continue their status as a royal holding, directly dependent on the crown. As they explained it, "the present happiness is exemplified to us by the freedom of yearly assemblies, warranted to us by his majesty's gracious instructions."[7] So in the early going, Virginia conceived an attachment to the king, linked to the practice of self-government. Its allegiance was to Charles, not to the Company or—most relevant to ensuing struggles—to the House of Commons.

The most significant feature of this history is that Virginia always enjoyed the right of self-taxation, and had no dealings in this regard, or almost any other, with the Parliament. This right was pointedly reconfirmed in 1643 by royalist Gov. William Berkeley, at the outset of the civil war in England. In this conflict, as might be guessed from the foregoing, Virginia was hostile to Westminster, and became the more so after the execution of the king. When the Roundheads informed the colony they would henceforth control its economic fortunes, Berkeley offered this analysis of Parliament's presumed authority:

"We are more slaves by nature than their power can make us if we suffer ourselves to be shaken by these paper bullets . . . The sun looks not on a people more free than we are from all oppression . . . The Londoners . . . would take away the liberty of our consciences, and our right of giving and selling our goods to whom we please . . . By the Grace of God, we will not so tamely part with our king and all these blessings we enjoy under him. And if they oppose us, do but follow me. I will either lead you to victory or lose a life which I cannot more gloriously sacrifice . . ."[8]

In the event, Virginia and the Parliament reached a stand-off, and came to an agreement that preserved much of the self-governing status of the province. By terms of this accord, signed in 1651, the colony's right of self-taxation was, again, expressly stated. The agreement said "*Virginia shall be free*

*from all taxes, customs, and impositions whatever, and none
to be imposed without the consent of the Grand Assembly."*
(Italics added.) Thus even at the height of Cromwellian power,
the Old Dominion had stood its ground for independence—
precedents well remembered by common lawyers of the revolutionary era. Jefferson, for example, referred to these events
in his *Summary View*, and included the text of the 1651 agreement in his *Notes on Virginia*.[9]

Equally conversant with this background was Richard Bland,
whose *Inquiry* in 1766 sounded one of the early trumpet calls
against taxation by Westminster. Bland recalled the history of
early attachment to the crown, the fact that Virginians had
never been dependent on the Parliament with respect to taxes,
and that they had renounced the commonwealth in favor of
Charles II a year before the restoration. Under this Charles as
well, Bland pointed out, it had been agreed that *"taxes ought
not to be laid upon the inhabitants and proprietors of the
colony but by the common assent of the General Assembly"*—
though it was conceded that Parliament could levy external
duties for purposes of regulating trade. (Italics added.)[10] Thus
the precedents of Virginia history with which Jefferson, Bland
and others were familiar all pointed in the same direction: the
colony had never been subject to a revenue by the House of
Commons.

Throughout this period, of course, Virginia was very much a
Stuart enclave, and hostile to Britain's Puritan legislature to
begin with. But it is remarkable to note that New England's
congregationalists expressed a like opinion on the subject, and
came up with the same conclusions on the underlying issues. As
is obvious from the matter already cited, the Puritan settlers
meant to be independent all along—as when they carefully
removed their charter, officialdom, and governing machinery to
Massachusetts, rather than leaving things to be meddled with by
Whitehall. With this accomplished, they proceeded to argue that
their royal charter gave them the privilege of self-government.

The Puritans' aversion to rule from London always included Parliament, even when it was being run entirely by their co-religionists. Singular proof of this was provided by the civil war, in which Massachusetts maintained a neutral stance between the Cavaliers and Roundheads, maneuvering with steady purpose to avoid subjection to Westminster. In one notable instance, Winthrop's government punished a parliamentary privateer that fired on a royalist vessel in Boston harbor. In another, it rejected proposals to send a legislative delegation to London, since "if we should put ourselves under the protection of the Parliament, we must then be subject to such laws as they should make."[11]*

The lesson of such episodes was not that the Massachusetts settlers were somehow partial to the Stuarts, which of course they weren't. It was rather that they had adopted an independent stance toward *all* authorities in England, including Parliament, were accustomed to doing things without its say-so, and meant to keep it that way. Self-government was the Boston method, and anyone acquainted with its history might have foreseen the troubles that developed at the revolution. Predictably, there were more such cases following the Stuart restoration, as in this pugnacious salvo from 1661:

"The governor, deputy governor, assistants and select representatives have full power and authority, both legislative and executive, for the government of all people here ... without appeal, excepting law or laws repugnant to the laws of England. *The government is privileged of all fitting means (yea,*

---

* The men of Massachusetts were full of such surprises, often disappointing expectations in their era, as well as ours. In 1647, Nathaniel Ward returned to London as a famous divine and author, and was invited to preach before the Parliament—whose army had recently captured Charles. Ward was the principal author of the Body of Liberties, a devotee of the common law and England's system of mixed government; he delivered a sermon defending the king, denouncing the army, and telling the astonished Parliament that if they could not control the soldiers, they should "give way to a new Parliament that could." (Samuel Eliot Morison, *Builders of the Bay Colony*, Houghton Mifflin, 1964, p. 242)

*and if need be, by force of arms) to defend themselves, both by
land and by sea, against all such person or persons as shall at
any time attempt or enterprise the destruction, invasion,
detriment, or annoyance of this plantation, or the inhabitants
thereof...*" (Italics added.)[12] *

In the latter part of the century, Charles II launched an exasperated effort to rein in the Northern colonists, including suspension of their charter and appointment of a royal governor to
subdue them. These events prefigured, to an uncanny degree,
the battles that would occur a century later. When Gov. Edmund Andros abridged the powers of its assembly, Massachusetts demanded taxation by consent and other rights of
Englishmen. The conflict ended in 1689, coterminous with the
Glorious Revolution, as the Puritans succeeded in ousting Andros and restoring their elective system, amid scenes of popular rejoicing. With this disreputable exception, the people of
New England, like the inhabitants of Virginia, had always enjoyed the privilege of self-taxation.

While Virginia and Massachusetts were the most obdurate of
the colonies, Rhode Island and Connecticut were not far behind, and all the "plantations" had something similar in their
outlook. They were, after all, three thousand miles from England; the official British presence in the colonies was slight;
and the settlers for the most part were left to fend for themselves in turning a wilderness into a civilized society. The habits
engrained by this experience, as several British ministries
would learn, were hard to alter.

---

* If that didn't sufficiently hint a mood of independence, the dispatch of British
agent Edward Randolph to Charles II in 1676 further clarified the situation.
Randolph reported the governor of the Bay as saying that "laws made by your
majesty and your Parliament obligeth them in nothing but what consists with the
interest of the colony, that the legislative power is and abides in them solely to
act and make laws by virtue of a charter from your royal majesty's father, and
that all matters in difference are to be concluded by their final determination..."
(Michael Hall, et al, eds., *The Glorious Revolution in America*, North Carolina,
1964, p. 19)

This history of spirited self-reliance and *de facto* independence, and the colonists' acute awareness of it, must be kept in mind if we want to understand the events that developed into the American revolution. The pivotal decade in this respect was the 1760s, marked by the accession of George III, the conclusion of the French and Indian War, and many other momentous changes. Most relevant to our discussion, the decade brought a decisive shift in imperial dealings with the colonies. Burdened with debt from their struggles with the French, the British executed an abrupt *demarche*—a concerted effort to tighten up on their American cousins and raise some added revenue for the crown. It was this drastic change of front that led inexorably to conflict, and ultimately to independence.

The new imperial program included three major tax bills, draconian restraints on trade, procedures for trying cases without juries, and suspension of colonial legislative powers. The British also moved to close off the Western spaces to immigration from coastal regions and install an Anglican bishopric in New England—the very thing the Puritans had fled the homeland to avoid. This last redoubled the Northern colonists' fears that some vast design had been concocted to "enslave" them. (It also suggested the continued power of religious motives in their thinking.)

There has been a good deal of debate among historians as to whether the Americans were justified in their alarmist views about all this, should have paid more for imperial upkeep, or held consistent views about the nature of the colonial system. While interesting as matters of detail, such speculations obscure the major point at issue, which is essential to any analysis of the Patriot reaction: *Namely, that the policies the British launched in this fateful decade were radical changes in the colonists' long-accustomed, and highly cherished, way of doing things.* Whatever the nuances otherwise, this was the most obvious feature of the British program, the proximate cause of all the conflict, and the central theme of all colonial agitation.

John Dickinson made the point in his historical survey, again suggesting the legalistic temper: "I have looked over every statute relating to these colonies from their first settlement to this time; and I find every one of them founded on this principle [of trade regulation], till the Stamp Act administration. All before are calculated to regulate trade . . . The raising of a revenue thereby was never intended . . . Here we may observe an authority expressly claimed and exerted to impose duties on these colonies, not for the regulation of trade . . . but for the single purpose of levying money upon us. This I call an innovation; and a most dangerous innovation . . ."[13]

On this score, it should be noted, there is no serious dispute, since both sides observed the novelty of what was occurring. Despite some obfuscations floated by Grenville and Townshend on "external" vs. "internal" taxes,* the change of policy was basically admitted by the English, whose idea was precisely to plant and harvest a brand-new system of taxation. British Treasury official Thomas Whately, for example, described the Stamp Act as "a great measure . . . on account of the important point it establishes, the right of Parliament to lay an internal tax on the colonies." Such also was Lord North's rationale for retaining the famous tax on tea—insignificant as a revenue measure, but all-important in the principle it would establish. "An acknowledgement of the right," one British spokesman argued, "was of more value than millions."[14]

That this was a reversal of long-standing practice was noted also by the British opposition. The Duke of Newcastle, for

---

* Grenville argued that the Americans had accepted the first, and therefore should accept the second. In fact, as is plain from Dickinson's statement, the distinction the colonists drew was between imposts levied for purposes of *trade regulation* and those intended to *raise a revenue*. While the line was perhaps difficult to draw, the principle was clear enough, and consistently stated. The only notable exception was an early statement by Franklin before the House of Commons; all the colonial manifestos made the trade-vs.-revenue distinction. The point was clearly acknowledged, e.g., by British spokesmen such as Gov. Bernard and Lord Hillsborough (Burke, op. cit., pp. 56, 66.)

example, held out at length against colonial levies, rejecting "any alteration that may be proposed in the present constitution, or received use and practice with regard to our settlements in America." Burke made the point in his famous speech in our behalf, reprising the history Dickinson had cited, and concluding with the essence of Burkean wisdom on such matters: "Leave the Americans as they anciently stood . . . Do not burthen them with taxes; you were not used to do so from the beginning. Let this be your reason for not taxing."[15]

What English officials were debating among themselves, the colonists were shouting from the rooftops. The American people, said the assembly of Massachusetts, *"had always judged by their representatives* both of the way and manner in which taxes should be raised within their respective governments . . ." Virginia's position was the same: "His majesty's liege people of his most ancient and loyal colony have enjoyed without interruption, the inestimable right of being governed by such laws, respecting their internal polity and taxation, as are derived from their own consent . . . *which right has never been forfeited or yielded, but has been constantly recognized by the kings and people of Great Britain."*[16] (Italics added.) As has been seen, these were entirely accurate statements of the situation.

The identical points were made by other assemblies, and by intercolonial meetings called to mobilize resistance. In all of the resulting manifestoes, the rights of "free-born Englishmen," the history of the British constitution, and long-established practice were cited in profusion. The Stamp Act Congress, for instance, put it this way: ". . . it is inseparably essential to the freedom of a people, and the undoubted right of Englishmen, that no taxes be imposed on them, but with their own consent, given personally, or by their representatives . . . The only representatives of the people of these colonies are persons chosen therein by themselves, and . . . no taxes ever have been, or can be constitutionally imposed on them, but by their respective legislatures."

As late as July of 1775, in declaring its right to take up arms (a manifesto jointly drafted by Jefferson and Dickinson), the Continental Congress was still denouncing the British for "meditated innovations": "Parliament was influenced to take up the pernicious project, and assuming a new power over them, have in the course of eleven years given decisive specimens of the spirit and consequences attending this power ... They have undertaken to give and grant our money without our consent, *though we have ever exercised an exclusive right to dispose of our own property.*"[17] (Italics added.)

There is a great deal more like this, all marked by an elaborate legalism, resort to precedent, appeals to history and ancient usage. In the literature of colonial protest, one encounters little suggesting visionary schemes of government, plans of social renovation, or overthrow of the established order. The presentation is just the other way around—an attempt to fend off changes and adhere to known procedures, by which they had historically been governed. What the colonists wanted was the *status quo ante*—before the Stamp Act, Townshend duties, abrogation of jury trials and patrolling redcoats. Above all, they wanted their accustomed right of self-taxation.

Americans of the era were thus traditionalist in two different, albeit overlapping, senses: They consistently appealed to their *British heritage* under the common law, which in their view entitled them to taxation only by consent, as well as to other legal rights and privileges; and they recurred to their *American experience*, extending back 150 years, in which revenue bills had been the purview of their own assemblies. In both respects, therefore, they fought to keep what was established and familiar. *It was the British policy, self-consciously aimed at destroying this layer-cake of precedent, that was authentically revolutionary.* Such was the constant argument of the colonists, and such also is the voluminous witness of the record.

Under the circumstances, the widespread habit of describing the Patriot spokesmen as "radicals" and defenders of the British program as "conservatives," is perverse to the point of total obfuscation. It is of a piece with our discussion of "conservatism" as a mere defense of reigning power, irrespective of all other factors. It neglects the traditionalism and legalism of the colonists, masks the radical changes attempted by the British, and distorts the issues that brought on the War of Independence. The terminology suggests the break with England resulted from a rage for innovation, when it in fact resulted from a desire to fend off unwelcome changes. A greater reversal of historical form would be difficult to imagine.

If the Americans were conservative in trying to keep accustomed practice, they were equally so in terms of the principles they defended. At this level, indeed, the clash with Britain was even more profound, since it involved not merely adhering to tradition, but the most fundamental attitudes about the state. Differences of this type became increasingly clear in the course of the prerevolutionary struggle, as the combatants were driven to define the basic theories on which their views were founded. The chasm revealed by this debate was so immense as to preclude, at last, all hope of reconciliation.

The point in conflict, as it happens, was exactly the issue considered in our earlier discussion: Whether the power of the ruler shall be unchecked and arbitrary, or subject to some exterior principle of constraint; whether law is merely the will of the sovereign, or the product of a constitutional-legal system that is controlling on official conduct. As noted, this is the foremost question in the history of Western statecraft, dating back to the *lex regia* of the ancients and its denial by the worldview of the Bible, and recurring thereafter down through the eons of constitutional struggle.

On this issue, the lines between the British and the Americans were drawn with utmost clarity, and, despite some nuances of detail, in substance never varied. In so many words, all leading spokesmen for the British interest said there were *no limits whatsoever on the power of Parliament*, other than its own discretion. The unanimity with which this concept was advanced is one of the more amazing aspects of the record—and was viewed with appropriate outrage by American pamphleteers and statesmen. They flatly denied that Parliament had such boundless power, or that its claims to do so were compatible with English freedoms.

The essence of British constitutionalism, the Patriots said, was that no man or group of men was entitled to wield unchecked authority over others. To be sure, this teaching had mostly been directed at ambitious kings, since they generally held the power that needed to be bridled. But from the standpoint of popular freedoms, the lesson would be the same applied to any species of power—be it a military junta, aristocracy, or assembly. Oppression from such sources would be just as bad as from a monarch. This very logic, as discussed, had been espoused by Coke and other judges, and some Puritans in Parliament, at the time of the early Stuarts.

By the era of Grenville and Lord North, however, a great sea change had occurred in British constitutional thinking. Under Cromwell, the House of Commons had swallowed up both king and Lords, enacting statutes that claimed far-reaching power over every aspect of the state, including the management of royal colonies (the change that caused John Dickinson to pinpoint 1650 as the year that started all the trouble). Thereafter, with the Lords in tow, the Commons had cashiered James II and replaced him with William and Mary, settling terms of their accession by statute. From these events it became accepted, by virtually everyone in Britain, that Parliament—meaning chiefly the House of Commons—was omnipotent.

This doctrine may be gleaned from many statements of the era, most notably Blackstone's view (exactly contemporaneous with the Stamp Act) that Parliament is "the place where that *absolute despotic power*, which must in all government reside somewhere, is entrusted." In relation to the colonies, according to Lord Mansfield, "the supremacy of the British legislature must be complete, entire, and unconditional." The Declaratory Act had said "the Imperial crown and Parliament of Great Britain" enjoyed "full power and authority to make laws and statutes . . . *to bind the colonies and people of America . . . in all cases whatsoever.*" (Italics added.)[18]

Not only were such claims rejected by the colonists, it was precisely this rejection that defined the Patriot interest—separating "Whigs" (American style) from "Tories." In contesting the writs of assistance, for example, James Otis had cited the authority of Coke to argue that acts of Parliament against the common law would be invalid. Otis said, "an act against the Constitution is void . . . if an act of Parliament should be made, in the very words of the petition [for writs of assistance], it would be void; the executive courts must pass such acts into disuse."* John Adams, as we have seen, made the identical case against the Stamp Act.[19] The purely common law approach had evolved into a system of unbounded legislative power; America stuck with the older view that held all authority subject to a higher standard—and focused the lens directly on the House of Commons.

"It is a vain and weak argument," said South Carolina's Thomas Tucker, "that the legislature being the representative of the people" need not be subject to constitutional limits. "With us it would be an absurd surrender of liberty, to delegate

---

* Coke had ruled as follows: ". . . it appears in our books that in many cases, the common law will control acts of Parliament, and sometimes adjudge them to be utterly void; for when an act of Parliament is against common right and reason, or repugnant, or impossible to be performed, the common law will control it, and adjudge such act to be void . . . some statutes are made against law and right, which those who made them perceiving would not put them in execution . . . because it would be against common right and reason, the common law adjudges the said act of Parliament as to that point void." Other English decisions to similar effect included a 1450 ruling of the court of common pleas (cited by Coke) asserting "this statute is void for it is impertinent to be observed." And one of 1615, *Day vs. Savadge*, ". . . even an act of Parliament, made against natural equity, as to make a man judge in his own case, is void in itself." (Pound, op. cit., pp. 173, 176, 133)

full powers to any set of men whatever, unless in case of most urgent necessity." Richard Henry Lee was of the like opinion: "It will not avail to say that these restrictions on the right of taxation are meant to restrain only the sovereign and not the Parliament. The intention of the constitution is apparent, to prevent unreasonable impositions on the people."[20]

Debate about this topic was incessantly joined—from John Adams' quarrel with Daniel Leonard in *Novanglus* to Wilson's repeated assaults on Blackstone. A fiery exchange occurred in 1773, when Governor Hutchinson delivered an oration to the Assembly of the Bay, counseling submission to the Parliament. The assembly answered by denying the colony had ever "consented that the Parliament of England or Great Britain should make laws binding upon us in all cases . . . *The question appears to us to be no other than whether we are subjects of an absolute, unlimited power, or of a free government, formed on the principles of the English constitution.*"[21] (Italics added.)

Thus, on the substantive point at issue, the British and American views were as distinct as the opposing sides could make them: Spokesmen for the English repeatedly stressed the concept of absolute authority in the Parliament, controlled by nothing but its own discretion. The Americans just as repeatedly said no earthly sovereign should or could possess such boundless power. These claims were so totally irreconcilable that it seems unlikely they could have been resolved by any method short of the one adopted—a test of arms resulting in submission or independence.

One oddity of this dispute was that the British view of the question—professed even by the pro-American Rockingham administration, Pitt and Burke—was at bottom the same as that propounded by Rousseau, and later practiced by the Jacobin Assembly. Though unlike in many other ways, the French and English both affirmed the concept of unbounded legislative power. Equally peculiar was the resemblance of British policy at this era to the conduct of the Stuarts. As these monarchs had tried to raise a revenue without consent, suspended legal rights, and resorted to martial law to enforce their edicts, Parliament did the same to the colonials. And when challenged on the matter, it gave aloof imperial replies that stressed its own supreme authority and the virtues of "submission."

The statements of Grenville and Townshend on this topic, indeed, are eerily like the assertions of James I concerning his absolute power and majesty, and his right to rule according to discretion; the only difference was that a rampant House of Commons had now been substituted for an unbridled king.* The ominous parallels escaped the English, but were fully visible in Williamsburg and Boston. Our ancestors fought these doctrines at every step along the road. Clinging steadfastly to the rule of law and older notions of constitutional freedom, the colonists were much better traditionalists than the English— and also much better libertarians.

---

* Grenville, in particular, was relentless on the themes of sovereignty and submission. He hoped, he said, "that the power and sovereignty of Parliament over every part of the British dominions for the purpose of raising or collecting any tax will never be disputed." "That this kingdom has the sovereign legislative power over America," he said, "cannot be denied." As to what this implied for colonial freedoms, as one American reported, Grenville said "the house will hear all our objections and would *do as they thought best.*" (Italics added.) (Edmund S. and Helen M. Morgan, *The Stamp Act Crisis*, Collier, 1963, pp. 76, 348; Knollenberg, op. cit., p. 205)

13

The Declaration of Independence

THE PRINCIPAL MANIFESTO of the American Revolution, and of American politics in general, is the Declaration of Independence. Though not a legal document strictly speaking, this is the closest thing we have to an official credo.* In its well-chosen words, the themes of freedom and equality, liberty under law, government by consent, and the right of resisting abusive power are set down with classic force and eloquence.

Because of its symbolic status, the Declaration has been the subject of relentless myth-making, some of it in the well-meaning but simplistic vein of Parson Weems, a great deal more in the form of tendentious pleading. Either way, we have been told a lot about the Declaration that isn't so. The effect has been to muddle understanding not only of the document itself, but of the action that it justified, and thus the origins of our republic. As with other matters we have considered, the main objective of such treatment is to prove the secular-Enlightenment basis of American freedoms.

In most efforts to show that our revolution was a radical undertaking, the Declaration is Exhibit A. Here, supposedly, is

---

* That is, the Declaration neither required, permitted, nor altered anything in legal sense, but rather explained the act of Congress (two days before) officially severing ties with England. It nonetheless appears in the U.S. Code, before the Articles of Confederation.

the analogue to the effusions of the French, the *a priori* appeal to abstract concepts, the secular-rationalist view of Thomas Jefferson, America's leading Francophile and skeptic. And since the Declaration is the most remembered statement of our revolution, it seems to follow that the people who waged the struggle were doing something like the saturnalia that occurred in France.

It is also here, of course, that emphasis is chiefly given to John Locke. The Declaration stated a theory of social contract and government by consent, and renounced allegiance to the King of England on this basis. Locke had stated a theory of social contract and justified resistance to another English king in the preceding century. The conclusion is that Jefferson read Locke and copied down his doctrines, and that on these grounds Americans decided they should opt for independence. Since Locke and Jefferson were both *philosophes* of the Enlightenment, the radical nature of our freedoms is established. *Q.E.D.*

This reading or something like it is accepted not only by the usual historians, but also by some otherwise fairly sensible people. A few iconoclasts have challenged the Lockean thesis, but even these have done so in order to tout some other Enlightenment source supposedly responsible for the Declaration. Whatever the variations, such analyses distort the meaning of the statement, and of the action that it defended. In fact, the Declaration and the colonial move to independence were fully continuous with the developments we have been describing.

While the facts that go to prove the point are legion, they are screened from view by the selective methods used in weaving the fabric of the standard history. Foremost among these is the device of fixating on "key" documents or people, to the exclusion of many preceding or contemporaneous data that establish context for what is being said. In this approach, doctrines and manifestoes seem to spring up without historical basis, and thus appear to be completely novel and surprising. Magna Carta, the *Vindiciae*, the Mayflower Compact, and Locke's *Second Treatise* are examples we have already met with.

Nowhere is this technique more commonly used than with the Declaration of Independence. In the usual teaching, the Declaration is treated as an abstract, philosophical statement, to be dealt with through methods of literary sleuthing, as a critic might parse the meaning of an abstruse poem. A whole library of books has been devoted to figuring out what Jefferson must have meant when he expressed himself in a certain way, where he might have come up with specific phrases, his relationship to the thought of Locke or other Enlightenment figures, what works he read (or owned), and so forth.

This approach leads to results that are sometimes astonishing. For example, "no taxation without representation," government by consent, social contract, and other concepts in the Declaration have all been portrayed as radical innovations dreamed up by Jefferson, or by the secular theorists he consulted. As we have seen, however, these ideas were rooted in centuries of British, and American, practice, and by the era of the Declaration were anything but new. Only by neglecting the growth of the English common law, religious-feudal contract doctrine, the covenantal theology of the Puritans, and a great deal else, could one arrive at these conclusions. Such are the intellectual wages of ignoring history.

With this in mind, a good place to begin analysis of the Declaration is with its own specific history, which is drastically different from the standard teaching. There is, for instance, the fact that the decision for independence was not in context very radical, considering what had been going on between the colonists and the English for upwards of a decade. As has been shown, the colonial protest against British power was in many respects the opposite of revolutionary. But even if the struggle for independence could be properly described as "revolution," the colonists were most reluctant revolutionaries. Rather than rushing headlong into things, they agonized, equivocated, and delayed before they took the plunge, and did so only after every other option had been considered and discarded.

The British effort to tighten the noose around the colonies had been in progress, after all, since the end of the French and Indian War. Repeated efforts to tax the Americans, the stationing of troops in Boston, suspension of jury trials, etc., had gone on throughout the 1760s, accompanied by the most expansive claims of parliamentary power. This provoked a torrent of manifestoes, concerted efforts at resistance, and demands for redress—but no move toward independence.

Nor were Americans quick to renounce allegiance even when it came to military conflict. Martial law had been imposed on Boston as of June 1774; the Continental Congress assembled that September; Lexington and Concord erupted the following April, Bunker Hill in June; in July the colonists declared the need for a resort to arms. Despite all this, Congress took no formal steps toward independence until May of 1776, casting its final votes to this effect two months thereafter. This was more than fourteen months from Lexington, two years after martial law arrived in Boston, and eleven years beyond the Stamp Act. Hardly a record of precipitous haste in making revolution.

We know from notes of the proceedings and the comments of Jefferson, John Adams, Ben Franklin, and Richard Henry Lee that many in Congress were loath to cut the tie with England, wanted compromise, or thought the colonies were not yet ripe for independence. An "olive branch" petition had been adopted in the summer of 1775, *after* the resolution on the necessity of resort to arms. At this juncture, as Jefferson would recall, "a separation from Great Britain and establishment of republican government had not yet entered into any person's mind . . ."[1] Contemporaneous comments from many other Founders say the same.

As late as the spring of 1776, in fact, the issue was being thrashed out daily in the Congress. That resistance was still

strong—but that things were moving in the right direction—
was indicated by a letter from Franklin at this period. "The
novelty of things deters some," he wrote Josiah Quincy, "the
doubts of success others, the vain hope of reconciliation, many.
But . . . every day furnishes us with new causes of increasing
enmity, and new reasons for wishing an eternal separation, so
that there is a rapid increase in that formerly small party, who
were for an independent government."[2]

What was in prospect here, it bears repeating, was not a
socio-political earthquake like the French Revolution, but the
highly specific act of cutting an already frayed colonial nexus
so Americans could keep existing freedoms. Yet even steps in
this direction were taken slowly, with such as John Dickinson
and Edward Rutledge opposing independence to the bitter end.
(Since Adams was Dickinson's main antagonist and the chief
"radical" in Congress—as usually depicted—his comments on
the subject are worth recording. "There was not a moment
during the revolution," he would write, "when I would not have
given everything I possessed for a restoration of the state of
things before the contest began."[3])

A review of these events is useful also in assessing the notion
that Jefferson was the chief guru of independence, and that
his opinions are the only ones that need to be consulted. This
is patently in error. This essay, as by now should be apparent, is
not bent on debunking Jefferson; if anything, our argument
is that his contributions have been both misunderstood and
under-rated. It is curious to note, however, that in the critical
months in Congress that led up to the decision for independence, Jefferson played no role whatever. This is a readily
ascertainable fact of record, albeit one that is seldom mentioned.

The main congressional struggle over independence extended from February through May of 1776, when the Adamses,
Richard Henry Lee, and others pushed hard to break the link
with England, against the go-slow tactics of Dickinson and

Rutledge. This effort reached an apogee of sorts in motions of May 10 and 15, declaring British power a nullity in America and urging the colonies to set up governments of their own devising. As John Adams exulted, this was independence in everything but name, though further steps would still be needed to formalize the separation. These three and a half months were thus the crucial period in which opinion was tilted in favor of independence.

The historical oddity is that Jefferson was gone from Congress for all this time, having left the previous December and not returning until May 14. Why he was gone is not entirely clear, but the fact that he was not around when most of the heavy lifting was being done for independence is well established. The true "Atlas of Independence," as Lee would put it, was John Adams, constantly in the forefront of debate, the drafting of the pivotal resolutions, and the maneuvering required to get them voted. Jefferson had been a part of the Patriot bloc in Congress the preceding year, but he was by no means the leader of it, and when the major push occurred for independence he was at home in Monticello.

In the drafting of the final Declaration, Jefferson's role was of course immense, justifying the view of Adams that he should be given the job because of his "peculiar felicity of expression." The enduring fame of the Declaration is testimony to his talents. Yet even here, the idea that the document was merely a statement of Jefferson's personal outlook misconceives the whole endeavor. Not only was the Declaration vetted by a committee (with Adams again the principal player); there is the more significant point that it was a corporate statement of the Congress, which assumed responsibility for what was said and took an active role in rewriting the final product.

In particular, Congress wasn't bashful about removing things it considered troublesome—such as Jefferson's convoluted accusations against George III concerning slavery—and adding others it felt to be important—such as two explicit references to a providential God. In all, Congress adopted more than eighty editorial changes and removed almost five hundred words of Jefferson's text. Whatever the merits of these excisions, they make it plain that anything the Congress or a substantial part of it saw as problematic would have been deleted. Conversely, what Jefferson privately believed, outside the boundaries of the agreed position, was no more relevant than the private opinions of other delegates who helped to shape its contents.*

This becomes the more important when we recall that Congress included many influential people senior to the youthful Jefferson (then thirty-three). Among these were the *antiphilosophe* John Adams, Presbyterian divine John Witherspoon, pious Calvinist Roger Sherman, old-fashioned Puritan Sam Adams, Tidewater conservative Carter Braxton, merchant princes Robert Morris and John Hancock, common lawyers James Wilson and George Wythe (Jefferson's own teacher), and so on. These were smart, experienced men who in temper and conviction were far from the unbuttoned theorizing of the French. That they were converted into *philosophes* at the dawn of independence, didn't know what they were signing, or were led into radical by-ways by their malingering colleague may all be doubted.

Congress, of course, was perfectly within its rights to make the changes that it did, since the Declaration was to be a corporate statement. This is apparent on its face, though neglected in much modern comment. John Adams was to write

---

* Jefferson wanted to condemn the king both for having permitted the development of slavery in America and for having urged that the slaves rebel—to fight against the colonists. (Jefferson himself was a slaveholder who would have been in considerable jeopardy from such an uprising.) That Congress made many changes in his draft, and that the document was materially different from what he had written, were matters that Jefferson took great pains to stress. His unhappiness with the changes was well known in Congress at the time, and he continued to advertise it for many years thereafter. He went to elaborate lengths to point out the differences between the two drafts, circulated copies among his friends, and included the comparison in his *Autobiography*.

that "there was not an idea in it but what had been hackneyed in Congress for two years before." Jefferson himself would basically confirm this, saying his object was "not to find out new principles, or new arguments, never before thought of, not merely to say things which had never been said before, but to place before mankind the common sense of the subject ... Neither aiming at originality of principles or sentiments, nor yet copied from any particular and previous writing, it was intended to be an expression of the American mind ...."[4]

It is against the backdrop of corporate purpose that the text of the document needs to be examined. Considered in this light, many aspects of the Declaration that otherwise seem strange become quite comprehensible. Taking the least philosophic portions first, since these may be handled rather briefly, the most obvious thing to be observed is that in form and content the Declaration closely resembles *other resolutions of the Congress*. All of these, for evident reasons, offer a similar mix of features: An assertion of belief or principles about the proper conduct of the state, a list of offending actions by the British, and conclusions about the measures required to get the harm corrected.

This is, of course, precisely the form of the Declaration. By far the greater part of it, roughly two-thirds, is taken up with a recital of the abuses supposedly committed by George III—some twenty-eight in all. These include such matters as suspending colonial governments, taxation without consent, denial of trial by jury, and so forth. None of this was in the least unusual. These charges had been made many times before—in newspapers, pamphlets, colonial resolves, and statements of the Congress.* (The form was also in keeping with the lists of

---

* For instance, the resolves of the first Congress (October 14, 1774) contained an enumeration of the acts of Parliament that allegedly violated the rights of the colonists, including the various revenue measures of the 1760s, suspension of jury trials, excessive bail, the closing of the port of Boston, rescission of the

particulars familiar in British constitutional history—the sixty-three articles of Magna Carta, thirty-three charges lodged against Richard II, twenty-five charges and provisos in the Declaration of Right, etc.)

As to the single novelty in the indictment—that the charges were leveled at the king instead of Parliament—there is no mystery at all, if the historical background is considered. A great deal of speculation about this subject would be obviated by a survey of the preceding record. As we have seen, the colonists denied that they had ever owed allegiance to Parliament, and had based their theory of resistance precisely on this denial. ("As to the people and Parliament of England," said the congressional advocates of separation, "we have always been independent of them."[5]) It was to the king alone that they had pledged allegiance, and it was this allegiance that had to be suspended. Given all the previous declamation on the subject, this was a perfectly obvious method of proceeding.*

As separation from England required the colonists to renounce the king, it also required a shift in philosophic focus. As has been shown, their protests from the Stamp Act forward had been intensely legalistic, and stayed that way until the hour of independence. The dispute was handled as a case of constitutional and imperial law, through addresses to the crown, state

---

Massachusetts charter, maintenance of a standing army, and other asserted abuses. A summary of these same actions was offered the following week in the resolves of Congress concerning nonimportation of British goods (October 20, 1774) and thereafter in an appeal to the inhabitants of Canada (May 29, 1775). (Henry Steele Commager, ed., *Documents of American History*, Appleton Century Crofts, 1963, pp. 83–85, 93)

* Oddly enough, this connection was one of the things that Congress edited out of Jefferson's draft, or rather condensed so much as to obscure its meaning. Jefferson's version said: "We have warned them from time to time of attempts to extend a jurisdiction over these our states . . . We had adopted one common King, thereby laying a foundaton for perpetual league and amity with them; but that *submission to their Parliament was no part of our constitution* . . . if history may be credited." Congress altered the first sentence slightly, and dropped the rest. (Koch and Peden, op cit., p. 26; italics added)

papers, and diplomatic missives. Once the decision had been made for independence, however, such legalisms became irrelevant—though the habit of thinking in terms of English constitutional history would continue. Since the colonists were leaving England altogether, it no longer served, and would have made no sense, to stress the "rights of free-born Englishmen." And since they were appealing for support from a "candid world," and not from the king or Parliament, they sought to phrase their case in terms persuasive outside of Britain.*

All of which meant the Patriots needed to couch their appeal in general maxims. This is the major difference between the Declaration and other colonial statements, and even so it is not that different. The colonists had previously talked this way, for instance, in disputes about the powers of Parliament; when the British said Parliament had become supreme by virtue of accepted precedent, the Americans answered that principle, not precedent, should be controlling. Likewise, a mix of legal and axiomatic appeals, drafted by John Adams, had been adopted in 1774—stressing "the immutable laws of nature, the principles of the English constitution, and the several charters or compacts"—as a way of covering all the argumentative bases.[6] The axioms had been there all along. The decision for independence merely pushed them to the forefront.

So much, perhaps, is obvious. What is obscure, given the emphases of the standard treatment, is where the axioms came from. As typically explained, the radicalism of the Declaration shines through the passages about these topics, specifically the famous opening creed: "We hold these truths to be self-evident, that all men are created equal, that they are endowed by their

* It is fairly clear from the statements of Lee and others at the time, indeed, that the "candid world" was the chief intended audience for the Declaration. The colonists were in search of foreign aid, which they could not hope to get until they were formally independent. And the principal source of expected help was France—where "the rights of free-born Englishmen" have never been considered a valid reason to do anything.

Creator with certain unalienable rights, and that among these are life, liberty, and the pursuit of happiness. That to secure these rights, governments are instituted among men, deriving their just powers from the consent of the governed."

If we are to believe the usual teaching, these were secular concepts that sprang full-blown from the brow of Jefferson—with an assist from Locke, or perhaps some other Enlightenment theoreticians. This construction is, at best, obtuse. In fact, there is nothing in the axiomatic passages of the Declaration that any *philosophe* invented. Everything expressed had been part of the mental equipment of the West from the Middle Ages forward, and part of the American outlook from the beginning And far from being secular, as we have seen, the principal sources of such thought were all religious.

Among the most notable features of the Declaration, indeed, is its theistic character. It both opens and closes with references to God—two at the outset in the draft that Jefferson handed over, two at the conclusion inserted by the Congress: "the Laws of Nature and Nature's God," "endowed by their Creator," "the Supreme Judge of the World," "a firm reliance on the Protection of Divine providence." While "Nature's God" and "Supreme Judge" are eighteenth-century natural theology phrases, the God referred to is clearly providential, superintending, and creative—the God, in sum, appearing in the Bible.

We need only consider in this regard the Declaration's clarion statements about equality and freedom as inherent attributes of human beings. While there has been debate about the application of these phrases,* the general pedigree of such ideas in Western thinking is not in doubt. They stem from the biblical view examined in Chapter VIII, repudiating the authoritarian doctrines of the Greeks and Romans. As noted there,

*E.g., as to whether the "equal" men referred to were enfranchised voters, or the American people *vis à vis* the English, as opposed to the more obvious facial meaning. This dispute is triggered by the well-known fact of slave-holding in America when the Declaration was adopted, and for ninety years thereafter.

biblical teaching rejected the pagan concepts of "great souled men" and "natural slavery," asserting instead that all human beings were the children of God, created in His image, but fallen and in need of grace—and thus in the most significant terms of their existence equal. This is so basic a tenet of biblical faith, and so radically different from the worldview of the ancients, that it is hard to believe the most dogged secularist could fail to see it.

On this point, the usual discussions of the Declaration verge on the absurd, when they do not cross the boundary altogether. Where, it is asked, could Jefferson possibly have got the idea that "all men are created equal"? Much speculation is devoted to this tremendous puzzle. Did he perhaps get it from Locke, or from the French by way of Joseph Priestley, or possibly from the more moderate *philosophes* of Scotland? All of this is propounded, worried over, and debated. Every conceivable source for this idea is minutely studied—except the one from which it is so obviously derived. Our secular historians are like an army of Clousseaus—pursuing every possible explanation of the mystery, except the one that is staring them in the face.

Missing the point about such matters is of course the essence of the standard history, but what we have here is especially feeble: The Declaration, after all, *says* the rights in question come from God, so the matter is not left to inference or ingenious speculation. The scriptural origin is apparent in the very wording: That "all men are *created* equal," that they are "endowed *by their Creator*," etc., are ideas and phrases that entered the vernacular of the West exclusively through biblical revelation. They are utterly distinctive, in the idea of creation that they express, and in the intrinsic value that they attribute to every human being—both in total contrast to the pantheist/statist systems of the ancients.

Had these notions been transmitted to America from Locke, from the English Dissenting Radicals, or from the Scottish "common sense" Enlightenment, their ultimate source in religious teaching would still be plain—since that is where these people got them. (Indeed, Christian theism is an obvious component of all the supposedly secular sources cited by the Founders, including not only Locke, but also Grotius, Pufendorf, and Sidney.[7]) The Founders, however, needed no intellectual brokers to come up with such doctrines. As we have seen, all the relevant ideas about God-given rights, and free government constructed on this basis, had been planted on our shores while Locke was still in swaddling.

Though the fervor of the original settlers had abated by the latter part of the eighteenth century, Americans continued to be a religious people. The degree to which religious attitudes and practices were prevalent at this era is one of the great untold stories of our founding, and will be discussed more fully in a later chapter. Here we pause only to note that, when the Patriot leaders were pressed to make an axiomatic case for freedom, they routinely did so on a religious basis. Their argument was, precisely, that individual liberty came from God, prior to any human documents or institutions, and that this transcended all the precedents of British history. They thus opposed to the purely glacial flow of custom the axioms from which that custom was descended.

As might be guessed, some of the most emphatic statements to this effect came from New England, where the Puritan heritage was a potent factor. Sam Adams and James Otis, for example, put it that, "the right of freedom being the gift of God almighty, it is not in the power of man to alienate this gift." Otis made the point as well in his discourse on *The Rights of the British Colonies Asserted and Proved*. Government, he said, "has an ever-lasting foundation in the unchangeable will of God, the author of nature, whose laws never vary. . . . There can be no prescription old enough to supersede the law of nature, and the grant of God almighty, who has given all men a natural right to be free. . . ."[8]

John Adams, whose writings abound with references to "an overruling providence," and "devotion to God almighty," likewise contended that human freedom was founded in the ordinance of the Creator. Recalling the accomplishments of the Puritan fathers, he urged a similar piety and dedication among their offspring. "Let the pulpit resound," he said, "with the doctrine and sentiments of religious liberty. Let us hear of the dignity of [man's nature], and the noble rank he holds among the works of God . . . Let it be known that British liberties are not the grants of princes and parliaments . . ."[9]

The New Englanders, of course, were not only descended from the Puritans, but also the most intransigent "radicals" in the battle for independence—a connection that is itself instructive. But similar views were expressed in other regions, by leaders more moderate than those of Massachusetts. John Dickinson, for instance, said of American freedoms: "We claim them from a higher source, from the King of Kings and Lord of all the earth. They are not annexed to us by parchments and seals. They are created in us by the decree of Providence, which established the laws of our nature . . . they are founded in the immutable maxims of reason and justice."[10] Hamilton and Jay were of the like opinion.*

With Jefferson himself, the evidence is much the same. Though it is frequently argued that Jefferson was a Deist, this is obviously mistaken. By his own repeated statement, he

---

* Hamilton's version was: "The sacred rights of mankind are not to be rummaged for among parchments and musty records. They are written, as with a sunbeam, in the whole volume of human nature, by the Hand of the Divinity itself, and can never be erased or obscured by mortal power." And: "The Supreme Being gave existence to man . . . He endowed him with rational faculties . . . and invested him with an inviolable right to personal liberty." Jay asserted that "we are . . . entitled by the bounty of an indulgent Creator to freedom," and that when "attempts are made to deprive men of rights, bestowed by the Almighty," resistance was in order. (Rossiter, op. cit., p. 107; Harvey Flaumenhauft, *The Political Science Reviewer*, Fall 1976; Commager, op. cit., p. 91)

believed in the creative, sovereign, and superintending God of
Scripture, but thought that the original monotheism of the
Bible had been corrupted by Platonic doctrine. While his uni-
tarian faith was hardly orthodox Christianity, there is no
doubt as to where he got his notion of the Deity.* We have
noted Jefferson's view that the only basis for American freedoms was a conviction among the people "that these liberties
are of the gift of God." As if to refute in advance the idea that
he merely thought *other* people should believe this, Jefferson
also stated: "The God who gave us life gave us liberty at the
same time; the hand of force may destroy, but cannot disjoin
them."[11]

From these and many other similar statements, it should be
evident that the notion of God-given human freedoms was not
exactly unprecedented in the founding era; this was, indeed, a
commonplace among the political leaders of the time. There
was accordingly nothing novel about Jefferson's using such
expressions in the Declaration, or the readiness of other members of the Congress to accept (and reinforce) them.[†]

This leaves us with a final candidate for radical/secular invention in the Declaration—the concept of social contract as
the basis of the state, and renunciation of allegiance to George

---

* Jefferson's writings are full of phrases such as "a benevolent creator," "a
superintending power," "infinite power who rules the destinies of the universe,"
"God is just," "an overruling providence," "the common father and creator of
man," "the creator, preserver, and supreme ruler of the universe," and so on. (See
Robert M. Healey, *Jefferson on Religion in Public Education*, Yale 1962, pp. 33–
38, 170)

† These matters are discussed at illuminating length, from somewhat different
angles, in Gary T. Amos, *Defending the Declaration* (Wolgemuth & Hyatt, 1992)
and Richard Vetterli and Gary Bryner, *In Search of the Republic* (Roman &
Littlefield, 1987). Also of interest in this regard is pamphleteer Tom Paine, whose
Common Sense worked powerfully on opinion during the critical months of '76.
Contrary to Paine's later (and scandalous) reputation as a Deist, this philippic
against kings is scriptural throughout—containing, e.g., an exposition of the
passages from Samuel discussed in Chapter VIII. (Philip S. Foner, ed., *The
Complete Writings of Thomas Paine*, Citadel, 1945, pp. 9 *et seq.*)

III brought on by his supposed violation of the compact. Here is the "right of revolution" *par excellence*, allegedly imported into our politics from Locke, then migrating into the mind of Jefferson. As already seen, however, this is a complete misreading of social contract, both as to its general provenance and as to its arrival in the colonies.

Again, the relevant precepts go back to the Middle Ages, and to those who took up the medieval doctrine at the era of the Reformation. All these spokesmen said political authority, under God, came ultimately from the people, that kings and other magistrates were their agents, that such officials could be disobeyed if they transgressed the law of God, and, if it came down to that, replaced. The reader may readily compare the many sources cited in Chapters X and XI to the statements by American clergy and statesmen at the revolutionary era:

". . . all government . . . is founded in compact, or agreement between the parties, between rulers and their subjects . . . rulers, receiving their authority solely from the people, can be rightfully possessed of no more, than these have consented to, and conveyed to them." (Rev. John Tucker, 1771) "Those only are to be esteemed lawful magistrates, and ordained of God, who pursue the public good by honoring and encouraging those that do well and punishing all that do evil." (Rev. Samuel West, 1776) "Power being a delegation, and all delegated power being in its nature subordinated and limited, hence rulers are but trustees, and government a trust." (Rev. Phillips Payson, 1778)[12]

Of similar import is the statement of the Massachusetts General Court in January of 1776, as the campaign for independence was starting up in earnest: "When kings, ministers, governors, or legislators . . . instead of exercising the powers entrusted with them, according to the principles established by the original compact, prostituting those powers to the purposes of oppression . . . they are no longer to be deemed magistrates vested with a sacred character, but become public enemies and ought to be resisted."[13] This is the doctrine of the medieval era, of Buchanan, the *Vindiciae*, and the Act of Abjuration—with scarcely so much as a change of wording.

While the religious basis of these notions is apparent, there is a further aspect of the matter that needs discussing. In terms of legal doctrine, the formula used in the Declaration shows the Founders were conversant also with the *feudal* component of social contract, as expressed at critical junctures in the constitutional history of England. Though this point seems universally neglected, it is all-important in grasping the American theory of resistance, and the language used in foreswearing loyalty to the king. The Founders' performance in this regard shows, once more, their penchant for British legal history— even at the moment of declaring independence from Great Britain.

As discussed, the feudal system assumed a tie of mutual obligation—protection on the one hand exchanged for loyalty on the other. If one was withdrawn, then the other was forfeit. This was the conceptual format in which the medieval English constitution had developed. King John had been brought to heel by barons and clergy and required to recognize their feudal rights in Magna Carta, itself a form of feudal contract. Richard II had been deposed in 1399 for assertedly violating his coronation oath and Magna Carta, and for saying "the laws were in his mouth." The estates of the realm accordingly renounced "liege homage and fealty" to him and declared the throne of England "vacant." This formula was adapted in 1689, in the statement, we have quoted, declaring that James had "withdrawn himself out of the kingdom," and justifying the accession of Prince William to a once more "vacant" throne.

This legal-constitutional background, now long forgotten, was well known to American lawyers of the revolutionary era. Feudal notions of allegiance, indeed, are widely evident in their statements of resistance. John Adams asserted, for example, "we are put out of the royal protection and thus discharged of our allegiance." James Wilson's version was: "The duties of the king and those of the subject are plainly reciprocal, and they can be violated on neither side unless they be performed on the other." The Virginia House of Burgesses informed the royal governor there: "By the frame of our constitution, the duties of protection and allegiance are reciprocal."[14] *

Among the most elaborate statements in this vein was the charge of Chief Justice William Henry Drayton to a South Carolina grand jury in April 1776, declaring formal independence from the king two months before the Congress got around to doing so. Drayton's performance on this occasion is usually portrayed as "radical," but this again results from ignorance of the legal record. Drayton had been a student at the Inns of Court, and was well familiar with the matters we have examined. His approach was entirely grounded on the British constitutional precedents.

In good common law fashion, Drayton listed the asserted misdeeds of George III, his denial of chartered freedoms, and the final blow of withdrawing his protection from the colonies, comparing all this to the activities of James II. The chief justice concluded with this peroration: "George III, king of Great Britain, has endeavored to subvert the constitution of this country; by breaking the original contract between king and people; by the advice of wicked persons, has violated the fundamental laws, and has withdrawn himself and his protection out of this country. From such a result of injuries, from such a conjuncture of circumstances—the law of the land authorizes me to declare

* Countless other statements might be cited to the same effect, but we shall rest content with two from Patrick Henry: "Government is a conditional compact between king and people . . . violation of the covenant by either party discharges the other from obligation." "A law of general utility could not, consistently with the original compact between king and people be annulled . . . a King, by disabling acts of this salutary nature, from being the father of his people, degenerates into a tyrant, and forfeits all right to his subjects' obedience." (Edward S. Corwin, *The Higher Law Background of American Constitutional Law*, Cornell, 1971, p. 76; Moses Coit Tyler, *Patrick Henry*, Cornell, 1962, p. 53) The latter statement is from 1763—thirteen years before the Declaration of Independence.

... that George III ... has abdicated the government, and that the throne is thereby vacant; that is, he has no authority over us and we owe no obedience to him."[15]

As may readily be seen by referring to page 182, this "radical" statement was as close as Drayton could make it to a verbatim rendering of the charges against James, themselves an adaptation of the allegations against Richard (whose language Drayton also borrowed). Drayton obviously didn't invent the phrases or ideas in question, nor did he get them from the French Enlightenment, or from Locke, or from any other rationalist theoretician. He took them directly from the annals of English constitutional history.

From notes provided by Jefferson himself, we know a similar discussion was conducted six weeks later at the Continental Congress, in the final debates about the impending Declaration. Now back from Monticello, Jefferson recorded the comments of the opposing sides, as advocates of independence sought to win over the still reluctant. Among those speaking for the Patriot interest were John Adams and George Wythe, both experienced common lawyers, also familiar with the precedents in question. This was the summation of the case for independence:

"That, as to the king, we had bound to him by allegiance, but that this bond was now dissolved by his assent to the late act of Parliament, by which he declares us out of his protection, and by his levying war on us, a fact which had long ago proved us out of his protection, *it being a certain position in law that allegiance and protection are reciprocal, the one ceasing when the other is withdrawn.* That James II never declared the people of England out of his protection yet his action proved it and Parliament declared it."[16] (Italics added.)

Against this background, the idea that the official formula renouncing allegiance to George III was the invention of either Locke or Jefferson dissolves into the ozone. The relevant passages in the Declaration read as follows: "The history of the present king of Great Britain is a history of repeated injuries and usurpations, all having in direct object the establishment of an absolute tyranny over these states ... *he has abdicated the government here, by declaring us out of his protection, and waging war against us ... These United Colonies, accordingly, are absolved from all allegiance to the British crown."* (Italics added.)

These citations show the reliance of the colonists on the Glorious Revolution as a precedent. They also suggest the degree of their affinity—or lack thereof—to its chief defender, Locke. As discussed, the cashiering of James II had been accompanied in the colonies by a similar rebellion, the uprising against Governor Andros that sought to restore the freedoms of New England. Americans thus saw in the events of 1688–89 an important phase of their own experience, as well as a structural parallel to the eighteenth-century contest. Mostly, of course, they saw an instance of contractual government at work, a change of magistrates based on the notion of violated compact.

As we have also noted, however, the colonists routinely denied the *other* main idea established by the Glorious Revolution—the notion of unbounded parliamentary power. For this idea, they had no use at all, and never countenanced it for a moment. Likewise, the Patriot leaders opposed the more generalized version of the doctrine advanced by Locke—in which he sang the praises of the "supreme legislative" as the chief locus of authority in the state.* The Americans were wholeheartedly with Locke when he expounded social con-

---

* ". . . there can be but one supreme power, which is the legislative, to which all the rest are and must be subordinate . . . In all cases whilst the government subsists, the legislature is the supreme power . . . The legislature must needs be the supreme, and all other powers in any members or parts of the society derived from and subordinate to it." (*Of Civil Government*, Regnery Gateway, 1955, pp. 109–110) Locke believed the legislature was in turn subordinate to the people, *via* election, and also that it should govern according to the laws. He suggested no method for ensuring this, however, except a right of rebellion against abuse of power. As shall be discussed, American ideas of constitutional government were entirely different.

tract, but ignored or rejected him when he defended unchecked "supremacy" in the legislative body.

This picking and choosing suggests, again, the primacy of axioms in American thinking, as opposed to mere reliance on British precedent. The basis for selection, moreover, was quite consistent, and left no doubt about the principles that were foremost. Social contract was congenial to the cause of freedom, when it imposed restraints on rulers and provided a basis for resisting their excesses. But the legislative theory was, the Founders saw, exactly the reverse: it could be used—and was—to justify completely arbitrary measures. Both in what they affirmed and what they denied, the Americans took their stand for liberty and limitations on coercive power.

These distinctions should be kept in mind when we are told the colonists received their ideas from Locke, or any other theoretician they happened to quote in the course of the dispute with England. Far from slavishly following Locke and/or the Glorious Revolution, the Americans selected what they wanted—no more, no less. More accurately, they received from these and other sources doctrines congruent with *what they already believed*, useful to their case, and familiar from their own experience. Only if this point is understood can we avoid the error of many, if not most, intellectual treatments of the era, with their "key" documents and people selected to fit a predetermined thesis.

All of this is pertinent, finally, to efforts at twinning our Declaration with the French Declaration of the Rights of Man—usually treated as emanations of the same ideas. In point of fact, our Declaration was notably different from the French, and the differences arose precisely over the points that are the focus of this essay: In their attitudes toward religion, and toward questions of concentrated power. Since the American Revolution was much admired in France, the verbal and conceptual parallels are not surprising. But beneath the glaze of surface similarity, the American and French ideas about the central issues are quite distinctive.

We have noted the biblical theism of our Declaration. Reference to such matters in the French Declarations (two versions were published during their revolutionary epoch) are very different. These put the "rights" in question, in truly revolutionary fashion, on a secular, rationalistic basis. They do *not* attribute them to man's status as a creature of God, but simply assert them as self-justifying concepts. There is, to be sure, a reference to the Deity in the French Declarations, but it is of a rather curious sort. They proclaim the "rights of man" "*in the presence of the Supreme Being,*" implying that God is a kind of witness to the event, perhaps in the character of a notary public.[17] At no point do the French manifestoes say these rights *derive* from God; the deliberate nuances of the wording (together with many other data on the subject) suggest that this was far from accidental.

The second major distinction between the French and American declarations concerns the matter discussed in our mention of the Glorious Revolution, and at many other places in these pages: The degree of power that should be vested in a legislative assembly, if it has been chosen by "the people." In the French view, as set forth in the Jacobin declaration (and accompanying constitution), this power was completely sovereign, with no restraint beyond its own discretion. Our manifesto was the climactic statement of a long political discourse which said the opposite: That legislative power, like any other, could be extremely hazardous to freedom. The essence of the American creed had been, and would remain, that *every* form of human authority must be subject to the most definite limits.

14

The Law of the Constitution

WILLIAM GLADSTONE DESCRIBED the American Constitution as "the most wonderful work ever struck off, at a given time, by the brain and purpose of man."[1] The tribute was deserved, but the suggestion that our founding document was the product of a particular moment was in error. In fact, the Constitution was the work not of a moment, an hour, or even a lifetime, but of two millennia of Western thought, political struggle, and hard-won knowledge about the state.

The Constitution is an almost perfect summation of the themes expounded in this essay. Virtually every doctrine, value, institutional development, and painful lesson gleaned through all the centuries since Magna Carta converged on the State-house in Philadelphia in the summer of 1787. Here were combined the notions of the law above the king, the need to impose restraints on power, the wisdom of diffusing authority instead of having it focused in one center, that were the chief political doctrines of the free society, annealed and tested in the fires of battle.

As noteworthy as the ideas that guided the convention were the men who held them. While perhaps not quite an "assembly of demi-gods," as Jefferson put it, the people who attended made an impressive muster: Washington and Franklin, Madison and Hamilton, Dickinson and Wilson, John Rutledge and Roger

Sherman, George Mason and George Wythe, Oliver Ellsworth and Elbridge Gerry. Despite the absence of Jefferson, Patrick Henry, and the Adamses, this was a company of heroes, distinguished for character, principle, and understanding. If one were looking for signs of providential care in the creation of America—and the framers often did—it would be found in the gathering of these men, with these particular qualities, at this juncture of our history.

Nor should we forget the factor of experience. These were not utopian dreamers like the French, who having lived under autocracy so long had no training in self-government, and formed all their doctrines from hazy speculation. The American framers had such training to the fullest. They were used to running their own assemblies, had conducted a gruelling but successful war with England, and managed the independent states of the Confederation. Their ranks included more than thirty members of the Continental Congress, seven former governors, and eight signers of the Declaration, plus numerous judges, legislators, and state convention delegates.

This background was reflected in the tenor of debate about the Constitution. Almost everything was discussed in terms of immediate past or historical experience, with little being said of an abstract or strictly theoretical nature. The most frequent references were to things that had happened in the states (or colonies) themselves, followed by comment on British or other European practice, then by observations on the classical republics (mostly by way of bad example). The standard used throughout was what had worked, and how, and whether it could be expected to work again.

As the collected experience of the delegates gave their labors a practical cast, their long immersion in public life supplied another key ingredient—that of *continuity*. This aspect of our founding is often overlooked, if not denied entirely. Yet the stability of leadership provided by the founding generation is one of its most remarkable (and conservative) features, removing it even further from the purges and murders that would ravage revolutionary France.

We need only note in this regard that the first five presidents of the United States had all been active in our revolution—albeit at many different levels—and in the case of Washington, Adams, and Jefferson this involvement dated from the Stamp Act. Among them they provided six consecutive decades of American leadership, from the 1760s to the 1820s, and all of them died peacefully in their beds.* These five are surrogates for many others whose fame is less exalted but who also made the orderly passage from the revolution to service as governors, senators, congressmen, diplomats, and judges under the federal Constitution.

The point is important because of numerous efforts to portray the constitutional era as *discontinuous* with the epoch of the revolution—supposedly featuring different leaders and, even more to the purpose, different ideas about the conduct of the state. In this analysis, the influence of the French model is again apparent, since in France there was precisely such a cleavage—a period of radical violence, followed by an authoritarian reaction, ending in the dictatorship of Napoleon. Considerable effort has been devoted to stuffing the history of America into this configuration.

While the needs of revolution-making and constitution-building are obviously quite different, and while the framers often quarreled among themselves, preoccupation with these matters obscures what was most significant, and enduring, about the founding era: the topics on which these leaders were *agreed*, and that accordingly formed the consensus on which our system was established. These areas of agreement, as it happened, were precisely the matters that had prompted con-

---

* Not to forget the historical grace note that Adams and Jefferson, having reconciled in their declining years, both passed away on July 4, 1826—fifty years to the day after they had fathered the Declaration of Independence.

flict with the British: The need to safeguard freedom, and a consequent effort to limit the reach of government compulsions. On both these points, the Constitution was clearly an extension, not a denial, of the ideas that spurred the War of Independence.

To grasp the libertarian implications of the Constitution, we once more have to get past the usual history—which tends to treat the founding as a case study in the growth and triumph of national power. This view of the topic, oddly enough, is promoted by schools of thought that otherwise are in opposition: Historians such as Charles Beard and Merrill Jensen, who have depicted the Constitution as a conspiracy of propertied interests against the common man, and those of a more "conservative" bent (Rossiter, Louis Hacker) who view it as a wise and necessary move to overcome the disorders of the preceding era.

The net assertion of these teachings is that the founding was, for good or ill, a grand *consolidation of authority*, over against the state-autonomy regime that had existed under the Confederation. In the now widely accepted version, the "nationalist" views espoused by such as Madison and James Wilson not only prevailed in 1787, but laid the predicate for stronger measures that would follow: The rulings of John Marshall, the views and actions of President Lincoln, the regulatory schemes of the "progressives," the epiphany of Franklin Roosevelt. In this treatment, the story of our Constitution is a romance of concentrated power.

As ever, the reasons for handling the subject in this manner may be found not in the past but in the present. It is a reading back into our beginnings of the big-government doctrines of the modern era: the "Whig theory of history" as written by a Schlesinger, Galbraith, or Rousseau—or maybe Hegel. The idea is to sanctify unfettered power as currently wielded in our gigantic welfare state, devoid of constitutional boundaries, by arguing that this was how our far-seeing Founders set it up.

If we consult the debates, orations, and specific measures of the constitutional age, however, we see that the reality was nothing like this. Rather than being some kind of distant overture to modern centralization, or even an effort to heap up such modest power as then existed, the point of the Constitution was altogether different. Its object, in keeping with the history we have examined, was to devise a system of authority sufficient to the tasks of order—*but controlled and limited, in a multitude of ways, in the interest of protecting freedom.*

The Founders, obviously, were anything but anarchists. They believed that government was a necessary institution, without which there could be neither peace nor liberty. The state was needed to provide defense, administer justice, and otherwise supply a zone of order in which people could go in safety about their business. The problem, as the framers saw it, was that government under the Confederation was *too weak* to accomplish these objectives; this was the view not only of the "nationalists," but also of people such as George Mason, Luther Martin, and Patrick Henry, who wound up opposing the Constitution.

These concerns did *not* mean that the framers opted for a regime of unchecked national power. While they believed that government was needed, they also believed that it was dangerous: unless its powers were strictly limited, it could threaten the freedoms it was founded to protect. The question was how to establish sufficient power to perform to the basic functions of the state, while ensuring it did not become excessive: to stop the pendulum at midpoint, rather than having it swing too far in the reverse direction. ("It is a melancholy reflection," James Madison would observe, "that liberty should be equally exposed to danger whether the government have too much or too little power.")[2] All of the discussions at Philadelphia took place inside this framework.

The notion that the Founders might have wanted or could have envisioned a system of unfettered federal power is, indeed, preposterous, as everything in their experience inclined them the other way. Their view of human nature, study of Coke and the common law, years of colonial self-government, and ardent defense of liberty against the British, all confirmed them in the belief that power was of "an encroaching nature." Such encroachments, in their analysis, had to be guarded against at every crossroads.

We have already examined the Founders' views concerning human sin and frailty. Those opinions were much in evidence at the convention, alluded to in one fashion or another by most of the major speakers. The words most typically used in this connection were "abuse," "corruption," "intrigue," "encroachment," "avarice," "ambition," "licentiousness," "vice," "discord," "bribery," and other epithets of the sort, and they were used repeatedly. Concern about these unpleasant matters led the framers to take a highly skeptical view of political power in all its aspects.

In this approach, among ruling politicians of the time, they were unique. Champions of elective politics in France and England at this era generally argued that only *some* kinds of power needed limits—the power wielded by kings and nobles. Power that emanated from "the people," "the nation," or "the commons," expressed in legislative bodies, did not require precautions. On the contrary, elected assemblies were thought to be omnipotent, entitled to do whatever they wanted. As suggested in the preceding chapters, the Founders had an entirely different theory on this question.

While the framers believed in the authority of "the people," they did not believe that simply conferring power on an elected body was in itself a solution to anything. From their standpoint, the ultimate issue was not where the power came from, or by whom it was wielded, but *what was done with it*. It was this that made the difference between freedom and oppression— and between the American and French conceptions of what it meant to found a political order on "the people."

The distinction appears at the time of the revolution—when

state assemblies, having carried the day against appointed governors and councils, moved to the ascendant. This period of legislative rule was the closest Americans of the constitutional era ever came to the French revolutionary model—and the founding fathers, with few exceptions, didn't like it. John Adams, for example, described the effects of untrammeled legislative power in the following caustic phrases:

"A single assembly is liable to all the vices, follies, and frailties of an individual; subject to fits of humor, starts of passion, flights of enthusiasm, partialities, or prejudices, and consequently productive of hasty results and absurd judgments. And all of these errors ought to be corrected and defects supplied by some controlling power. . . . A single assembly is apt to be avaricious . . . [and] ambitious and after a time will not hesitate to vote itself perpetual . . . is unfit to exercise the executive power . . . [and] still less qualified for the judicial power . . ."[3]

This was written, it should be noted, in 1776, when Adams was in the midst of being a "radical" revolutionary; it was a pretty good forecast of what would happen in France a decade later, and also a measure of how far America's constitutional Founders were from Jacobin opinion. Similar notions were voiced by Jefferson in his critique of "elective despotism," and by such as Randolph and Gerry at the convention. Madison, likewise, was eloquent on the topic: "There is no maxim . . . which is more liable to be misapplied than the current one, that the interest of the majority is the political standard of right and wrong." "Bodies of men are not less swayed by interest than individuals, and are less controlled by the dread of reproach and other motives felt by individuals."* [4]

---

* While Madison felt this way about unchecked majority rule through the assemblies, it by no means followed that he was complacent about the exercise of executive power. On the contrary, he also said, "some provision should be made for defending the community against the incapacity, negligence or perfidy of the chief magistrate. The limitation of the period of his service was not a sufficient security . . . He might pervert his administration into a scheme of

These statements are hard to reconcile with the idea of aggregating power in the national government, then simply letting matters take their course, and no such idea was ever considered by the Founders. Their endeavor was just the other way around: To devise a system in which every form of political power was subject to the most careful limits. On this point we see once more the linkage between the revolution and the Constitution: The struggle with the British showed the Americans the dangers of untethered power; the constitutional settlement was their solution to the problem.

The Founders, be it noted, weren't content with general pieties about the rule of law; they wanted limits that were *fixed and certain*. This is incomparably the most important point about American thinking in the constitutional era, and the key to understanding what the framers were trying to accomplish. In pursuing definite, unchangeable boundaries around the power of the state, they departed notably from the conceptions of the English, as well as from all other previous systems of which we have any record. And to achieve the limits that they wanted, they came up with governing methods completely distinctive to the United States.

As the Founders saw it, a system in which the ruling power could alter the constitution as it pleased, and thus expand the scope of its authority, was a system in which freedom was imperiled. James Otis had argued the point, for instance, in voicing opposition to the Stamp Act. "No legislative supreme or subordinate," he said, "has a right to render itself arbitrary ... The supreme legislative cannot justly assume a posture of ruling by extempore arbitrary decrees, but is bound to dispense justice by known settled rules, and by duly authorized judges ... These are their bounds, which by God and nature are fixed; hitherto have they a right to come, and no further."[5]

---

peculation or oppression. He might betray his trust to foreign powers..."
(*Elliot's Debates*, op. cit., p. 317)

The notion of *definite constitutional boundaries* is evident in this, but was made even more explicit by Sam Adams. He was, indeed, a virtuoso on the subject, offering several different versions of it in protesting British efforts at taxation. *"In all free states,"* he wrote in 1768, *"the constitution is fixed;* it is from thence that the supreme legislative as well as the supreme executive derives its authority. Neither, then, can break the fundamental rules of the constitution without destroying their own foundation."6* (Italics added.) This was an excellent statement of the doctrine. Unfortunately, as we have seen, it was not the doctrine that prevailed in London.

The problem, of course, was that in England the constitution *wasn't* fixed; operating on purely common law assumptions, it had absorbed the precedent of unfettered legislative power, subject to no control except its own discretion. Having experienced the effects of this, the Founders were anxious to avoid it in their new republic. They wanted a system that could guarantee their freedoms, established in such a way that *people wielding power couldn't change it.* Though generally ignored (for obvious reasons) in modern comment, this was a recurrent theme throughout the revolutionary-constitutional era.

An evident corollary of this view, as the Founders saw it, was that the constitution could be neither made nor altered by the legislative body. As the town of Concord put it, in the year of independence: "the supreme legislative . . . are by no means a proper body to form and establish a constitution . . . because the same body that forms a constitution have of consequence a power to alter it . . . A constitution alterable by the supreme legislative is no security at all to the subjects against any en-

---

* Underscoring this line of thought, in American theory, was the idea of social contract. After all, if there is a *contract* between officials and the people, then its terms should be plain and certain, not subject to one-sided, arbitrary changes. Thus Rev. Jonas Clark, in 1781: "No man, party, order or body of men have any right . . . to alter, change, or violate the social compact. Nor can any change, amendment or alteration be introduced, but by common consent." Thus also Rev. John Tucker, already quoted: "[power] can be exercised only within certain

croachment by the governing part, on any or on all of their rights and privileges."[7] The town of Pittsfield, and other Massachusetts spokesmen, said the same.

In Virginia, both Jefferson and Mason would also propound the doctrine, arguing that a constitution established by the legislature really wasn't a constitution. Since such an enactment could be changed by any succeeding legislative body, Jefferson wrote, it "pretends to no higher authority than ... other ordinances," and thus could not be "perpetual and unalterable." "We well know," he said, "that this Assembly, elected by the people for the ordinary purposes of legislation only, have no power to restrain the acts of succeeding assemblies, constituted with powers equal to our own." A constitution had to be higher than, and unchangeable by, the legislative power.[8]

A final example in this vein is provided by South Carolina's Tucker. A law made by a legislature, he asserted, "can only be of force during the pleasure of those who made it," whereas a constitution "should be the first and most fundamental law of the state, and should prescribe the limits of all delegated powers": should be, in sum, the opposite of the British system in which the legislature could make and unmake the constitution at its pleasure. What was needed was a constitution devised by the express authority of the people—"superior to the legislative power, and therefore not alterable by it."* [9]

The principle expressed is plain enough, but so is the nature of the problem: How does one establish a government

---

limits, and to a certain extent, according to agreement.... These limits are marked out, and fixed, by the known established, and fundamental laws of the state ... by which ... the very lawmaking power is limited, and beyond which it cannot pass.... (Andrew McLaughlin, *The Foundations of American Constitutionalism*, Fawcett, 1961, p. 106; Hyneman and Lutz, op. cit., pp. 162–169)

* This author clearly drew our distinction between purely common law approach prevailing in England and the very different view that would be adopted in America. "Their constitution," he observed, "is established only on precedents or compulsory concessions ... They hold it as a maxim, that whatever they have once done (however improperly) they have a right to do again."

supposedly accountable to a "fixed" unalterable higher law, while avoiding the kind of thing that had occurred in England? How do you vest authority in a legislature, or any other governing body, and prevent it from absorbing still more authority once it is up and running? The Founders devoted a lot of attention to these questions, suggesting again how distant they were from any concept of unfettered power. The answers that they came up with drew on the tradition we have examined, but also included two contributions to libertarian thought and practice that were unique to the American system.

The first of these was the idea of a specially called convention, whose purpose was to draft a constitution, submit it for ratification to the voters, and then disperse. In the usual history, the purpose of this now-familiar American institution is neglected or blurred over, if not misstated outright. The point was not only that a convention thus assembled was to represent "the people," but also that it was different from, and superior to, the ordinary legislature. Moreover, the convention *was not a continuing body*. Once its work was completed, it no longer existed. It would not be around to alter what had been agreed to, and since the component parts of the government were subordinate to the compact, they couldn't change it either. Hence the constitution would be "fixed."*

In this respect as in so many others, the Founder who arguably did the most to set our constitutional standards was John Adams. As early as 1775, he had propounded the idea of such conventions to delegates at the Continental Congress; five years later he took a leading role in drawing up a constitution

---

* The rationale for this approach, and its implications for the American view of statecraft, were well expressed by Jefferson. The American states, he wrote, "have been of the opinion that to render a form of government unalterable by ordinary acts of assembly, the people must delegate persons with special powers. They have accordingly chosen special conventions to form and fix their governments." (The ironic exception was Virginia, about which Jefferson was complaining.) The absence of such arrangements, he added, would "expose us to the hazard of having no fundamental rights at all."

for Massachusetts, adopted by the convention/ratification method (after a draft proceeding directly from the legislature had been rejected). New Hampshire followed suit, as did most of the other states, all on the premise that a constitution should be superior to the legislative body. Not only was the principle of an unchangeable fundamental law affirmed in theory, but a method had been devised for putting the notion into practice.

Only if this conceptual-historical background is understood can we grasp the significance of the ratification process approved at Philadelphia—which was, precisely, to submit the newly drafted Constitution to specially called conventions in the states. This is usually treated as a scheme to get around the state assemblies, presumably hostile to the new proposal, and such motives were undoubtedly present. The larger issue, however, was the need for definite, "fixed" arrangements. As Mason explained it on the floor of the convention:

"The legislatures have no power to ratify it. They are the mere creatures of the state constitutions, and can be no greater than their creators . . . Whither then must we resort? To the people, with whom all power remains that has not been given up in the Constitution derived from them. It was of great moment . . . that this doctrine should be cherished as the basis of free government . . . *[even] admitting the legislatures to have a competent authority, it would be wrong to refer the plan to them, because succeeding legislatures having equal authority could alter the acts of their predecessors . . .*"[10] (Italics added.)

These matters are of utmost importance in understanding the objectives of the framers. The goal throughout was to achieve a system that would be separate from, and superior to, all forms of political power—and that could not be altered at the discretion of officials. This is the soul and essence of the founding theory. It is also, of course, directly opposite to the current teaching which says we should have an evolving, ever-changing Constitution, after the fashion of Justice Brennan, in which officeholders wielding power decide from time to time how much is needed. The Brennan thesis, indeed, is exactly the thing the Founders were trying to banish from our system.

This background is also essential in understanding what the Founders meant when they discoursed about "the people"—and how different their notions were from those that would prevail in France: When Madison, Jefferson, Wilson, Mason, et al. invoked this phrase, they meant the *authority of the public to set up a constitutional system through the convention/ratification method,* superior to and controlling on the legislative body. "The people" in revolutionary France meant unchecked power for the assembly that governed in their name. In America it meant exactly the reverse: A sharp curtailment, not an extension, of legislative—and all other—power.*

Coordinate with the convention method, indeed intrinsic to it, was the idea of having a *written constitution,* setting forth the boundaries, as well as the powers, of the newly created government. This may sound obvious, and is, but in the fashionable treatments of the Constitution-as-wise-consolidation is frequently forgotten. That is, the Constitution was written down, not simply to *authorize* the federal government and start it going, but also to spell out the *limits on its powers.* On even a cursory reading of the debates in the convention, state ratification proceedings, or *The Federalist,* this is impossible to miss, but it still gets left out of standard treatments.

The idea of appealing to a written constitution occurred quite naturally to the Founders, who were accustomed to dealing with written materials of all types pertaining to government

---

* This point is frequently misunderstood in construing, e.g., the thought of James Wilson. He is sometimes depicted as a majoritarian democrat, since he discoursed often on the "sovereignty of the people." But Wilson meant by this precisely the kind of constitutional check upon the legislature we have been discussing. E.g.; "it is ... proper to have efficient restraint upon the legislative body ... under this constitution, [such restraints] may proceed from the great and last resort—from the people. I say, under this constitution, the legislative may be restrained, and kept within its prescribed bounds; by the interposition of the judicial department." (*The Debate on the Constitution,* op. cit., Vol I, p. 822.)

activity and their freedoms. Such was the heritage of Magna Carta and the Petition of Right, the colonial charters, the compacts of Plymouth and Connecticut, and the constitutions and bills of rights of the states themselves. (Such was also the heritage of "men of the Book," and not only in New England, who were used to consulting Scripture as a source of guidance.) With social contracts, as with others, they thought it advisable to get the particulars down in writing.

Good realists that they were, however, the Founders were not content to write something on a piece of paper and trust that its terms would be respected. We have seen the fallacy of this notion in our era, which has abounded in written constitutions whose guarantees are worthless. Madison and the others were fully alert to this sort of problem, having no faith in merely "parchment barriers." The greater part of their effort at Philadelphia was devoted to fashioning "auxiliary precautions," in which checks and balances would provide more realistic safeguards—constraining one kind of power with another. As Madison expressed it:

". . . the great security against a gradual concentration of the several powers in the same department consists in giving to those who administer each department the necessary constitutional means and personal motives to resist encroachments of the others. . . . Ambition must be made to counteract ambition. The interest of the man must be connected with the constitutional rights of the place . . . [so] that the private interest of every individual may be a sentinel over public rights."[11]

In obedience to this idea, the Constitution abounds with checks and balances of all descriptions: The tripartite division of authority among the executive, legislative, and judicial branches; a bicameral legislature, the electoral college, the executive veto, provisions for advice and consent, and other complications. This was the feature of the American system that puzzled Turgot and Condorcet: wheels within wheels, different principles of representation, multiple negatives, and hindrances to action. It was the very opposite of the simplicity, vigor and dispatch of the all-powerful French Assembly, concentrating all the authority of "the nation" in a single chamber.

The complexity baffling to these sages would have been equally so to anyone who approached our Constitution without the aid of further information. Why make it so hard to get things done? Why impose so many restraints? For those who argue that the genius of the Constitution was simply to pile up authority—and make more accretions possible in the future— there is no good answer to that question. The answer, however, is quite well known, and it is a good one: As with the device of the convention and the written Constitution, the point was to impose constraints on power by every possible method, consistent with the order-keeping mission of the state.

Madison's comments referred specifically to the three-way division of official functions—which was the orthodox opinion of the age. That government was naturally divided into executive, legislative, and judicial branches—made famous by Montesquieu as a (mistaken) rendering of the English system—was accepted by all the framers. Adams was especially voluble on the concept, and put it in the Massachusetts constitution. Madison called it "the sacred maxim of free government."[12] Washington expounded it in his Farewell Address. Had the Founders been operating simply in terms of theory, this would have been the extent of their precautions.

The framers, however, weren't theoretical politicians, and weren't dealing with a theoretical situation. They had a real-world problem on their hands, and it was a large one: thirteen separate, independent, and headstrong states, who could not be dragged into the union against their will, but had to be persuaded. And there was no way that this could be accomplished unless the system being formed took into account their powers, interests, and ambitions. Being the practical statesmen that they were, the Founders proceeded to do exactly that.

This requirement produced their second distinctive contribution to political science, and also the master complexity of our system—the *federal* balance between the states and central government. The foremost compromise arrived at in this respect was to make the states an integral part of the new republic: In the chief concession by the "nationalists," the states were given equal representation in the Senate, set over against the popularly elected House; they were also made the units of voting for the presidency, authorities on questions of the franchise, and ultimate arbiters on amendments to the basic law—as well as the entities that, via their conventions, would authorize the Constitution to begin with.

These concessions, however, weren't sufficient for small government men such as Mason, Lee, and, above all, Patrick Henry. They conducted a fierce campaign against the Constitution, in the course of which they became the "anti-Federalists." According to the standard history, they lost the battle, and their cause went down in flames—deservedly in some versions, unjustly according to some others. But in fact they won some important victories—the net effect of which was to push the system even further toward limits on the reach of power.

The main complaints against the new arrangement were that it would "swallow up" the states, and that it contained no Bill of Rights to guarantee the freedoms of the people. These issues were contested vigorously in the debates over ratification, especially in Pennsylvania, Virginia, and New York, and led to outcomes that were, at least initially, congenial to the cause of freedom. The most obvious was the Bill of Rights, which Wilson, Madison, and Hamilton and many others had said was superfluous and undesirable (and they had some good arguments for their view) but which the Federalists finally accepted as the price of ratification—to be enacted after the new regime had been established.

Such was the first great victory for the anti-Federalists; the

second was equally significant, although generally less understood. This was the fact that by their challenge they forced the
Federalists to provide a highly detailed discussion of all the
clauses, words, and nuances of the document. It is to this
pressure that we owe the expositions provided by Wilson, Madison, Sherman, Ellsworth, and others in the ratification struggle. The principal effort in this regard was, of course, *The
Federalist*, which among its other virtues leaves no doubt at all
about the intended scope of powers in the system.

What emerged from this discussion was a clear delineation
of the federal balance, explaining the state and national jurisdictions and the relationship between them. It was to be a
system of *dual sovereignties*, each with its appropriate powers
and field of action. The message repeatedly hammered home,
by all the leading advocates of the Constitution, was that the
federal government would tend to tasks that were authentically
national in scope, such as defense and diplomacy, foreign commerce, and interstate relations, while the states would control
affairs of a domestic nature.

This formula, it should be stressed, concerned not only the
original *distribution of authority* in the system, but also the
rules of construction that would apply thereafter. Wilson stated
the basic premise early on, when he asserted that "everything
which is not given is reserved."[13] Hamilton and Madison put it
that the central government would be one of "enumerated
powers," with definite functions assigned it, and thus confined
in its activities. The states would retain their power over everything not delegated in this fashion. In undesignated or doubtful
areas, therefore, the presumption would be in favor of the
states.

The Federalist made these points not once, but over and
over. Hamilton argued that "the states will retain all preexisting
authority which may not be exclusively delegated to the Federal head." The reason a Bill of Rights was not required, he said,
was that the powers it would guard against weren't in the

federal government anyway; "why declare that things should not be done which there is no power to do?" (Wilson made the identical plea in Pennsylvania.) Madison said the federal jurisdiction "extends to certain enumerated objects only, and leaves to the several states a residuary and inviolable sovereignty over all other objects."[14] And again:

"The powers delegated by the proposed constitution to the federal government are few and defined. Those which remain to the state governments are numerous and indefinite. The former will be exercised principally on external objects, as war, peace, negotiation, and foreign commerce; with which last the power of taxation will, for the most part, be connected. *The powers reserved to the states will extend to all the objects, which, in the ordinary course of affairs, concern the lives, liberties, and properties of the people, and the internal order, improvement, and prosperity of the state."* (Italics added.)[15]

While this was the construction anti-Federalists were after, they still weren't reassured, and insisted that it be written into the Constitution. Such is the origin of the Tenth Amendment, which says, "the powers not delegated to the United States by the Constitution, nor prohibited by it to the states, are reserved to the states respectively, or to the people." (Language of this sort had been demanded by a majority of the states in their instruments of ratification—usually at the top of the list of amendments that were requested.)

From all of which, the character of the new arrangement could hardly be in doubt. *The framers sought to establish sufficient power to deal with tasks of national scope, but to hedge that power around with every possible safeguard:* the convention method of conferring and defining power, the written Constitution, the trisection of the federal authority, the bicameral legislature, the state-federal balance, the doctrine of "enumerated powers," the reserved authority of the states, a Bill of Rights. It takes incredible ingenuity to read into this a plan for unchecked consolidation of national power.

Comparing all this to what we have today, the obvious question is—how did we get from there to here? No one familiar
with our current federal government would dream of calling its
powers "few and defined"—or describing the boundaries of its
authority as "unalterable" and "fixed." The situation, as everyone knows, is the reverse. How has it been possible to deduce a
system of *unlimited national power* from these arrangements,
and still maintain that we are living under the federal Constitution? The answer to this question, as provided by liberal
scholars and the courts, is more ingenious yet.

The favored approach in this regard, already noted, has been
to take particular phrases in the Constitution—"general welfare," "necessary and proper," "commerce"—and construe
these as independent grants of power, affecting all kinds of
things that weren't confided to the national jurisdiction. Since
these phrases might be made to mean anything whatever, there
is little in this doctrine that is exempt from federal preemption,
subsidy, or regulation. What may *not* be done, for instance, that
doesn't affect the "general welfare," or "commerce," in some
fashion? Thus has our system of supposedly limited government, under a binding Constitution, become a regime of dominant power.

As it happens, such arguments were fully anticipated in the
ratification struggle, since opponents of the Constitution had
said these phrases *might* be interpreted in this way and the
supporters categorically denied it. This discussion makes it
clear that the phrases had no such meaning, and could not
conceivably have done so—precisely because the system was
one of limited powers. Hamilton said, for instance, that "necessary and proper" was a "tautology," not an independent grant of
power.[16] Madison called the protest over "general welfare" a
measure of anti-Federalist desperation—"stooping to such a
misconstruction."

*"For what purpose could the enumeration of particular
powers be inserted,"* he asked, *"if these and all others were*

meant to be included in the preceding general power?" The identical phrases had been included, more than once, in the Articles of Confederation: "Construe either of these articles by the rules which would justify the construction put on the new Constitution, and they vest in the existing Congress a power to legislate in all cases whatsoever." Viewing "general welfare" as an independent grant of power, he concluded, was an "absurdity."[17] (Italics added.)

So it was—and is. Yet this absurdity has long since become the ruling theory of our courts, and the premise for a boundless exercise of federal power. It is in consequence of such reasoning that the national government today involves itself in welfare spending of all types, extensive regulation of the economy, employment training, health care programs, education, criminal justice, care of children, and countless other functions that were, by the repeated witness of the Founders, to have been the jurisdiction of the states, and were understood that way by the people who ratified the Constitution.

The practical effects of this are beyond the scope of our discussion. For present purposes, we may simply note the *sophistry* of what has been done, and its implications for the very idea of having a constitutional system. For the plain reality is that the Constitution as originally adopted, and expounded in *The Federalist,* is no longer with us; the forms and titles remain, there are still entities called states, and there are divisions of administrative function. But the system of *limited powers* that was supposed to be the palladium of our freedoms has been consigned these fifty years and more to the dustbin of forgotten doctrines.

This transformation involves a double denial of what the Founders thought they were achieving—and, for a considerable period, did achieve in fact. First, the nature of the system has been inverted; we have in operation now exactly the kind of top-heavy, arbitrary power that the framers wanted to forestall, with the central government routinely dictating to both states and individuals what is permissible and what is not. And we have rules of construction, used to justify such power, that have turned the federal-state relationship effectively on its head.

Second, as discussed in Chapter IV, *we no longer have a rule of law*. By this I mean the idea of definite, ascertainable rules of conduct that are controlling on both the government and the citizen, and that are not subject to arbitrary changes at the whim of those who are in office. There are known *procedures*, to be sure, but no certain limits on the reach of federal power. Once we enter zones of purely ingenious, subjective interpretation, in which words and phrases are made to mean whatever people in authority may wish, in the manner of Justice Brennan, the rule of law goes out the window.*

This, too, was something the Founders sought to avoid—was, in fact, what they had feared the most: a system in which the ruling powers are bound by no exterior principle, claim authority as they will, and decide in arbitrary fashion which freedoms will be honored or negated. This was a prerogative that medieval constitutionalists denied to kings, that Parliament refused the Stuarts, and that our forefathers refused to Parliament itself—fighting a war of independence to make the point emphatic. The federal government that we have today deploys exactly this kind of power.

The distance we have travelled in these matters can be measured by recalling another comment made by Jefferson: "I had rather ask an enlargement of power from the nation, where found necessary, than to assume it by a construction which

* Anyone who wishes to test this proposition may readily do so by getting and reading a recent opinion or two of our Supreme Court, on almost any subject whatsoever. In such a ruling he is likely to discover multiple plurality opinions, purely subjective interpretations, "line drawing" that defies ready comprehension, distinctions among cases that to the lay mentality are identical, and a great deal more of similar nature. On abortion, civil rights, criminal justice, pornography, religious issues, and much else (as dissenting Justices have noted), there is no telling what our "constitutional law" may be from one court session to the next.

would make our powers boundless. Our peculiar security is in the possession of a written Constitution. Let us not make it a blank paper by construction."[18] Where the essentials are concerned, our peculiar security has long since vanished; blank paper is what we have remaining.

15

An Establishment of Religion

NOWHERE IS THE CULTURAL CONFLICT of the modern era more apparent than in dispute about the place of religion in the civic order. Here the battle is overt, relentless, and pervasive—with traditional belief and custom retreating before a secularist onslaught in our courts and other public institutions.

Over the past three decades, the Supreme Court of the United States has handed down a series of rulings that decree a "wall of separation" between affairs of state and the precepts of religion. In the most controverted of these cases, in 1962, the Court said an officially sponsored prayer recited in the New York public schools was an abridgement of our freedoms. This prayer read, in its entirety: "Almighty God, we acknowledge our dependence on Thee, and we beg Thy blessings upon us, our parents, our teachers, and our country." In the Court's opinion, this supplication triggered the First Amendment ban against an "establishment of religion," logic that was later extended to reading the Bible and reciting the Lord's Prayer in the classroom.

In adopting the First Amendment, according to the Court, the Founders meant to sever all connection between religious faith and government, requiring that religion be a purely private matter. As Justice Hugo Black put it in an oft-quoted statement: "The 'establishment of religion' clause of the First Amendment means at least this: Neither a state nor the federal government can set up a church. Neither can pass laws which aid one religion, aid all religions, or prefer one religion over another . . . No tax in any amount, large or small, can be levied to support any religious activities or institutions, whatever they may be called, or whatever form they may adopt to teach or practice religion."[1]

This doctrine has been affirmed and amplified in many rulings since. In support of it, Black and his successors (most recently Justice David Souter) have offered a reading of our history that supposedly shows the intentions of the people who devised the First Amendment. This tells us, in a nutshell, that the Founders chiefly responsible for the Constitution's religion clauses were Madison and Jefferson; that they held views intensely hostile toward any governmental backing for religion; and that the amendment was a triumph for their separationist position.

While presented as an argument at law, this thesis is clearly part of the philosophic conflict we have examined—the practical outcome of the standard history lesson. We are invited to view the Founders as *philosophes* who shared the anticlerical passions of the French, sought to diminish the influence of religion in our public life, and tried to set up a purely secular republic. In obedience to these notions, we have undergone a revolution in our legal theory, educational system, and religious practice—including such departures as barring Christmas manger scenes from tax-supported settings. In these teachings, also, we see the basis for the on-going attack against the "religious right" and its political involvements.

That the usual treatment of such matters is off the mark has been stated often in these pages. In the case of judicial rulings on religion, this comment is more appropriate than ever, since we are dealing not merely with conceptual linkage but with an official public record—and, in the case of the First Amendment, a legislative transcript. If we consult this background, which may be done quite readily, we find the Court and its supporters have misstated the material facts about the issue in every possible fashion.

Although mainly important as background to the legal history, we begin with some of the broader assumptions about the era which produced the First Amendment. Foremost among these is the idea that the Founders were skeptics, secularists, or "Deists," and that it was from attitudes of hostility or indifference to revealed religion that they framed our institutions. Something like this is either assumed or stated in most discussions of the subject, not only by liberal secularists who like the notion but also by some conservative theorists who don't.

If we review the available data about the Founders, however, we once more find a different picture. Several scholars have examined the religious beliefs and/or affiliations of the founding fathers, and they tell us that the vast majority of the men at Philadelphia were church-going Christians.* Even more to the point, perhaps, these researches suggest the framers were people of strong religious conviction. In this respect, some excellent work has been done by W. W. Sweet, Rene D. Williamson, and M. E. Bradford, indicating that the Founders were not only members of Christian churches but in many cases quite devout. This was most obviously so in New England, bulwark of the Congregational interest, but was also true in other regions of the country.

Among the framers well known for religion were Roger Sherman and Oliver Ellsworth, staunch Congregationalists from Connecticut, which had an official, tax-supported church, and was famous for the continued vigor of its Puritan tradition. In

---

* In his review of the framers' church affiliations, for instance, W.W. Sweet concludes that nineteen of them were Episcopalians, eight Congregationalists, seven Presbyterians, two Roman Catholics, and two others Quakers. He also finds that there was one Methodist, one member of the Dutch Reformed Church—and one Deist. (Concerning the Deist, see below.) Daniel Boorstin cites the collateral point that, "of the more than a hundred members of the Virginia Constitutional Convention in 1776, only three were not vestrymen [of the Episcopal Church]." (*The Americans*, Vol. I, Vintage, 1964, p. 131.)

the Continental Congress, Sherman had objected to holding Sunday sessions as impious; Ellsworth, for his part, had been a chief defender of the Connecticut establishment. Also believing Calvinists, according to Williamson and Bradford, were Caleb Strong and Elbridge Gerry of Massachusetts, William Livingston of New Jersey, and Abraham Baldwin of Georgia (formerly of Connecticut), who had served as a chaplain with the revolutionary army.

Other Founders known for their religious interests were Rufus King of Massachusetts (later warden of New York's Trinity Church), David Brearly of New Jersey (delegate to the Episcopal Convention of 1786), Richard Bassett of Delaware (a "religious enthusiast" and supporter of Methodist Bishop Francis Asbury), Hugh Williamson of North Carolina (a former Presbyterian preacher), Charles Cotesworth Pinckney of South Carolina (longtime president of the Charleston Bible Society), John Dickinson and Thomas Mifflin of Pennsylvania (Quakers), William Few of Georgia ("a staunch believer in revealed religion"), and so on.[2] *

If any delegation at Philadelphia harbored secret Deists, according to the standard teaching, it would have been Virginia's. There has been speculation that George Washington was a Deist—based chiefly on "architect of the universe" phrasing that was the eighteenth-century manner. Yet he was publicly, and consistently, devout; his official utterances were explicitly Christian (see below); and he supported taxpayer subsidies for religious teaching. It is believed that George Mason was a Deist, which may be so, even though he was a vestryman of Truro parish (Fairfax County) and professed himself a Christian in his will. The one Virginian we know for certain *was* a Deist was Edmund Randolph—since he acknowledged it—but

---

* If none of the above was a likely candidate for French revolutionary sympathies, we may safely conclude that the two Roman Catholics at the convention— Charles Carroll and Thomas FitzSimons—were equally distant from the secular furies of that revolution, aimed specifically at their religion.

he had by this time been converted to Christianity by his wife.

Madison's views are stressed in these discussions because he was the sponsor of the Bill of Rights in Congress. Though he is often portrayed as a Deist, the known particulars of his life do not support this. He was the protegé of the Calvinist John Witherspoon at Princeton, read theology with his mentor, and maintained his interest in the subject for many years thereafter. Between 1772 and 1775, he undertook an extensive study of Scripture, and conducted family prayers at Montpelier. His papers include notes on the Bible made at this period, and a pocket booklet on *The Necessary Duty of Family Prayer, with Prayers for Their Use.* He also engaged in theological correspondence with his friends, advising one to "season" his studies "with a little divinity now and then."[3]

Among the Philadelphia framers, Franklin was at least a fellow traveler of the Enlightenment, and is often referred to for this reason. On the other hand, he proposed at midpoint in the proceedings that the convention resort to prayer—asserting that "the longer I live, the more convincing proof I see of this truth—*that God governs in the affairs of men.*" The motion was opposed by Hamilton, who said it might create the impression that things were going badly. While this exchange gives rise to the suggestion that *Hamilton* was the skeptic, the evidence is to the contrary. (Indeed, the proof could hardly be more conclusive—or more poignant. Hamilton refused to fire at Burr in the fatal duel, as he explained in his final letter, because "the scruples of a Christian have determined me to expose my own life to any extent rather than subject myself to the guilt of taking the life of another.")[4]

From this survey it is readily apparent that many of the framers were professing Christians—active in church affairs, engaged in prayer, avowing a belief in God and Scripture. One Ben Franklin, even if assisted by a Mason, does not a French Enlightenment make. As Tocqueville would observe about American faith, no one can search the human heart, but on the public record the framers were overwhelmingly believers in the revealed religion of the Bible. The point is relevant since the chief progenitors of the First Amendment are included in this group, and also because it suggests the general temper of the era.

Also germane to our inquiry are the public customs of the time—in which all aspects of government and politics routinely acknowledged biblical religion, the truth of Scripture, and the providence of God, and made such belief part of official practice. Indeed, if we go by the state papers, legal arrangements, and political comment of the founding generation, we can only conclude that American culture at this period was suffused with religious doctrine.*

The point is made, ironically, by the very concept of an "establishment of religion." This term had a definite meaning in England and the colonies, and this is critical to understanding the debate about the First Amendment. It signified an official church that occupied a privileged position with the state, was vested with certain powers denied to others, and was supported from the public treasury. Such was the Church of England in Great Britain, and such also were numerous churches in the colonies at the beginning of our revolution.

In 1775, no fewer than nine colonies had such arrangements. Massachusetts, Connecticut, and New Hampshire had systems of local church establishment, in favor of the Congregationalists. In the Southern tier of states, from Maryland on down, the establishments were Episcopalian. In New York, there was a

---

* Preceding chapters have discussed the religious passages in the Declaration of Independence and other statements of the time that founded the idea of human freedom on a religious basis. Such references were not unusual during the revolution, and were in particular not unusual for Thomas Jefferson. In May of 1774, for instance, he had been in the forefront of a group in the Virginia House of Burgesses that proposed a resolution for a day of fasting and public prayer, in solidarity with the beleaguered city of Boston. It was resolved, without a dissenting vote, that the House should march in a body to church to hear a sermon on the subject.

system of locally supported Protestant clergy. Because of growing religious diversity within the states, pressure mounted to disestablish these official churches—successful when the dissenting interests were strong enough to force the issue. Increasingly numerous Baptists and Presbyterians made particular headway against the Anglican position, which was further weakened by the identification of many Episcopal ministers with the English.

Even so, at the time of the Constitutional Convention, the three New England states still had their Congregational establishments. In other states, there remained a network of official sanctions for religious belief, principally the requirement that one profess a certain kind of Christian doctrine to hold public office, or enjoy other legal privilege. With local variations, these tended generally in the same direction, and they make instructive reading alongside the statements of Justices Black and Souter about the supposed history of our institutions.

In South Carolina, to pick an example more or less at random, the Constitution of 1778 said that "the Christian Protestant religion shall be deemed . . . the established religion of the state." It further said that no religious society could become a church unless it agreed "that there is one eternal God and a future state of rewards and punishment; that the Christian religion is the true religion; that the Holy Scriptures of the Old and New Testaments are of divine inspiration." South Carolina also asserted that "no person who denies the existence of a Supreme Being shall hold any office under this Constitution."[5]

Similar statements can be gleaned from other state enactments of the period. The Maryland Constitution of 1776 decreed, for instance, "a general and equal tax for the support of the Christian religion." New Jersey that year expressed its idea of toleration by saying that "no Protestant inhabitant of this colony shall be denied the enjoyment of any civil right." Massachusetts, in 1780, authorized a special levy to support "public

Protestant teachers of piety, religion and morality"—a formula adopted verbatim by New Hampshire.[6]

Vermont, which was admitted into the Union in 1791, was one of the more liberal states of the founding epoch, both politically and theologically. Nonetheless, this was the oath of office one had to take to assume office there: "I do believe in one God, the Creator and Governor of the Universe, the rewarder of the good and punisher of the wicked. And I do acknowledge the Scriptures of the Old and New Testaments to be given by divine inspiration and own and profess the Protestant religion." Quaker Pennsylvania was likewise famous for its toleration. Its latitudinarian view of religious matters, expressed in the constitution of 1790, said "no person who acknowledges the being of God and a future state of rewards and punishments, shall, on account of his religious sentiments, be disqualified to hold any office or place of trust under this commonwealth."[7] Such were the *liberal* jurisdictions of the era.

In Supreme Court decisions, reliance is placed mainly on Virginia, and in particular on Madison's role in moving for disestablishment of the Anglicans and opposing tax assessments for the support of churches. As noted, however, these measures reflected neither secularism nor indifference— chiefly because the political pressures to this effect came from other religious bodies, but also because Madison himself believed in such a policy for religious reasons. He maintained (as did Edmund Randolph) that in addition to being unfair to other denominations, establishment weakened a church instead of making it stronger (and had plentiful evidence to support his view from the ecclesiastical history of Virginia).

Nor, it should be added, did Madison as legislator take the doctrinaire approach imputed to him by the Court. It is a little noted fact, for instance, that on the same day that he introduced his bill in the Virginia legislature for disestablishment of the Episcopal church (October 31, 1785), he also introduced a

bill *to punish those who broke the Sabbath* (plus another providing for days of prayer and thanksgiving). This spelled out the
penalties that would be imposed on people who conducted
other than household duties on the Sabbath, or had their employees do so. Needless to remark, the Court's "wall of separation" thesis doesn't mention this Madisonian plan for backing
religion with the force of law.[8] *

Official support for religious faith and state religious requirements for public office persisted well after adoption of the First
Amendment. The established church of Massachusetts was not
abolished until 1833. In New Hampshire, the requirement that
one had to be Protestant to serve in the legislature was continued until 1877. In New Jersey, Roman Catholics were not permitted to hold office until 1844. In Maryland, the stipulation that
one had to be a Christian lasted until 1826. As late as 1835, one
had to be a Protestant to take office in North Carolina; until
1868, the requirement was that one had to be a Christian; thereafter that one had to profess a belief in God.

The official sanction for religious belief provided by the
states was equally apparent at the federal level, during and after
the revolution. Appeals for divine assistance, days of prayer
and fasting, and other religious observance were common in
the Continental Congress. Among its first items of business, in
1774, the Congress decided to appoint a chaplain and open its
proceedings with a prayer. When it was objected that this might
be a problem because of diversity in religious doctrine, Sam
Adams answered: "I am not a bigot. I can hear a prayer from a
man of piety and virtue, who is at the same time a friend of his
country."[9]

On June 12, 1775, the Congress called for "a day of public
humiliation, fasting and prayer," wherein "[we] offer up our

---

* The bill for days of thanksgiving required ministers to cooperate and levied
fines on those who didn't. These proposals are of further interest in that they
resulted from Jefferson's efforts at "revisal," discussed in Chapter XII.

joint supplications to the all-wise, omnipotent and merciful disposer of all events." In observance of this fast day, Congress attended an Anglican service in the morning and a Presbyterian service in the afternoon. Elsewhere around the country, religious ceremonies in response to this appeal were many and reiterated. (One of the most famous of patriotic utterances—a sermon preached by Witherspoon at Princeton in May 1776—was delivered on such a congressionally appointed fast day.)[10] *

Among the more notable ventures of the Congress was an effort to print an American Bible, as the supply from England had been cut off. On October 26, 1780, Congress adopted a resolution stating that "it be recommended to such of the states who may think it convenient for them that they take proper measures to procure one or more new and correct editions of the Old and New Testaments to be printed . . ." (In response to this suggestion, a Philadelphia Presbyterian named Aitken undertook to print up an American edition. Congress referred the matter to its chaplains, who found it "executed with great accuracy.")[11]

In addition to appointing chaplains, resorting to prayer, and seeing about the printing of a Bible, Congress took still other measures to advance the interests of religion. It passed, for instance, the Northwest Ordinance to manage the territories beyond the Ohio River, saying it did so, among other reasons, for purposes of promoting "religion and morality." The committee approving the legislation (with Madison as a member) stipulated that, in the sale of lands in the territory, Lot N29 in each parcel "be given perpetually for the uses of religion." Congress also appropriated money for the Christian education of the Indians.[12]

---

* As noted, religious utterance was the common idiom of the Congress. The 1775 Declaration of the Necessity of Taking Up Arms says, for instance: "We gratefully acknowledge, as signal instances of the divine favor toward us, that His providence would not permit us to be called into this severe controversy,

During the war, special efforts were made to promote religious observance in the army. Chaplains were appointed to conduct religious services. The Articles of War recommended that officers and men attend divine service, and that if any behaved improperly at these gatherings they should be court-martialed. Washington sought diligently to enforce such rules, explaining that "the blessings and protection of heaven are at all times necessary, but especially so in times of public stress and danger. The General hopes and trusts that every officer and man will endeavor so to live and act as becomes a Christian soldier defending the dearest rights and liberties of his country."[13]

In the new Congress under the Constitution, the peacetime measures for the support of religion were reenacted. The chaplains were reestablished, prayers were conducted, and days of thanksgiving were voted. The Northwest Ordinance, with its "religion and morality," was readopted. Also, and for many years thereafter, money was appropriated for the Christian education of the Indians—a policy explained as follows by John Quincy Adams: "They were considered as savages, whom it was our policy and duty to use our influence in converting to Christianity and in bringing within the pale of civilization . . . We endeavored to bring them to the knowledge of religion and letters . . . We have had the rare good fortune of teaching them the arts of civilization and the doctrines of Christianity . . ."[14]

Such was the body of doctrine and official practice that surrounded the First Amendment—immediately predating it, adopted while it was being discussed and voted, and enduring long after it was on the books. The resulting picture, obviously,

---

until we were grown to our present strength . . . We most solemnly before God and the world declare, that, exerting the utmost energy of those powers, which our beneficent Creator hath graciously bestowed on us, etc. . . . With an humble confidence in the mercies of the supreme and impartial judge and ruler of the universe, we most devoutly implore his divine goodness to protect us happily throughout this conflict." (Commager, op cit., p. 95)

is very different from any notion of America as a country being run by secularists and Deists. Nor does it look very much like a country in which the governing powers were intent on creating a "wall of separation" between church and state, denying official support to the precepts of religion. What it looks like, instead, is exactly the reverse.

How is it possible to reconcile these many practices with the Supreme Court's reading of the First Amendment? How can this history be squared with Justice Black's assertion that, under the amendment, *"no tax in any amount, large or small, can be levied to support any religious activities or institutions"*? The answer, of course, is that it can't. And the reason for this is that the First Amendment depicted by Black and other liberal jurists is a fabrication. The Court's alleged history is a complete misrepresentation of the record—a prime example of picking and choosing elements from the past to suit the ideological fashions of the present.

As seen in the preceding chapter, there were some very specific and pressing reasons for adopting the Bill of Rights, including what would become the First Amendment. Agitation to this effect had been mounted by such as Patrick Henry, who feared that the new government would "swallow up" the states. Most of the amendments that were proposed reflected this concern, including the provisions dealing with religion—all aimed at putting limits on the new consolidated government.

Madison had argued that a Bill of Rights would not be needed, since the new government would be one of "enumerated powers," but Henry and the anti-Federalists were so vociferous that the Federalists agreed to subsequent amendments. When Madison thereafter ran for Congress, Henry escalated the pressure further, supporting James Monroe against him on the thesis that Madison was an "enemy" to a Bill of Rights. It was in response to this campaign that Madison pledged to introduce just such a bill if he were elected to the House.

This was the background to Madison's motion on June 8,

1789, introducing a set of amendments to the Constitution, culled from the proposals of the state conventions. Among the measures that he offered (number four on the original list) was this pertaining to an "establishment of religion": "The civil rights of none shall be abridged on account of religious belief, nor shall any national religion be established . . ."[15] In view of the weight that has been given to Madison's *personal opinions* on the subject, his comments on this occasion are of special interest. For example, challenged by Roger Sherman as to why such guarantees were needed, given the doctrine of "enumerated powers," Madison said:

"*. . . he apprehended the meaning of the words to be,* that Congress shall not establish a religion and enforce the legal observation of it by law, nor compel men to worship God in any manner contrary to their conscience. *Whether the words are necessary or not, he did not mean to say, but they had been required by some of the state conventions, who seemed to entertain an opinion that* [under the 'necessary and proper' clause] . . . Congress . . . might infringe the rights of conscience and establish a national religion; to prevent these effects *he presumed the amendment was intended,* and he thought it as well expressed as the nature of language would admit."[16] (Italics added.)

In this and other exchanges, the House debate made two things clear about the Bill of Rights and its religion clauses: (1) Madison was introducing the amendments, not because *he* thought they were needed, but because others did, and because he had promised to act according to their wishes (a pledge that was frequently referred to in debate); (2) the object aimed at was to prevent *Congress* from establishing a "national" religion that would threaten the religious diversity of the states. Since they had the varied practices we have noted, ranging from establishments and doctrinal requirements for public office to relative toleration, any "national" religion would have been a source of angry discord.

Despite this obvious context, the usual history treats the First Amendment as Madison's private statement—and thus averse to all official backing for religion—because it was *his* language that was adopted. Though the point is secondary, it is worth observing that it is also false; in point of fact, the specific language voted by the lower chamber was offered by Fisher Ames of Massachusetts, a conservative from a state with an established church. If purely personal authorship is in question, then the Court and liberal scholars should be devoting their analyses to Ames. But since neither he nor Massachusetts fits the secularist scenario, this interesting project is not attempted.*

As it happened, this wasn't the final version anyway; the formula that got enacted was a compromise with the Senate, worked out in a conference committee, exactly the way that things are handled now. In deducing possible legislative motives for the language that was adopted, it is noteworthy that this six-man committee included Roger Sherman and Oliver Ellsworth, whom we have already encountered. As observed, these were stalwart Calvinists from Connecticut—a state with an established church. (In fact, in Connecticut at the time a law existed that you could be fined 50 shillings if you didn't go to church on Sunday.)

Sherman and Ellsworth also were experienced political and legislative hands, having served in both the Continental Congress and the Constitutional Convention. We may be certain they did not go into conference and devise an amendment that was hostile to religion generally, and even more certain they did

---

* Historian Irving Brant, biographer of Madison and archliberal on these topics, provides a priceless comment on this detail of constitutional history. Madison *must* have written the language, Brant insists. Ames couldn't have done it; he doesn't fit. (*"There can be little doubt that this was written by Madison . . . Ames had taken no part in the debate,* etc." *James Madison, Father of the Constitution*, Bobbs-Merrill, 1950, p. 271.) Such is the caliber of information that we are given on these important matters.

not assent to anything that would have remotely threatened the religious practices of their still strongly Puritan state.

Against that backdrop, the meaning of the "establishment" clause as it came out of conference should be crystal clear: *"Congress shall make no law respecting an establishment of religion."* The agency prohibited from acting is the national legislature; what it is prevented from doing is passing any law *"respecting"* an establishment of religion. In other words, Congress was forbidden to legislate at all concerning church establishments—either for or against. It was prevented from setting up a national established church; equally to the point, *it was prevented from interfering with the established churches in the states.*

Though this history is blurred over or ignored, it is no secret, and in its general features at least sometimes acknowledged by liberal spokesmen. It may be conceded, for example, that the First Amendment was intended to be—and on the face of it obviously is—a prohibition against the *federal* government. But that guarantee was supposedly broadened by the Fourteenth Amendment, which "applied" the Bill of Rights against the states. Thus what was once prohibited only to the federal government is now also prohibited to the states.

To enter into this terrain we must grasp the Orwellian concept of "applying" a protection of the states *as a weapon against them*—using the First Amendment to achieve the very thing it was intended to prevent. The legitimacy of this reversal has been convincingly challenged by Raoul Berger, Lino Graglia, and James McClellan, but that issue is too complex for our consideration here. For present purposes, let us simply *assume* the First Amendment restrictions on Congress were "applied" against the states. What then? What did this prohibit?

One thing we know for sure is that *it did not prohibit officially sponsored prayer.* As we have seen, Congress itself engaged in officially sponsored, tax-supported prayer, complete with paid official chaplains, from the very outset—and continues to do so to this day. Indeed, in one of the greatest ironies of this historical record, we see the practice closely linked with passage of the First Amendment—supplying a refutation of the Court's position as definitive as could be wished.

The language that had been debated off and on throughout the summer and hammered out in conference finally passed the House of Representatives on September 24, 1789. *On the very next day*, the self-same House of Representatives passed, by a better than two-to-one majority, a resolution calling for *a day of national prayer and thanksgiving*. On First Amendment day-plus-one, here is the language the House adopted: "We acknowledge with grateful hearts the many signal favors of Almighty God, especially by affording them an opportunity peacefully to establish a constitutional government for their safety and happiness."[17]

The House accordingly called on President Washington to issue a proclamation designating a national day of prayer and thanksgiving (the origin of our present holiday to this effect). This was Washington's response: "It is the duty of all nations to acknowledge the providence of Almighty God, to obey his will, to be grateful for His benefits and humbly to implore His protection and favor . . . That great and glorious Being who is the beneficent author of all the good that was, that is, or that ever will be, that we may then unite in rendering unto Him our sincere and humble thanks for His kind care and protection of the people . . ."[18]

Such were the sentiments officially pronounced, by president and Congress, immediately after adoption of the First Amendment. As may be seen by comparing the language quoted on page 270, these statements are far more doctrinal and emphatic than the modest prayer schoolchildren are forbidden to recite because it allegedly violates the First Amendment. If we are to accept the reasoning of the modern Court, as Robert Cord observes, both *Congress and George Washington violated the intended meaning of the First Amendment from the moment of its inception.*[19]

The more logical conclusion, of course, is that Congress knew much better what it meant by the language adopted the preceding day than does our self-consciously evolving Court two centuries in the future. And, all too plainly, in the view of Congress, there was nothing either in law or logic to bar it from engaging in officially sponsored, tax-supported prayer, then or ever. It follows that the amendment can't possibly bar the states from doing likewise—even if its prohibitions are "applied" against them.

To all of this, the liberal answer is, essentially: James Madison. Whatever the legislative history, we are informed, Madison in his subsequent writings took doctrinaire positions on church-state separation, and these should be read into the First Amendment. This, however, gets the matter topsy-turvy. Clearly, if the Congress that passed the First Amendment, and the states that ratified it, didn't agree with Madison's more stringent private notions, as they surely didn't, then these were *not* enacted. It is the common understanding of the relevant parties, not the ideas of a single individual, especially those expressed in other settings, that defines the purpose of a law or constitutional proviso.

In this regard, also, the Court's obsession with the individual views of Madison is highly suspect; it contrasts strangely with judicial treatment of his disclaimers in the House debate, and also of his opinion on other constitutional matters, all systematically ignored by modern jurists. As we have seen, Madison held strict-constructionist views about the extent of federal power, arguing that the Constitution reserved undelegated authority to the states. This was a point he made repeatedly in debates about the Constitution, spelled out in *The Federalist*, and stressed throughout his long career in politics. *These* views of Madison, as has been noted, are dismissed entirely by the

Court—scarcely ever being mentioned, much less relied on as a point of doctrine.

Thus we get a curious inversion: Madison becomes the Court's authority on the First Amendment, even though the notions he later voiced about this subject were not endorsed by others involved in its adoption. On the other hand, he isn't cited on the residual powers of the states, even though his statements on this topic were fully endorsed by other supporters of the Constitution and relied on by the people who voted its approval. It is hard to find a thread of consistency in this—beyond the obvious one of serving liberal ideology.

As peculiar as the Court's selective use of Madison is its resort to Jefferson. The anomaly here is that Jefferson was not a member of the Constitutional Convention, or of the Congress that considered the Bill of Rights, or of the Virginia ratifying convention. However, he had strongly separationist views (up to a point), and had worked with Madison for disestablishment and religious freedom in Virginia. For the Court, this proves the First Amendment embodied Jefferson's statement in 1802 about a "wall of separation," in a letter to the Baptists of Connecticut.

Again we pass over the Lewis Carroll logic—in this case deducing the intent of an amendment adopted in 1789 from a letter written thirteen years thereafter, by a person who had no official role in its adoption. Rather than dwelling on this oddity, however, we shall simply go to the record and see what Jefferson *actually said* about the First Amendment and its religion clauses. One such utterance appears, for instance, in his second inaugural address, as follows:

"In matters of religion, I have considered that its free exercise is placed by the Constitution independent of the powers of the general government. I have therefore undertaken on no occasion to prescribe the religious exercises suited to it. But I have left them as the Constitution found them, under the direction or discipline of state or church authorities acknowledged by the several religious societies."[20]

Jefferson made the identical point a few years later to a Presbyterian clergyman, who inquired about his attitude on Thanksgiving proclamations*: "I consider the government of the United States as interdicted from intermeddling with religious institutions, their doctrines, discipline, or exercises. This results from the provision that no law shall be made respecting the establishment of religion or the free exercise thereof, but also from that which reserves to the states the powers not delegated to the United States. Certainly no power over religious discipline has been delegated to the general government. It must thus rest with the states as far as it can be in any human authority."[21]

The irresistible conclusion is that there was no wall of separation between religious affirmation and civil government in the several states, nor could the First Amendment, with or without the Fourteenth Amendment, have been intended to create one. The wall of separation, instead, was *between the federal government and the states*, meant to make sure the central authority didn't meddle with the customs of local jurisdictions.

Considered as a matter of constitutional law, the Court's position in these religion cases is an intellectual shambles—results-oriented jurisprudence at its most flagrant. An even greater scandal, if such a thing were possible, is the extent to which the justices have rewritten the official record to support a preconceived conclusion: a performance worthy of regimes in which history is tailored to the interest of the ruling powers. In point of fact, America's constitutional settlement—up to and including the First Amendment—was the work of people who believed in God, and who expressed their faith as a matter of course in public prayer and other governmental practice.

---

* Among the early presidents, Jefferson was the only one who refused to issue such proclamations, though Madison later expressed regret for having done so.

16

The Economics of Freedom

WE HAVE TO THIS POINT considered freedom as a constitutional-legal matter, and tried to trace its philosophic origins. At this level, it has been argued, ideas of liberty and limited government are not only compatible with but products of the religious heritage of the West, and are dependent on its insights for their survival.

This constitutional treatment does not, however, address a common critique of libertarian statecraft, offered on what is said to be a religious basis. In the realm of economics, we are informed, Christianity rejects expansive notions of individual freedom, and consequent restrictions on the power of the state. Western faith condemns the money-grubbing of free markets, rampant materialism, ideas of "economic man," and so forth. Such has been the view of Christian socialists, promoters of the social gospel, and welfare-staters of vague religiosity—as well as many cultural critics on the Right.

While political liberty may be sanctioned by our religious values, therefore, a different standard is applied to economics. This division of the subject matches a widely accepted secular thesis, which holds that liberty of speech and press should be protected, but that merely economic liberties may be over-ridden with impunity. The constitutional doctrine of our courts, for instance, routinely approves compulsion in matters of economics but gives "preferred position" to other rights.*

The confusions embedded in this line of thought are many, and need to be disentangled if we want to prevent still further erosion of our freedoms. In fact, as may be shown, economic liberty is integral to the free society, cannot be divorced from libertarian policy in general, and is recommended by religious precept. If we would understand the provenance of our freedom, seeing this connection is of the essence. Since this is a major point of conflict between "classical liberals" and traditional conservatives, it needs consideration for that reason also.

A threshold difficulty with this subject is that many people are indifferent to, or ignorant of, the principles of economics. This is most notably so with liberal planners and collectivists, who assume that economic laws do not exist, are simply matters of opinion, or can be suspended by official fiat. The baleful effects of these assumptions have been noted in preceding chapters. In some conservative circles, the situation is not a good deal better, since many of traditionalist bent incline to view the dismal science as unworthy—the intellectual version of doing windows. The result of these conceptions is that a lot of us don't pay attention to economics, and are convinced that we don't need to.

For reasons already touched on, this is a great and serious error. Economic ignorance translated into policy can generate the most awful suffering—as happened in the countries of Eastern Europe, collectivist regimes in Asia, African nations racked by famine. One would think that neither conservatives

---

* Discerning readers may have noted that this distinction is drawn by professional verbalizers, and that the liberties to be "preferred" are those involved in verbalizing. Thus the freedom of a writer, professor, or lawyer to say or publish what he wants is of the first importance, while that of a farmer, businessman or factory worker to be exempt from coercive measures is dismissed as insignificant. If farmers, *et al.*, were in charge of making the distinctions, it is possible that these priorities would be reversed.

nor liberals could view all this misery with indifference, decline to remedy it if they could, or calmly accept the emergence of similar horrors in our own society. Yet calamities of this type can be neither forestalled nor cured without some understanding of economics.

Even short of such disasters, economics is important. We are talking, after all, about the ability of people to earn a living, feed themselves, own or rent their homes, pay for medical care and schooling. Failure of economic policy can lead to serious problems in all of these departments. We need only recall the energy crisis of the 1970s, the bout of double-digit inflation and interest rates occurring at the conclusion of that decade, or recent agitation about the problems of our health care system. All these troubles stemmed from policies that disregarded economic concepts—price constraints on energy, rapid expansion of the supply of money, subsidies and controls that distort incentives in the health care market.

The centrality of economics is reflected also in the daily round of debates in Congress and other public policy forums: Budgets and taxation, employment and rates of interest, agriculture and transportation, urban policy and the environment—the vast majority of domestic issues are economic. The same is increasingly true in matters of foreign policy—dealings with the former Soviet bloc, Third World hunger, free trade and protection, and many others. In the circumstances, the notion that conservatives should ignore or disparage the principles of the market is a formula for conceding the field to liberal ideology and/or the inertia of the going system—thereby conferring greater power on an already huge and intrusive state.

The likely effect of such default may be assessed by noting the degree to which we presently display the features of collectivist malaise in our society. At this writing, health care is the salient topic, but there are others that come instantly to mind—the condition of our schools, the debacle of public housing and urban renewal, the welfare subculture in our cities. Despite their differences, these problem areas have one obvious trait in common: Each has been removed from the disciplines, incentives, and options of the market, and placed under a regime of government subsidy and planning. It should accordingly not surprise us that they produce outcomes resembling those in Eastern Europe.

Note also the social effects of these "merely economic" troubles. Because of perverse incentives in our health care system, we have adopted a scheme of official rationing that denies access to needed services, and threatens further denial in the future. Because our public schools are a monopoly, with all the ills that this is heir to, we have students completely unequipped to work as functioning members of society. Because the array of welfare benefits is mainly triggered by the absence of the father, we have witnessed an almost total destruction of the family in our inner cities. These are social disasters of immense proportions.

Obviously, the problems cited are *not* "merely economic," either in effect, or in their causes. The failure of public education, the rise of illegitimacies, the rampant crime of our major cities all have an ethical-intellectual component that is hard to miss, and that has been a principal focus of our discussion. Yet no realistic analysis of the world we live in can omit the fact that people respond to incentives in terms of costs and benefits, and in these cases the incentives are almost exactly the reverse of what they should be. There can be no hope of improvement in these matters if economic factors are neglected.

All of this is significant in itself, but if we turn to the subject of political freedom its importance is redoubled. The notion that our political liberties can be divorced from economic factors is one of the strangest delusions in modern thinking— again suggesting pervasive ignorance of the subject. Whether considered in terms of Western history or the experience of the modern era, the facts of record are always and everywhere to the contrary. It is quite clear that political freedom and economic freedom go together, and have to do so, and that where economic freedom is denied political liberty will also be imperiled.

In fact, the prevalence of *economic* issues is one of the most striking features of the Anglo-American political record. Consider the saga of the British common law, examined in Chapters V and IX. Nothing could be plainer from this history than that English political liberties are founded on an economic basis— primarily limits on the financial power of the crown. A few minutes devoted to the study of Magna Carta will readily confirm the point, since this historic manifesto is first and foremost an economic document. Roughly two-thirds of its guarantees have to do with property rights and economic liberties— taxation, free commercial passage, property takings, rights of inheritance, use of waterways and forests, and similar provisos.

If we consider the rise of Parliament in the centuries after Magna Carta, the story is essentially the same. The issue that above all others led to the growth of representative institutions was the economic necessity of the crown—the inability of kings to "live of their own," efforts to seize the property or income of their subjects, resistance to such measures by the Lords and Commons. As we have seen, the principal issue in the early Parliaments was the question of taxation, and the leverage this provided against the authority of the king. Guarantees about this topic were frequently demanded, while grants of money were used to safeguard other rights and privileges. Conversely, it was when kings tried to raise a revenue without consent that the most bitter constitutional quarrels erupted.

Nor was this the only economic aspect of English freedoms. Almost as prominent as the question of taxation was the more general topic of economic intervention—monopoly, trade restrictions, and other interference with the rights of property. To take the obvious case in point, the great siege of thirteenth-

century legislation under Edward I was almost entirely economic: sorting out and securing private rights concerning the
sale and inheritance of property, foreign commerce, debt collection among merchants, and the like. The great bulk of the
common law, indeed, is economic. Fortescue's comparison of
the French and English systems, for example, is expansive on
the subject:

> ... the king of France does not permit any one to use salt, but
> what is bought of himself, at his own arbitrary price ... the
> peasants live in great hardship and misery. Their constant drink
> is water, neither do they taste, throughout the year, any other
> liquor; .. their clothing consists of frocks, or little short jerkins
> made of canvas no better than common sackcloth ... The
> women go barefoot, except on holidays ... And if it happen that
> a man is observed to thrive in the world, and become rich, he is
> presently assessed to the king's tax, proportionably more than
> his poorer neighbors, whereby he is soon reduced to a level with
> the rest ...
>
> [In England, conversely] ... every inhabitant is at his liberty to
> use and enjoy whatever his farm produceth, the fruits of the
> earth, the increase of his flock, and the like; all the improve-
> ments that he makes ... are his own to use and enjoy without
> let.... the inhabitants are rich in gold, silver and in all the
> necessaries and conveniences of life.... They are fed, in great
> abundance, with all sorts of flesh and fish, of which they have
> plenty everywhere ... Everyone, according to his rank, hath all
> things which conduce to make life easy and happy.[1]

Such issues came to the forefront in the parliamentary battle
with the Stuarts. James complained about the "eating canker of
want," and this would be a decisive factor in the policy of
Charles—forced loans, ship money, and the sale of monopoly
patents to raise a revenue without consulting Parliament. Also,
though less noted than the subject of taxation, the general
question of economic interference was a constant grievance

against the Stuarts. Ideas of high prerogative in the crown were joined with measures of extensive business regulation—including bars to competition and innovation, wage and price controls, commercial and industrial restrictions.

The degree to which the Stuarts and their party were committed to such meddling, and the resemblance of their policy to much that has happened in the modern era, are nontopics in the usual history. An exception is Prof. Christopher Hill, who provides a lengthy list of the official monopolies that impeded competition in Stuart England. In 1621, for instance, there were seven hundred monopolies extant, along with countless other interventions that stifled the economy. "Throughout the early Stuart period," Hill observes, "governments thought it their duty to regulate industry, wages, and working conditions. In times of dearth, they ordered Justices of the Peace to buy up corn and sell it below cost price; they forbade employers to lay off workers whose products they could not sell."[2]

Monopolies had been a particular target of the medieval clerics, and were condemned by the common law courts and Parliaments of the Stuart epoch. In 1603, Coke had ruled that a monopoly was "against the common law," "against the freedom of trade and traffic," and "against diverse acts of Parliament." In 1624, Parliament said monopolies were opposed to the "fundamental laws of this . . . realm." Charles accordingly sought to enforce his policy through the prerogative courts, beholden to the crown, where ancient safeguards could be evaded. A side effect of the ensuing revolution was to sweep away many economic regulations of the Stuarts, permitting the growth of private enterprise and the development of markets.*[3]

---

* "Employment and entrepreneurs were freed from government control and regulation in various ways. Attempts to supervise quality of manufactures and to fix prices were abandoned; industrial monopolies were abolished. Greater freedom was established in relations between employers and workmen. The government stopped trying to regulate wages, to compel employers to keep their employees at work in time of slump . . . The common law, so favorable to

The earliest American settlements were by-products of
Stuart monopolistic practice, which would prove to be a source
of distress and conflict, but also of economic lessons for the
future. In both Virginia and Plymouth, for slightly different
reasons, initial arrangements with the sponsoring London merchants prevented the colonists from owning and reaping the
benefits of private property. Predictably enough, the communal
set-up proved disastrous in terms of incentives and resulting
output, so that both infant states were threatened with starva-
tion. The upshot in both cases was that the settlers converted
as soon as they were able to a system of private ownership, and
reward for private effort.

Captain John Smith described the beneficial effects of this
transition in Virginia, which had suffered grievously from the
communal system. "When our people were fed out of the common store," he wrote, "and labored jointly together, glad was he
who could slip from the labor, or slumber over his task, he
cared not how; nay, the most honest among them would hardly
take so much true pains in a week, as now for themselves they
will do in a day." Plymouth's Governor Bradford gave an almost
identical verdict on the shift to private property there: "This
had very good success, for it made all hands very industrious,
so as much more corn was planted than otherwise would have
been by any means the governor or any other could use . . ."[4]

In Massachusetts and Connecticut, private property existed
from the beginning, but a variety of economic regulations were
attempted. These included wage and price controls, as well as
schemes of government subsidy to encourage manufactures
and mining ventures. By the latter 1630s, the programs of wage
and price control had so obviously failed that they were progressively dismantled—the price of corn, e.g., being "left at
liberty to be sold as men can agree."[5] Though systematic study

---

absolute property rights, triumphed over the prerogative courts." (Christopher
Hill, *The Century of Revolution.* Norton, 1966, p. 146)

of such matters lay well in the future, the early colonists learned many lessons of private property and free markets at the outset. What they didn't already know from doctrines they brought with them, they gleaned from hard experience on the ground.

The importance of property rights and taxes in the American Revolution is of course well known and was an extension of the British emphasis on these topics. "No taxation without representation" was not simply a slogan or pretext with the Patriot spokesmen, but a bedrock principle of their theory. The Americans believed that if Parliament could tax them even a little without their consent, it could thereafter make incursions on their property at its leisure. Every manifesto of the revolutionary era focused on this issue, in keeping with the tradition of Magna Carta, the Petition of Right, and other milestones of British history. We have quoted Burke on the subject of America and religion; he was equally cogent on the issue of taxation:

"It happened . . . that the greatest contests for freedom in this country were from the earliest times chiefly upon the question of taxing . . . On this point of taxes the ablest pens and most eloquent tongues have been exercised, the greatest spirits have acted and suffered . . . They took infinite pains to inculcate . . . that in all monarchies the people must in effect themselves, mediately or immediately, possess the power of granting their own money, or no shadow of liberty could subsist. The colonists draw from you, as with their life-blood, these ideas and principles. Their love of liberty, as with you, fixed and attached on this specific point of taxing."[6]

In the struggle that led to independence, there was a further consideration concerning taxes—analogous to the contests that had occurred between the British crown and Parliament. When the colonies wielded control of funding through the power of taxation, they had some degree of leverage over royal governors, councilors, and other officials whose salaries were paid from public coffers. Unleashed from this restraint, as all participants in the struggle were aware, royal officials could rule in true imperial fashion; much of the conflict, *e.g.*, about the Stamp Act, was prompted by these considerations. As in England, power over the purse-strings was decisive in establishing the locus of authority in the system.

The importance of defending property against arbitrary power remained a preoccupation of the Founders at the era of the Constitution. Hamilton and Madison were emphatic on the subject, as was John Adams: "The moment the idea is admitted into society that property is not as sacred as the laws of God and that there is not a force of law and public justice to protect it, anarchy and tyranny commence." Nor was this simply Federalist opinion; arch-"radical" Sam Adams believed the same. "It is an essential, natural right," he wrote, "that a man shall quietly enjoy, and have the sole disposal of his own property . . . The Utopian schemes of leveling, and a community of goods, are as visionary and impracticable, as those which vest all property in the crown . . ."[7]

In the framers' view, the point was not that property had "rights," but rather that *people* had a right to property, and that this was an essential aspect of a free society. The common concern among the founding generation was that a government which could at its discretion take private property could thereby control every aspect of existence. Property was thus a condition, and a product, of a regime of freedom. Such was the lesson of British constitutional history, the meaning of taxation by consent, and a principal reason for the Founders' high regard for Locke—who was above all a defender of the rights of property.

We are frequently told things have "evolved" since the old-fangled era of the Constitution, that the lessons considered relevant then are now no longer binding. But all experience since bears out the Founders' warnings on this subject. "A power over a man's subsistence," as Hamilton put it, "amounts to a power over his will."[8] Far from being disproved by latter-day developments, this maxim has been repeatedly confirmed in the political history of our era. This has been most obviously the case with the totalitarian systems. As we have seen, all of these regimes set out to control or dominate economic life, and through that control to dictate all other facets of behavior: Where one could live and work, go to school or travel, worship or assemble, speak or publish one's opinions.

Such consequences have been apparent well short of the totalitarian outcome. To take an obvious example, authoritarian governments have found it a simple matter to control the press, merely by controlling the supply of newsprint. In our own society, government control in matters of finance or the material elements of communication has been used to inhibit voices of dissent—as in the "fairness doctrine" imposed by the Federal Communications Commission, antitrust actions against unfriendly media, or timely investigations by the IRS.

How do these considerations affect the ethics of economic freedom, and its relationship to our religion? One obvious answer is that if our ethical system supports the idea of political liberty, as most people would agree it does, then it must support as well the material factors by which that liberty can gain expression. To argue that freedom of the press is sanctioned by the Western ethic, but that the material elements needed to have a press are not, is a hopeless contradiction. The first is conditioned on the second, and to approve of one entails approval of the other. So likewise with other First Amendment liberties that have an economic basis.

These thoughts about the press translate to a more general consideration: The exercise of freedom in all its forms requires some kind of private space—a sphere in which the individual can enjoy a degree of independence, and thereby exercise his own ideas and judgments. A state that controls the material elements of life can, at its whim, deny this. Hence the need in a regime of freedom for a *material spot* on which the individual can stand, and which cannot arbitrarily be taken from him.

That spot is "private property," if not in land, then in material possessions of some kind, or personal income. Take these away—as our Founders understood, but we so obviously do not—and the space required for freedom is abolished.

If we consider the specifically religious aspect of the subject, a number of linkages become apparent. Most obviously, perhaps, the biblical worldview encouraged economic freedom because of what it did in the realm of politics. The principal thrust of Western religion, in political terms, was to impose effective boundaries on the power of the state. The result was, *eo ipso*, to give rise to market economics. "Free markets," after all, are what happens when government doesn't interfere with the transactions of private parties; to the degree that the powers of the state can be curtailed, to that degree free markets will develop.

An interesting illustration of the point—again directly counter to the usual teaching—is provided by the Middle Ages, long before the advent of market doctrine. The clerical spokesmen of the era were skeptical of earthly power in economic as well as political affairs, for essentially the same causes. This is ironically apparent with regard to pricing, where we have been taught that medieval sages favored official regulation for religious reasons. In fact, as shown by Viner, Berman, and other students of the issue, the "just price" of medieval theory generally meant "the common estimation of the market"—as opposed to the dictated prices of state monopolies. (Likewise, the clerical theorists were generally hostile to tax-supported poor relief, since this invaded the charitable, voluntary jurisdiction of the church.)[9]

The connection between religion and the market was not, however, simply a matter of negative correlation. There is a positive relationship as well. This arises from aspects of the biblical outlook concerning nature, man, and society, discussed in Chapter VIII, which had important consequences in the realm of economics. Obviously, biblical religion is anything but "materialistic" in the conventional meaning of the term. For reasons already stated, it rejects all notions of economic determinism, condemns preoccupation with worldly things, and opposes concepts that would elevate the secular to the status of divinity.

There is, however, another side to the equation—a sense in which biblical religion *is* "materialistic." Judaism and Christianity, after all, confirm the goodness of the created order, since this is the handiwork of God. Nature is not divine, but neither is it evil or illusory—concepts pervasive in the mystery religions of the East. When Manichean doctrines threatened the teaching of the early church, Christian orthodoxy rejected them emphatically. Likewise, the biblical view affirms the harmony and regularity of the created world, showing forth the wisdom and authority of God. We see the combination quite clearly in the writings of Augustine:

"The good and simple . . . reason of the world's creation [is] that a good God made it good; and that the things created, being different from God, were inferior to Him, and yet were good, being created by none other than He . . . 'And God saw everything that He had made, and, behold, it was very good.' (Gen. I 31) . . . When in the case of any creature the questions are put, Who made it? By what means? Why? . . . it should be replied, God, By the Word, Because it was good . . . The world itself, by its well-ordered changes and movements, and by the fair appearance of all visible things, bears a testimony of its own . . . that it has been created, and also that it could not have been created save by God . . ."[10]

To the idea of a created universe that is both good and orderly, the Christian outlook added yet another: The intelligibility of this universe to the mind of man. Since the world and humanity both spring from the same creative principle, the orderly motions of the cosmos are harmonious with and accessible to the human intellect. The sum of these conceptions was a mindset radically different from the usual psychology of the ancients. Rather than submitting fatalistically to the mystical potencies of nature—or fleeing from it as the source of evil—the biblical view leads to an active engagement of the mind with the created order. As noted in Chapter VIII, this in turn gives rise to a distinctive concept of human nature, affecting every aspect of behavior.*

In the Christian outlook, man though sinful is a rational creature, capable in obedience to God of negotiating the world he lives in, making decisions, coordinating his activities with others. "As man has a rational soul," Augustine wrote, ". . . his intellect may have free play and may regulate his actions, and . . . he may thus enjoy the well-ordered harmony of knowledge and action . . . and arrive at some useful knowledge by which he may regulate his life and manners." St. Thomas's version was the same: "the rational creature is subject to divine providence in a most excellent way, insofar as it itself partakes of a share of providence, by being provident for itself and for others . . . This participation of the eternal law in the rational creature is called the natural law . . ."[11]

If human beings are "rational creatures" capable of self-regulating conduct, the implications for the social order are profound. This is a notion contrary to the normative view among the ancients and other devotees of top-down power. From the *lex regia* of the Romans to the plans of modern-day collectivists, the premise has always been that order occurs at the expense of freedom. Without a despotism of some kind, it is assumed, there will be chaos in society. Such was the rationale of the pagan state, the theories of Rousseau and Hobbes, divine

---

* In Pythagorean/Platonic thought, great stress was placed on celestial harmonies and the numerical/geometric ratios of the cosmos. What was lacking in these systems, however, was the *realism* of the biblical view, with its emphasis on the nonmagical, objective character of the created order—an outlook required for economic and scientific progress, as opposed to number mysticism or *a priori* speculation.

right monarchs and the French Revolution, the authoritarian systems of the modern era.

Assume that people can regulate their conduct on a rational basis, however, and an entirely different arrangement is suggested: A natural harmony based on volition, in which order arises through the interactions of freely choosing individuals. This notion of a spontaneous order has appeared repeatedly in our conspectus of Western history: the idea of the common law or custom as consent, medieval theories of government by compact, the covenantal precepts of the religious settlers of our country—all assuming an ethical-rational basis for the decisions taken. This was, indeed, what Americans of the founding era meant by a republic based on virtue—in phrases that frequently echo Augustine or Aquinas.*

In most intellectual histories, these concepts are acknowledged as they apply to politics—government by consent, the idea of social contract, popular elections. Less often noted is the degree to which they apply to economics. For the concept of natural harmony or spontaneous order in the realm of economics is, of course, the idea of the market. As spelled out by the Physiocrats of eighteenth-century France, developed thereafter by Ricardo and Adam Smith, and expounded in the modern era by such as Hayek and Mises, the market is the epitome of spontaneous order: an arrangement in which the free decisions of many people produce a structured outcome—of a type that top-down planners could not envision, much less accomplish.

---

* Cf. Rev. Daniel Shute, in an election sermon of 1768: "The plan of the Creator being thus manifestly adapted to promote the happiness of his creation, his conduct herein becomes a pattern to his creatures that are rational moral agents, and the rule of their duty, according to their measure . . ." "It being so evidently the will of God, from the general constitution of things, that the happiness of his rational creatures should be promoted, all such are under moral obligation in conformity thereto, according to their ability, to promote their own, and the happiness of others." (Hyneman and Lutz, op. cit., Vol. I., p. 111)

The connection between the idea of the market and the precepts of our faith is not mere speculation. The Physiocrats, who first expounded the notion of comprehensive economic harmonies, were explicitly theistic, seeing in the symmetrical operations of *laissez faire* the hand of the Creator. (In fact, as noted by Hume and Halevy, the basic ideas were taken almost verbatim from theological doctrines of natural harmony, most notably those of the priest-philosopher Malebranche.) The theistic basis is also evident in Adam Smith, who alluded often to the "Author of Nature" and "Providence" in his writings, and summarized his conception of the universal harmonies as follows:

". . . all the inhabitants of the universe, the meanest as well as the greatest, are under the immediate care and protection of that great, benevolent, and all-wise being, who directs all movements of nature, and who is determined, by his own unalterable perfections, to maintain in it at all times the greatest possible quantity of happiness . . . The idea of that divine Being, whose benevolence and wisdom have from all eternity contrived and conducted the immense machine of the universe . . . is certainly, of all the objects of human contemplation, by far the most sublime."[12]

The same conjunction appears in Frederic Bastiat, the most notable French exponent of free markets in the nineteenth century. In his *Economic Harmonies*, Bastiat compares the social to the natural order, seeing in both the operations of "the universal mind of God," but with this difference: "the social world presents an additional and stupendous phenomenon: its every atom is an animate, thinking being enforced with marvelous energy, that source of all morality, of all dignity, of all progress, that exclusive attribute of man—freedom."[13] Such are the conceptual underpinnings of market theory.

Though it lies outside the political province of this essay, I offer a final comment concerning the impact of biblical doctrine in the realm of science, since this connects quite closely to the foregoing topic. Here, even more than in matters of economics, the conventional history paints a picture of conflict and opposition. Christianity, it is alleged, is otherworldly, obscurantist, and antiscientific. Hence the supposed need at the time of the Enlightenment to throw off the shackles of religion, before advancing to the age of reason. From what has been said about the Christian view of man and nature, the accuracy of this portrait may be doubted.

In fact, as shown at length by Stanley Jaki and A. C. Crombie, the rise of modern science, like that of political freedom and economic progress, has been coterminous with Christian-European thought, and for like causes. The biblical worldview that posits a *harmonious objective order intelligible to man* is an obvious prerequisite of modern science. Of similar import are biblical teachings concerning man's dominion over nature, rejection of pantheistic magic, the idea of progress over linear time, a contingent rather than eternal cosmos. Pagan ideas of submission before the deities in nature, antagonistic precepts of form and matter, and recurring cycles in which everything simply starts all over, are of the opposite implication. It is for these reasons, as Jaki argues, that modern science developed in Christian Europe and not elsewhere. As with so much else considered in these pages, modernity has taken the relevant concepts out of their religious frame, and attempted to set them up on a self-validating basis. Their religious origins are nonetheless apparent.

A few examples may be briefly cited to illustrate the point. One such is the prevalence in pagan and neopagan eras of astrology, alchemy, and other varieties of nature mysticism, which for obvious reasons inhibit the advance of science. In the normative pagan view, nature is thought to have intentions and purposes of its own, to be propitiated by acts of magic rather than by grasping the notion of comprehensive, objective laws imparted by the hand of the Creator. This animistic view is evident even in the works of the philosophers, who conceived of physical nature in "teleological" terms—in terms, that is, of having purposes of its own.

The effects of this may be seen in the cosmologies of Plato and Aristotle, whose ideas of science suggested that celestial bodies were pushed from one place to another by intelligences and spirits. Such notions have obvious affinities to pagan astrology, but none at all to the Newtonian concept of a self-sustaining system, in which the planets traverse their orbits by inertial motion. Compare, however, the theistic view of Jean Buridan (ca. 1320): "One could say, in fact, that God, when he created the universe, set each of the celestial spheres in motion as it pleased him, impressing on each of them an impetus that has moved it ever since."[14] The resemblance to the Newtonian thesis is apparent.

The difficulties with the pagan mindset appear quite plainly in the case of Galileo, forced to recant his observation that the earth revolved about the sun, rather than the other way around. This is cited in the usual histories as an instance of Christian obscurantism, since the recantation came at the hands of the Roman Curia. Neglected in the standard treatment, however, is that the church authorities of the day were defending Aristotle's *Physics* and *On the Heavens*—the principal sources of geocentric theory in the West—while Galileo invoked the authority of St. Augustine in his rebuttal.* These points are made not only by Jaki but also by Giorgio de Santillana in his definitive study of the subject.[15]

The hostility of pagan animism to ideas of systematic science is further evident in the modern epoch—most notably in disputes about environmental questions. The extreme environ-

---

* Galileo cited Augustine's view that the physical facts of God's creation should be derived from observation, which he held would be compatible with Scripture. The theological case for geocentrism was founded on biblical passages such as Joshua's commanding the sun to stand still—implying it was normally in motion. Such a statement, however, hardly required a geocentric view, since the sun could move without the earth's being the center of the cosmos. The hard-core geocentric dogma came from Aristotle's *On the Heavens*.

mentalists, as has been seen, are essentially neopagan, and their attitudes of nature worship result in hostility to science and economic progress—enforced by ever more rigorous compulsions from the state. The more traditional outlook of the West, grounded in the biblical idea of man's dominion over nature, is hospitable both to new technology and economic freedom. It is Christianity, not paganism, that is congenial to Western science.

None of this, be it said, means Christian doctrine would approve of many things that have been done in the modern era in the name of either science or economics; far from it. The *philosophes* of the Enlightenment, the utilitarians and positivists, liberals of all descriptions, and other modern schools of thought have wrenched these and other concepts from their theological moorings, and put them to uses that by scriptural lights are erroneous and harmful. The point is rather that all of these conceptions, from personal freedom and limited government to ideas of economic and scientific progress, come to us from the religion of the Bible.

17

The Need for Limits

SIMPLY PUT, the achievement of freedom in the Western world has been a matter of imposing limits on the power of the state. This may seem a fairly obvious point, but in our academic discourse it tends to get neglected. For Americans in particular, given the recent drift of things, it can't be emphasized too strongly, or too often.

This formula of course is not only simple, but overly so, and needs to be refined and sharpened. A total limitation of government power, after all, would be no government whatever, which translates into anarchy. What is needed is something more complex—to establish a particular kind of government: big enough to handle the tasks of keeping order, so that people may go in peace about their business; not so big that it can destroy their freedoms.

Finding the equilibrium that will achieve this, and ways to keep the system balanced, is the crucial issue of "free government." It was a problem that defeated the empires, city-states, and philosophers of the pagan era, when authoritarian power always seemed to be the price of order. Likewise, the usual cure for despotism among the ancients was a species of disorder—assassinations, *coups d'état* or other violence—which generally led to yet another arbitrary ruler. Avoiding this oscillation between the extremes of anarchy and tyrannical power is the essence of the matter.

The preceding chapters have briefly sketched the events of Western history in which this puzzle was worked out. Indeed, it is fair to say that Western Christendom not only solved the problem (albeit intermittently), but conceptualized and named it. The cosmology and mindset of the pagans were such that ideas of limited government and personal freedom could scarcely be envisioned, which was the reason for all the authoritarian outcomes. It took the biblical view of Deity, nature, man, and state to make the free society even a mental possibility.

In the pagan epoch, as has been seen, political power embraced the whole of life—in the Greek city states as well as in the Egyptian, Babylonian, or Roman empires. Government was church and state rolled into one, so that there were neither upper limits on its powers nor competing agencies to oppose it. Even in the profoundest works of Greek philosophy—indeed, especially in these—theoretical limits on the power of the state and ideas of personal freedom were sadly lacking. "Freedom" in the classical world meant, essentially, participation in the conduct of the state, rather than imposing definite limits on its powers.

Under Judaism and Christianity, all of this was changed. In the biblical view, the state is no longer divine, and is not a church; it doesn't absorb the whole of our existence. A separate source of spiritual awareness appears, moreover, to challenge its authority—the prophets in Israel, the Catholic Church in the Christian era. Most to the point, the king or emperor is neither the law incarnate nor a divinity to be worshipped; rather, in the phrase of Bracton, he "is under God, and under the law." The entire course of Western constitutional history has been a series of footnotes to this concept—attempting to translate its theory into practice.

Among the institutions that acted as a counterpoise against the power of kings, first and foremost was the church itself.

Through defense of its prerogatives, the message of a higher law above the state, and influence on the minds and emotions of the people, it exerted a tremendous countervailing leverage against the secular power. The effects in terms of limited government are acknowledged even by those who differ from the church on questions of liturgy and doctrine. "Had the Christian church not existed," as Guizot observed, "the whole world must have been abandoned to purely material force." Cardinal Manning, for evident reasons, put it in more positive fashion: the medieval church, politically and otherwise, "is the mother of us all."[1]

While the church became the principal limit on the power of kings, Christian Europe also provided others: the baronage claiming its feudal rights, and wielding military force to get them; contractual theories of the state; the diffusion not only of weapons but of wealth, which meant that kings, whatever their ambitions and claims to majesty, had to truck and barter with their subjects. From these constraints arose the major features of constitutional statecraft—the concept of the higher law, written guarantees in the spirit and form of Magna Carta, the development of representative bodies.

These medieval ideas and customs survived in England when they were largely being extinguished elsewhere, by a revival of the pagan view of kingship, at the onset of the modern era. For Americans, it was extremely fortunate that they did, as English limited-government notions reached their apex precisely when the American colonies were being settled. The colonists thus brought with them well-developed views about the rule of law, protections against the power of the state, government by consent, and limits on taxation, drawn from the practice of the homeland.

Even so, constitutional government as we conceive it was not attained in England. On the contrary, the principal lesson English Whigs derived from struggling with the Stuarts was that Parliament should wield the supreme, unchecked authority that had been wrested from the crown. While constitutional-ism and the rule of law continued to be talked of, the British concluded, in so many words, that Parliament could do what-ever it wished, up to and including making changes in the constitution. The king accordingly was "under the law," but Parliament wasn't—since law was whatever Parliament de-cided.

As we have seen, this idea was never accepted by the Ameri-cans, and it became the focus of bitter conflict with the English. In the American theory, *all* political power was subject to a higher law, and this included legislatures as well as monarchs. In constitutional terms, the War of Independence was fought about this issue, and the political arrangements arrived at in the aftermath of fighting reflected the identical thesis. "In all free states," Sam Adams put it, "the constitution is fixed." Hence the method of establishing and tightly controlling power through conventions, the written Constitution, federalism, the doctrine of "enumerated powers," and other techniques for limiting all authority whatsoever.

Why the Americans arrived at these particular notions, as opposed to the purely common law approach, is an intriguing question, though one omitted in the usual treatment. Part of it no doubt is the "freezing" effect of colonial living, which tends to keep political (and other) thought close to the baseline at the era of departure. Also important was the reliance of the settlers on written documents: colonial charters, the New England compacts, the constitutions and bills of rights adopted in the revolutionary era. While certainly not immune to change, as we well know, a document defining government powers is less susceptible to slippage than an evolving scheme of precedents and customs.

Undergirding this reliance on written agreements, also, was the habit of consulting Scripture. And while this too is open to variant readings, the Scriptural-theological element was a major prop of "fixity" in colonial doctrine. By keeping the original sources of the tradition to the forefront, this axiomatic stress restrained the drift inherent in a purely common law approach, which goes wherever precedent leads it.[1*] "Fixity" thus became the distinguishing feature of our founding epoch, and in limited-government terms was as much an advance beyond the British system as that was beyond the absolutism of the French. Rather than affirming the "rule of law" as a sentiment or theory, the Americans made it a definite principle of statecraft, enforced and strengthened by as many devices as they could muster.

Viewed this way, American constitutional doctrine is the product of an immensely long development, unfolding over two millennia of Western thought and practice. It starts with the religious insight that there is a higher law above the state; finds backing for this stricture in the church, and thereafter in the feudal order; deduces from these a system of contractual statecraft, representative bodies, and written guarantees of freedom—all translated to our shores and undergirded by the methods we have examined. Taken as a whole, this history tracks a *series of ever-narrowing and more definite limits on the reach of secular power*—of which the American Constitution is (or was) the ultimate expression.

So construed, the measures adopted at our founding were an extension of the medieval outlook—though modified by religious changes, the colonial setting, and years of struggle with the British. Self-professed traditionalists that they were, the framers were more conservative than they knew. They were in a sense the last survivors of the feudal-medieval order, insisting that all earthly power must be subject to some limit. And, like their medieval forebears, they backed this up with pluralist, decentralized arrangements that gave practical content to the doctrine.

---

* Such axioms, of course, are subject to hazards of their own, most obviously that of diverging into extreme *a priori* politics—the opposite danger from the pure traditionalism of the English.

If this reading be accepted, a number of important conclusions are in order. One is that the chief political tradition of our culture *is*, above all else, a tradition of limited government, in the interest of protecting personal freedom. Those who profess this view today accordingly defend a legacy passed down to us, at considerable hazard, through many generations. The oft-stated conflict between traditional values and libertarian practice in our politics is therefore an illusion—a misreading of the record, or an artifact of special pleading. In the Anglo-American context, "big government conservatism" is the oxymoron—whatever its vogue among paternalists in Europe.

Also, it is worth repeating that this tradition is rooted in religious faith, not secular abstraction. The very concepts of the limited state and personal liberty, and the institutions that gave these practical force, grew from the religious vision of the West. Likewise, the specific ideas and political methods of our republic were products of this background—as seen in the theology of the early settlers, the arrangements they derived from this, and the religious customs of the founding era. All this is irrespective of whether Americans have always lived up to their faith, whether religious people have resorted to oppression, and other charges brought (sometimes correctly) in the conventional treatment. The point is rather that the conceptual building blocks and main political features of the free society were derived from these religious sources.

If we compare this history and resulting institutions to what exists today, the most remarkable thing to be observed is how totally different our system has become. This is true concerning both the larger issues and the everyday details. If the essence of our tradition up through the founding (and for a lengthy span thereafter) was to establish limits on the reach of power, the essence of modern statecraft has been, precisely, removal of those limits. America's Founders did everything they could to stuff the genie of state coercion into the bottle of constitutional safeguards; their successors of the modern era have been equally zealous in letting that genie out again, to work what is supposed to be its special magic.

The reversal of form is obvious in many ways, but is most apparent perhaps in federal-state relations. The record as to the intended diffusion of powers in our system is unequivocal— having been spelled out repeatedly by Hamilton, Madison, Wilson, and other advocates of the Constitution. Madison through the years provided a dozen extensive commentaries on the subject—all affirming the statement, in *Federalist* No. 45, that the powers of the federal government were "few and defined" while those remaining to the states were "numerous and indefinite." The main endeavor of "constitutional" reasoning in the modern era has been to deny this, by any sophistry that will serve the purpose.

The effects in terms of economic and social questions have doubtless been talked about enough already. Suffice it here to reemphasize the point made in our opening chapter: That while the former USSR, Eastern Europe, and many other nations are struggling to escape the errors of top-down control and governmental planning, we continue to embrace them in heedless fashion. We seem as oblivious of lessons from the recent past as we are of those derived from our beginnings.

As to the implications for personal liberty, these also are plain enough to need no great elaboration. All experience teaches, as does the doctrine of our Founders, that concentrated power threatens freedom. This is more obviously the case when power is held to be on principle unaccountable to any kind of limits. We need only recall the insistence of Sam Adams, Jefferson, et al., that the very definition of a constitutional system is one in which the governing powers can't change the rules at their discretion. Compare this with the modern thesis that the judges may rewrite the Constitution as they please, in line with their evolving sensibilities. The first is a formula for limited government and the rule of law; the second a recipe for arbitrary power.

In this respect as in several others, the relativism of the epoch leads irresistibly to authoritarian practice, because it destroys all hope of standards. The liberal jurists and their academic allies regard the Constitution as a kind of verbal protoplasm, without definite form or content, which may be manipulated at their leisure. There are no universals, no commitments that are binding, no meanings that are certain. The Constitution may be made to say whatever five Justices at any given moment can agree on; the question is merely, as Humpty Dumpty put it, "Who shall be master?"

The evident solipsism in all of this, and its significance for the rule of law, suggest again the central fallacy of liberal thought, in all its guises: The idea that a libertarian system can be constructed on relativist assumptions. This fond delusion is everywhere disproved by history, as it is by common logic. The most conclusive examples are the totalitarian movements, all based, as has been seen, on relativist value theory; but the trend of liberalism itself has for decades been in the same direction—albeit at a slower pace, thanks to a lingering regard for Western institutions.

The essence of this liberalism, it has been argued, is to affirm the secular by-products of our faith, imagining them to have been invented by purely rational methods, and to suppose that they can be set up as self-sustaining concepts. The derivative pattern is repeated throughout the liberal canon: The goodness and harmony of the created order become a faith in mechanistic, or evolutionary, science; the concept of the "rational creature" becomes the idea of unaided, sovereign reason; the notion of history moving toward fulfillment over time becomes a belief in ceaseless progress; love of one's neighbor becomes humanitarianism; and so on. All are attempts to harvest and use the worldly aspects of our religion, divorced from the theology that gave them life and meaning.

As noted in our discussion of John Stuart Mill, this effort has been a colossal failure. Sever the roots, and eventually the branches wither. One by one, the features of Western thought and practice conceived as purely rational constructs have faded, along with the faith of our opinion-moulding classes: Ideas of "natural right," equality before the law, protection for the helpless, crusading zeal for science. All of these, by slow degrees, have been losing ground as well, replaced by ideas and values that are not only different from, but sharply antithetical to, the guiding precepts of our culture.

The meaning of this transition has been suggested in several places. It is a reversion to paganism, dressed up as secularism or value-free instruction. In essence, as the grip of Western faith has weakened, the old gods have come back. Hence not only astrology and Eastern cults, but abortion and euthanasia, the nature-worship of the environmental movement, homosexuality as an "alternative life style," the jihad against expressions of our religion. Hence also, and most relevant to our central theme, the reemergence of the unlimited state and reduction of the individual. All bespeak a resurgence of the pagan world-view, and behaviors common to the pagan era.

Specifically, we have seen a return to pagan ideas of social order. The Western concept of volitional harmony, in which free people regulate and adjust their conduct in peaceful fashion, has been progressively enfeebled, most obviously in the realm of economics. In its place we meet the notion that order must be imposed top-down, as with the *lex regia* of the ancients. If government doesn't control and regulate, it is assumed, there will be chaos. The concept of a free, spontaneous order, in the "grown institutions" of tradition or workings of the market, has been abandoned, in favor of edicts by social engineers and planners.

Also tending to fade away is the very *idea* of freedom as we have defined it—as the absence of coercion. In place of this we are getting once more the pagan view of freedom as inclusion in the circle of power, which is an entirely different matter. This is the common theme of much modern talk of "rights"—which generally means that if you are able to *vote on* something, or be included in it, it doesn't matter what level of power is being wielded. In this view, the salient issue is *who will have the power*, in what proportions, as opposed to *definite limits on its scope*. The Greeks and Romans believed this, more or less, but our founding fathers didn't. "An elective despotism," as Jefferson put it, "is not the government we fought for."*

Having doubtless deplored all this sufficiently, we must now consider the question of what might be done to make things better. From what has been said, it should be apparent that the religious issue is central to any such inquiry. The evidence plainly shows that our free institutions proceed from our religion, and are dependent on its teachings. The axioms of Western faith concerning the nature of human beings and the functions of the state gave birth to freedom, both conceptually and in terms of working institutions. Equally important, those axioms must have continuing force if liberty is to survive and flourish.

This connection was well understood by America's Founders and such advocates of the free society as Burke, Tocqueville, and Lord Acton. When John Adams said our Constitution was "made only for a moral and religious people [and] wholly inadequate to the government of any other," he meant that a people devoid of religious-ethical guidelines was incapable of sustaining a regime of freedom.[2] Such guidelines tell us how we should behave toward one another, establish norms of justice and fair dealing, and provide the framework of shared belief that must be the basis of any culture. Also to the point, interior standards

---

* Confusion on this point, indeed, is one of the most salient features of modern politics, and has been for a considerable period. It is most evident in panegyrics to "democracy," used as a synonym for freedom. But "democracy," defined as a method of voting, is obviously not the same as freedom, and very often can be the opposite. Fifty-one percent of the population, after all, might vote to put the other 49 percent in jail. The distinction was apparent to our Founders; though believers in popular elections, they went to considerable lengths to ensure that "democracy" didn't destroy individual freedom.

are needed for self-reliant conduct—standards that give purpose to our lives and supply the basis for our choices. Remove these benchmarks, and ordered freedom becomes impossible. "Men of intemperate minds," as Burke observed, "cannot be free. Their passions forge their fetters."[3] America's founding fathers said the same.

All of this, again, is amply borne out by the record. Careful students of the modern holocaust, such as Arendt and Friedrich, trace the rise of the totalitarian movements to the absence of interior guidelines in modern populations, who looked to the state to provide them with criteria for living. A similar pattern is evident in our own society, with government power growing as religious conviction has abated. While we are not so far down the road as the totalitarian movements, the resemblances are apparent: A paternalistic state, confronting ever more dependent people, increasingly making decisions for them, assuming control over every facet of their lives—sustenance, shelter, health care, schooling, and a great deal else.

The resulting tableau was sketched for us by Tocqueville, in an eerie passage, foreseeing the rise of "an immense and tutelary power" which minutely regulated every aspect of existence and reduced its citizens to drone-like status.[4] In many respects, this vision was prophetic—an accurate forecast of what the managers of the welfare economy have been trying to accomplish, and what has happened to many welfare clients caught up in its workings. The resulting symbiosis between powerful state and normless people suggests, once more, the reciprocal nature of inner conviction and outer freedom. Loss of belief goes hand in hand with loss of self-reliance, and thus the rise of statist practice.

From these reflections it should be apparent that we need, above all else, a reinfusion of religious precept in our national life and public custom. In this regard, the growth not only of the "religious right" but of evangelical churches generally should be applauded, as should the active engagement of traditional Catholics in questions of social value and public policy. Likewise, believers in traditional Judaism are increasingly heard from on such issues, and this too is to be welcomed. The distinctive values of Western culture, based on the message of the Bible, urgently need concerted defense against the onslaught of secular, neopagan doctrine.

In saying this, I am mindful that social and political questions are from a religious standpoint distinctly secondary—that our religious belief is justified not by its social effects but by its intrinsic truth and relation to the life hereafter. Much of the preceding essay is a disquisition on this subject. But it is also a part of Western faith that the world and human society are not simply to be abandoned to the forces of nonbelief. On the contrary, the consistent message of our religion is that God's law is governing in this world as in the next, and we are enjoined to stand fast for its teachings.

It is important to note in this respect that what is being talked of is not "imposing" belief on others, but rather defending it against an aggressive and relentless opposition. If anything is evident in our recent cultural struggles, it is that traditional believers are very much on the defensive, trying to protect their ideas and values, lives and families, from a secularist blitzkrieg in the schools and other public institutions. The notion that these religious people are engaged in censorship of others, or attempting to launch some kind of inquisition, is a preposterous reversal—a classic instance of portraying the victim as the villain.

Though less significant than faith itself, we also need to know the history of our institutions, and their connections to religion. The American educational system at every level is suffused with mistaken teachings about the nature and success of libertarian practice—all geared toward the disparagement of Western faith. This is wrong for secular as well as religious reasons, since it cannot be in the interest of our society to be plied with misinformation about the nature of our freedoms.

These considerations argue the need for deep-going changes in the system—not only in terms of procedures and skills, but even more so in terms of content. We need accurate, substantive teaching about the distinctive aspects of our faith, the relation of these to the development of our freedoms, and the decisive role of religious value in Western history—American history most of all. The fact that such topics are generally banished from our public institutions suggests the need for further growth in private education, religious instruction, and home-schooling. Right knowledge cannot be a substitute for faith, but as Ambrose, Jerome, and Augustine all remind us, it can at a time of cultural struggle be a handmaiden and support.

Strictly political "reforms" lie well beyond the province of this essay, yet some general principles concerning these are worthy of brief mention. Most obviously, if the essence of our political system and safeguard of our freedoms is *limitation on the powers of government*, then reestablishing such limitation should be a major object of our striving. Since the genie has long been out of the bottle, this is no easy task, yet there are some guideposts that can be followed.

The most obvious, perhaps, is that further extensions of federal power should be everywhere resisted. For people of conservative outlook, this is an evident conclusion, at least on most domestic issues. Added taxes and regulations, expansion of entitlement programs, health care legislation, or more federal intrusion in the realm of education can only compound existing problems. Apart from the demerits of such programs on other grounds—which are extensive—whatever increases the size of the Leviathan should be prevented.

While this may seem plain enough where economic topics are concerned, there is a class of issues on which conservatives have been partial to the centralizing impulse. These have primarily to do with "law and order"—crime, drugs, and cultural issues of one type or another. Under Republican administrations of recent decades, there has been a tendency to favor increased federal power in these areas, both because of the subject matter and because Republicans were sponsoring the measures. Whatever the motive for such programs, they contribute further to centralization in the system. Granted that some aspects of the problem are national in scope, dealing with crime is overwhelmingly a state and local matter, and friends of limited government should look askance at increasing federal powers in this regard, as in most others.*

Beyond the question of preventing further extensions of federal power, there is the more difficult—but obviously necessary—goal of seeking a devolution of the power that is already there. Although generalization about such matters is hazardous, and doubtless someone will come up with cases to make me regret my rashness, I would venture to say that *anything which can decrease the power of the federal government should be encouraged.*

This is, I think, the principal merit of tax-credit programs, school choice plans, medical IRA's and other "privatization" schemes that have recently been mooted. These programs are often advanced on grounds of increased efficiency and satisfaction, through better educational outcomes, controlling health care costs, and so on, all of which seems true enough. It is, however, the change that would be effected in terms of social power that is the most appealing feature. All these proposals

---

* None of this is to say the issue of "law and order" should be disparaged. On the contrary, it is of the greatest import, involving the most primordial purpose of the state, and one that has been disgracefully neglected. It is an oddity of the welfare mindset that as government seeks to do all of the things it shouldn't, it correspondingly fails to do the things it should. This inversion of functions is more than merely ironic. Prevailing ideas concerning lack of personal responsibility, blaming criminal conduct on "conditions," lenient policies of probation and parole, and court rulings tilted heavily toward defendants, all reflect the liberal ethic (imposed, in the usual instance, by federal authority on the states). The tendencies that make government a menace to the law-abiding also make it a patron of the average felon.

would transfer decision-making and control from Washington to parents, homeowners, and taxpayers, and for that reason above all others should be supported.*

These comments bring us to a most difficult subject of reform—the courts. By all odds the federal courts of the modern era have been the major force in favor of consolidation. By their elastic reading of the Constitution and yen for social engineering, they have done more to centralize our system than all other official agencies combined. Judicial review is an indispensable aspect of the limited state, since the courts are supposed to ensure that other agencies of government are abiding by the Constitution. But when the courts themselves disdain the rule of law, suggest the Constitution is so much silly putty, and routinely devote themselves to breaking down its limits, they too must be subject to the balances of the system.

Limited government notions, finally, should also be our guides in sorting out the realm of foreign policy. Many confusions could be mitigated here if we began discussion by asking the question that arises (or should) in considerations of domestic matters: *What is the proper role of the federal government, according to the Constitution?* The obvious answer is that its job is to serve and defend the people of the United States, in this case from foreign powers that may do things adverse to the security interests of the nation. If these interests are engaged, there is a reason for U.S. action; if not, then not.

Even here, of course, there are plenty of grey areas and grounds for disagreement. Using a "national interest" standard,

---

* For identical causes, programs of economic and other deregulation ought to be encouraged—as occurred with airline, trucking, and communications in the 1970s and 1980s (since then we have tended pretty strongly in the opposite direction). Likewise two reforms that have been in the news of recent years—a tax limitation-balanced budget amendment and the move for term limitations on congressmen and senators. Again, discussion of practical detail is not my purpose here and I leave the policy merits of these ideas to some other venue. Enough to say, to the degree that such reforms would achieve a reduction of federal power, they could be hugely beneficial.

one could argue endlsessly about Vietnam, the Gulf War of 1991, or other matters. There is no escaping these complexities and confusions. On the other hand, some of the things that have been occurring in recent years would automatically be excluded by such a standard. All forms of globalism, creating a "new world order," foreign aid as tax-paid philanthropy, "nation-building" in third world states, subordinating American forces to the United Nations, would be summarily rejected on this basis. Though the constitutional requirements in some respects are different, mostly in terms of executive powers, adhering to a limited government rule would be as useful in foreign policy as domestic.

Clearly, to work out the details about such questions is a topic for another essay. These thoughts are offered merely to suggest the general direction in which reforms should be attempted. The object would be to change the existing situation in a fundamental way, rather than continuing to drift in our accustomed manner. For conservatives, at least, true reform cannot consist of simply replacing Democrats with Republicans, using power for "our" purposes instead of "theirs," proposing slightly smaller increases of government spending as substitutes for larger ones, or pledging to manage existing programs in more efficient fashion. What is needed is a determined rollback of federal power across the board, when and wherever this can be accomplished.

None of the foregoing, be it said, would be sufficient in itself to restore our freedoms—even assuming that such a platform could be adopted. In every sense, the spiritual and intellectual vision must be foremost. Recovery of our religious faith and its teachings should be our first and main concern. Without it, nothing much by way of practical improvement can be accomplished. With it, all the rest might readily be added.

Notes

1. *The Liberal History Lesson*

1. Cited in Peter Rutland, "Sovietology: Notes for a Post-Mortem," *The National Interest*, Spring 1993
2. Quoted in Skousen, p. 3. This book is an excellent antidote for the problem we—and Franklin—are addressing.
3. Clinton Rossiter, *Conservatism in America* (Vintage, 1962), pp. 204–211
4. Loren Eiseley, *Darwin's Century* (Anchor, 1961), p. 141

2. *In Search of Freedom*

1. *Selected Writings of Edmund Burke* (Modern Library, 1960), p. 420 (hereafter cited as Burke)
2. *The Federalist* (Modern Library, 1937), p. 337
3. Christopher Dawson, *The Historic Reality of Christian Culture* (Harper, 1965), p. 35
4. Burke, p. 477
5. Anton C. Pegis, ed., *Introduction to St. Thomas Aquinas* (Modern Library, 1948), pp. 530, 542
6. *Ibid.*, p. 622
7. Harold Berman, *Law and Revolution* (Harvard, 1983), p. 145
8. Gertrude Himmelfarb, ed., Lord Acton, *Essays on Freedom and Power* (Meridian, 1955), p. 91 (hereafter cited as Acton)
9. F.W. Maitland, *Selected Historical Essays* (Beacon, 1957), p. 112
10. Benjamin Hart, *Faith and Freedom* (Lewis and Stanley, 1988), p. 69; Christopher Hill, *The Century of Revolution* (Norton, 1966), p. 81
11. Perry Miller and Thomas Johnson, eds., *The Puritans* (Harper, 1963), pp. 212–213

12. Saul Padover, ed., *The Washington Papers* (Harper, 1955), pp. 318–319
13. Commager and Morris, eds., *The Spirit of Seventy-Six* (Harper, 1967), p. 379
14. Koch and Peden, eds., *The Life and Selected Writings of Thomas Jefferson* (Modern Library, 1944), p. 278
15. Alexis de Tocqueville, *Democracy in America* (Vintage, 1955), Vol. 1, p. 316

3. The Age of the Despots

1. *The Philosophy of David Hume* (Modern Library, 1963), p. 391
2. Peter Gay, *The Enlightenment: An Interpretation* (Vintage, 1966), p. 163
3. Lewis Feuer, ed., *Marx and Engels* (Doubleday, 1959), p. 272
4. R.N. Carew Hunt, *The Theory and Practice of Communism* (Penguin, 1964), pp. 113–114
5. Gary North, *Marx's Religion of Revolution* (Craig Press, 1968), pp. 33, 85, 86, 100
6. V. I. Lenin, *The State and Revolution* (Penguin, 1992), pp. 59, 56–57
7. This transition is made entirely clear in Lenin, *ibid.*, quoting Marx and Engels extensively to justify both violent revolution and dictatorial rule.
8. Crane Brinton, *Nietzsche* (Harper, 1965), p. 119; Friedrich Nietzsche, *The Will to Power* (Vintage, 1968), pp. 505–506 (hereafter cited as Nietzsche)
9. *Ibid.*, pp. 511, 80, 112, 119
10. *Mein Kampf* (Reynal and Hitchcock, 1939), pp. 613, 661, 670
11. *Ibid.*, p. 576; E.B. Wheaton, *The Nazi Revolution* (Doubleday, 1969), pp. 395–396
12. Michael Oakeshott, ed., *The Social and Political Doctrines of Contemporary Europe* (Cambridge, 1949), p. 227
13. *Ibid.*, pp. 190–193
14. Brinton, p. 209
15. Franz Neumann, *Behemoth* (Harper, 1966), pp. 462–463
16. Oakeshott, pp. 166–167, 176, 178

17. Nietzsche, pp. 9, 37

18. Brinton, pp. 146, 120, 132; Nietzsche, p. 33

19. Henri de Lubac, *The Drama of Atheist Humanism* (Meridian, 1966), p. 45; Nietzsche, p. 32; F.A. Hayek, *The Counter-Revolution of Science* (Free Press, 1952), pp. 108, 121

20. Hayek, pp. 140, 130, 200

21. *Ibid.*, p. 121; Brinton, p. 218

22. Herbert Marcuse, *et. al.*, *A Critique of Pure Tolerance* (Beacon, 1970), p. 109

23. E.g.: "Tolerance is a loaded virtue, because you have to have a base of power to practice it. You cannot ask a certain people to 'tolerate' a culture that has historically ignored them at the same time that their children are being indoctrinated in it." Quoted in Dinesh D'Souza, *Illiberal Education* (Vintage, 1992), p. 10. See the more sophisticated but parallel views of Stanley Fish, in *Are You Politically Correct?* p. 54.

4. *From Champagne to Ditch Water*

1. *Essential Works of John Stuart Mill* (Bantam, 1961), pp. 99, 102

2. *Ibid.*, p. 418

3. Max Lerner, ed., *The Mind and Faith of Justice Holmes* (Modern Library, 1943), p. 415

4. *Ibid.*, p. 97

5. John Dewey, *Individualism Old and New* (Capricorn, 1962), p. 182

6. Evans, *Clear and Present Dangers* (Harcourt Brace, 1975), p. 82

7. *Ibid.* p. 38. Chapter III quotes numerous other statements to this effect by liberal spokesmen from the 1920s through the 1970s.

8. Robert B. Reich, *The Work of Nations* (Vintage, 1992), p. 313

9. Doris Kearns Goodwin, Ralph Nader, Robert Kuttner, Robert Reich, *et. al.*, "The Logic of Public Investment. . . . Can We Do It Again?" *The American Prospect*, Fall 1992

10. Quoted in Robert Bork, *The Tempting of America* (Simon and Schuster, 1991), pp. 219–220

11. Evans, pp. 48–49

12. Carl Becker, *The Heavenly City of the Eighteenth Century*

Philosophers (Yale, 1962), pp. 14–15. See the virtually identical statement of Bertrand Russell in E.A. Burtt, *The Metaphysical Foundations of Modern Science* (Doubleday, 1954), p. 23

13. Brendan F. Brown, *The Natural Law Reader* (Oceana, 1960), p. 119. This book contains many other statements by Holmes to like effect.

14. Evans, "The Death of Liberalism," in Dorothy Buckton James, ed., *Outside Looking In* (Harper, 1972), p. 24

15. *Ibid.*, p. 25

16. *Ibid.*, p. 28

17. See Evans, *et. al.*, "Denying Health Care to the Elderly," *Consumers' Research*, July 1992; Binstock and Post, eds., *Too Old for Health Care?* (Johns Hopkins, 1991)

5. The Uses of Tradition

1. Acton, p. 164

2. Burke, pp. 270, 397; Peter J. Stanlis, *Edmund Burke and the Natural Law* (Ann Arbor, 1965), p. 165

3. J.G.A. Pocock, *The Ancient Constitution and the Feudal Law* (Norton, 1967), p. 35

4. *Ibid.*, p. 172

5. J.R. Tanner, *English Constitutional Conflicts of the Seventeenth Century* (Cambridge, 1962), p. 37

6. Edward S. Corwin, *The 'Higher Law' Background of American Constitutional Law* (Cornell, 1962), p. 4

7. Roscoe Pound, *The Development of Constitutional Guarantees of Liberty* (Yale 1967), pp. 141–142

8. Corwin, p. 43; Tanner, p. 20

9. *Diary and Autobiography of John Adams* (Harvard, 1961), Vol. I, p. 55

10. Pound, p. 73

11. *The Political Writings of John Adams* (Liberal Arts Press, 1954), pp. 23–24 (hereafter cited as Adams)

12. *Ibid.*, p. 68

13. C.H. McIlwain, *The American Revolution* (Cornell, 1958), p. 23

14. Pocock, p. 33
15. Hyneman and Lutz, eds., *American Political Writing During the Founding Era* (Liberty Press, 1983), Vol. II, pp. 1278–1284

6. *If Men Were Angels*

1. Stanlis, pp. 63, 74, 245
2. Acton, pp. 335–336
3. Bradley Chapin, *Provincial America* (Free Press, 1966), pp. 75–76
4. Bernard Bailyn, *Ideological Origins of the American Revolution* (Harvard, 1973), pp. 97, 94; *The Ordeal of Thomas Hutchinson* (Harvard, 1974), p. 183; Max Beloff, ed., *The Debate on the American Revolution* (Harper, 1965), p. 65
5. *Ideological Origins of the American Revolution*, pp. 60, 57
6. *The Federalist*, pp. 92–93
7. Jackson Turner Main, *The Anti-Federalists* (Quadrangle, 1964), pp. 127–128
8. Bailyn, ed., *The Debate on the Constitution* (Viking, 1993), Vol. I, pp. 466–470; Albert J. Beveridge, *The Life of John Marshall* (Houghton Mifflin, 1916), Vol. I, p. 389
9. Main, p. 105; Winton Solberg, ed., *The Federal Convention and the Formation of the Union of the American States* (Liberal Arts Press, 1958), p. 87
10. Koch and Peden, p. 237
11. *The Political Writings of Thomas Jefferson* (Liberal Arts Press, 1956), p. 161
12. *The Federalist*, pp. 57, 337; McClellan and Bradford, eds., *Elliot's Debates* (James River Press, 1989), p. 262
13. J. J. Rousseau, *The Social Contract* (Everyman, 1935), pp. 15, 27
14. *Ibid.*, pp. 17, 25, 18
15. G.W.F. Hegel, *Reason in History* (Liberal Arts Press, 1954), p. 53. Hegel's related statements on the subjection of the individual to the state not only parallel Rousseau but are remarkably like Plato. See Chapters VII and VIII.
16. Saul Padover, ed., *The Complete Madison* (Harper, 1953), p. 49

7. *The Rise of Neopaganism*

1. Rousseau, p. 121–122; Mill, p. 424; Lubac, p. 17
2. Teilhard de Chardin, *A New Synthesis of Evolution* (Paulist Press, 1965), p. 30
3. Julian Huxley, *Evolution as a Process* (Collier, 1963), pp. 13–14
4. Senator Al Gore, *Earth in the Balance* (Houghton Mifflin, 1992), pp. 259–264
5. *Eco-Tactics* (Pocket Books, 1970), pp. 86–87
6. Alston Chase, *Playing God in Yellowstone* (Harcourt Brace, 1987), pp. 304, 345
7. *Ibid.*, pp. 349, 348
8. *The Environmental Handbook* (Ballantine, 1970), pp. 20–21
9. *Roe v. Wade*, January 22, 1973, Part VI
10. Dennis Prager, "Homosexuality, the Bible, and Us," *The Public Interest*, Summer 1993

8. *The Birth of Liberty*

1. While many such books are named in the bibliographical section, three in particular may be useful as introductions to the subject: Will Herberg, *Judaism and Modern Man* (Meridian, 1953), Etienne Gilson, *The Spirit of Medieval Philosophy* (Scribners, 1940), and Charles N. Cochrane, *Christianity and Classical Culture* (Oxford, 1957). For the influence of biblical presupposition on specific aspects of Western thought, as opposed to pagan metaphysics, see Cornelius Van Til, *A Christian Theory of Knowledge* (Presbyterian and Reformed Press, 1969), and Stanley Jaki, *The Road of Science and the Ways to God* (Chicago, 1978).
2. The point is made, *e.g.*, in Pegis, pp. xxvii–xxix.
3. Richard McKeon, ed., *The Basic Works of Aristotle* (Random House, 1941), pp. 1132, 1133, 1137, 1182, 1279, 1305
4. T. R. Glover, *The Conflict of Religions in the Early Roman Empire* (Beacon, 1960), p. 18
5. Fustel de Coulanges, *The Ancient City* (Doubleday, 1956), p. 181
6. F.M. Cornford, ed., *The Republic of Plato* (Oxford, 1957), p. 234

7. Fustel de Coulanges, p. 220; Gustave Glotz, *Ancient Greece at Work* (Norton, 1967), p. 193

8. W.G. Forrest, *The Emergence of Greek Democracy* (McGraw Hill, 1966), p. 26. An extended version of this argument is offered by Zimmern, who adopts the historical-cultural relativist view in saying we shouldn't judge Athenian slavery harshly. (*The Greek Commonwealth*, Modern Library, 1931, pp. 398 *et seq.*)

9. Edward Gibbon, *The Decline and Fall of the Roman Empire* (Thompson and Thomas, 1900), Vol. I, p. 91; Jerome Carcopino, *Daily Life in Ancient Rome* (Yale 1962), p. 65

10. Gerard Uhlhorn, *The Conflict of Christianity with Heathenism* (Scribners, 1892), p. 133

11. Cochrane, p. 31

12. Sir Ernest Baker, *Greek Political Theory* (Methuen, 1960), p. 325

13. Henri Frankfort, *Kingship and the Gods* (Chicago, 1969), pp. 342–343

14. Herbert J. Musurillo, S.J., ed., *The Fathers of the Primitive Church* (Mentor, 1966), p. 151

15. Stanley Jaki, *Science and Creation* (Scottish Academic Press, 1974), p. 168

16. St. Augustine, *The City of God* (Modern Library, 1950), p. 177

17. *Ibid.*, p. 693

18. Lubac, p. 106

9. *The Making of Magna Carta*

1. Otto Gierke, *Political Theories of the Middle Age* (Beacon, 1960), p. 86

2. C.H. McIlwain, *The Growth of Political Thought in the West* (MacMillan, 1950), pp. 164, 174, 173

3. Brian Tierney, *The Crisis of Church & State* (Prentice Hall, 1964), pp. 13 *et seq*; Milton Viorst, ed., *The Great Documents of Western Civilization* (Bantam, 1967), p. 13

4. Marc Bloch, *Feudal Society* (Chicago, 1964), Vol. 1, p. 234; Michael Curtis, ed., *The Great Political Theories* (Avon, 1964), pp. 160–164

5. James Ayar, *We Hold These Truths* (Viking, 1977), p. 24

6. David Hume, *The History of England* (American News Company, n.d.) Vol. II, p. 15

7. A.R. Myers, ed., *English Historical Documents* (Oxford, 1969), Vol. IV, p. 362; Jean Froissart, *Chronicles* (Penguin, 1978), p. 440

8. J.C. Holt, *Magna Carta* (Cambridge, 1969), p. 321

9. George Haskins, *The Growth of English Representative Government* (A.S. Barnes & Co., 1960), p. 72

10. Most famously, this phraseology is quoted in the opening passage of the Petition of Right. See Pound, p. 166

11. Holt, pp. 78–79

12. C.H. McIlwain, *Constitutionalism: Ancient and Modern* (Cornell, 1958), p. 70

13. Henry Hallam, *The Middle Ages* (A.C. Armstrong and Son, 1882), Vol. I, p. 356

14. McIlwain, *Constitutionalism*, p. 103; Hallam, *The Constitutional History of England* (A.C. Armstrong and Son, 1882), Vol. I, p. 55

15. *The Constitutional History of England*, Vol. I, p. 277

16. J.E. Neale, *Elizabeth I and Her Parliaments* (Norton, 1966), pp. 318 *et seq*; Pound, p. 144

17. Justus Buchler, *et al.*, *Introduction to Contemporary Civilization in the West* (Columbia, 1947), p. 702

18. Tanner, p. 20

19. *Ibid.*, p. 30; *The Constitutional History of England*, Vol. I, p. 360

20. Tanner, p. 62

21. *Ibid.*, p. 63

10. *The Social Contract*

1. F.A. Ogg, ed., *A Source Book of Medieval History* (American Book Company, 1907), p. 221

2. Bloch, p. 228

3. Berman, p. 504; Holt, pp. 65–66

4. McIlwain, *Growth of Political Thought*, pp. 209–210

5. J.W. Allen, *A History of Political Thought in the Sixteenth Century* (Methuen, 1960), p. 312

6. Harold Laski, ed., *A Defense of Liberty Against Tyrants* (Peter Smith, 1963), pp. 67–68, 120, 199

7. John Lothrop Motley, *The Rise of the Dutch Republic* (Harper, 1858), Vol. III, p. 513
8. *Ibid.*, p. 509
9. *The Middle Ages*, Vol. II, pp. 364–365
10. *Ibid.*, Vol. I, p. 428
11. *English Historical Documents*, p. 414
12. Allen, p. 339
13. *Ibid.*, pp. 339–340
14. *Complete Prose of Milton* (Odyssey, 1948), pp. 323–324. (Milton reproduced Goodman's comments in an appendix to the *Tenure of Kings and Magistrates.*)
15. Alf Mapp, Jr., *The Virginia Experiment* (Open Court, 1974), p. 16
16. Macaulay's account of these events is the classic Whig version; the same conflict of principles is discussed, however, in Hume (Vol. VI, pp. 385 *et seq.*) and Hallam (*The Constitutional History of England*, Vol. II, pp. 308 *et seq.*)
17. Tanner, p. 265
18. The religious framework of Locke's analysis is more readily understood if the *Second Treatise* is read in conjunction with the (much neglected) first, which is entirely biblical in nature. See Chapter XIII, note 7.

11. *The Dissidence of Dissent*

1. Burke, p. 125
2. Ralph Barton Perry, *Puritanism and Democracy* (Harper, 1964), p. 108
3. Perry Miller, *Orthodoxy in Massachusetts* (Beacon, 1959), p. 77
4. Hill, p. 81
5. Perry, p. 108
6. Miller, pp. 117–118
7. James Truslow Adams, *The Founding of New England* (Little Brown, 1949), p. 132
8. Clinton Rossiter, *Six Characters in Search of a Republic* (Harcourt Brace, 1964), pp. 24–25
9. Miller and Johnson, pp. 199–200

10. Samuel Eliot Morison, *Builders of the Bay Colony* (Houghton Mifflin, 1963), p. 38 (hereafter cited as Morison).
11. Charles E. Rice, *The Supreme Court and Public Prayer* (Fordham, 1964), p. 160
12. *Ibid.*, p. 161
13. Verna G. Hall, ed., *The Christian History of the Constitution* (American Christian Constitution Press, 1962), p. 253
14. *Ibid.*, p. 248
15. Edmund S. Morgan, *The Puritan Dilemma* (Little Brown, 1958), p. 100
16. *Ibid.*, p. 110; Morison, p. 86
17. T. J. Wertenbaker, *The Puritan Oligarchy* (Grosset, 1947), p. 45
18. Morgan, p. 160
19. Miller and Johnson, p. 204
20. *Ibid.*, p. 227
21. Sumner Chilton Powell, *Puritan Village* (Doubleday, 1965), pp. 127–129; B. Katherine Brown, "Freemanship in Puritan Massachusetts," in *Pivotal Interpretations of American History* (Harper, 1966), pp. 17 *et seq.*; Morison, p. 380
22. Michael Hall, *et al.*, eds., *The Glorious Revolution in America* (North Carolina, 1964), p. 10
23. Robert Brown, *Middle Class Democracy and the Revolution in Massachusetts, 1691–1780* (Cornell, 1955), p. 110

12. The American Revolution

1. Adrienne Koch, ed., *The American Enlightenment* (Braziller, 1965), p. 192
2. Hyneman and Lutz, Vol. I, pp. 46, 173–174, 333
3. Corwin, p. 24
4. Koch and Peden, pp. 46–47
5. Bernard Knollenberg, *Origin of the American Revolution* (Collier, 1962), p. 152; Jack P. Greene, ed., *The Reinterpretation of the American Revolution* (Harper & Row, 1968), p. 157
6. Mapp, p. 47
7. *Ibid.*, pp. 123–124
8. *Ibid.*, pp. 126–128

9. Koch and Peden, p. 233
10. Hyneman and Lutz, Vol. I, pp. 78–83
11. Morison, p. 97. Further details are provided in Daniel Wait Howe, *The Puritan Republic* (Bowen-Merrill, 1899), pp. 324 *et seq.*
12. Michael Hall, *et al.*, p. 13
13. Forrest McDonald, ed., *Empire and Nation* (Prentice Hall, 1962), pp. 7–10
14. Edmund S. and Helen M. Morgan, *The Stamp Act Crisis* (Collier, 1965), p. 87; Knollenberg, p. 208
15. Knollenberg, p. 23; Burke, pp. 100–101
16. Greene, p. 158; *The Stamp Act Crisis*, pp. 128–129
17. Henry S. Commager, *Documents of American History* (Appleton, 1963), p. 93 (hereafter cited as Commager)
18. Beloff, p. 90; Esmond Wright, ed., *Causes and Consequences of the American Revolution* (Quadrangle, 1966), pp. 51, 219; McIlwain, *The American Revolution*, p. 51
19. Corwin, p. 77
20. Hyneman and Lutz, Vol. I, pp. 622–623; Knollenberg, p. 173
21. McIlwain, *The American Revolution*, p. 137

13. *The Declaration of Independence*

1. Koch and Peden, p. 239
2. Edmund Cody Burnett, *The Continental Congress* (Norton, 1964), p. 150
3. *The Spirit of Seventy-Six*, p. 271
4. Carl Becker, *The Declaration of Independence* (Vintage, 1958), pp. 25–26
5. Koch and Peden, p. 17
6. *The Spirit of Seventy-Six*, p. 57
7. On the theism of Grotius, see Richard Vetterli and Gary Bryner, "Hugo Grotius and Natural Law: A Reinterpretation," *Political Science Reviewer*, 1993; excerpts from Grotius' "The Truth of the Christian Religion" are given in Verna Hall, ed., *Self Government With Union* (American Christian Constitution Press, 1962), pp. 245 *et seq.*; this volume also contains extensive selections from Pufendorf, showing his strong religious views, pp. 263 *et seq.* As

to Sidney, his response to Filmer is pervasively biblical. (See his *Discourses Concerning Government*, Liberty Press, 1990, *passim*.) Locke's critique of Filmer is even more so, consisting entirely of an argument about the descent of kingship to the posterity of Adam. (*Two Treatises of Government*, Everyman, 1993)

8. Wilson Clough, *Intellectual Origins of American National Thought* (Corinth, 1961) p. 267; Beloff, pp. 53–58
9. Adams, pp. 19–20
10. Clinton Rossiter, *The Political Thought of the American Revolution* (Harcourt Brace, 1963), p. 107
11. Koch and Peden, p. 311
12. Hyneman and Lutz, Vol. I, pp. 162, 430
13. Hezekiah Niles, *Chronicles of the American Revolution* (Grosset, 1965), p. 224
14. Adams, p. 88; Beloff, p. 179; Rossiter, *The Political Thought of the American Revolution*, p. 141
15. Niles, pp. 234–235
16. Koch and Peden, p. 17
17. Mendenhall, Henning, Foord, *et al.*, eds., *The Quest for a Principle of Authority in Europe* (Holt, 1961), pp. 60, 70 *et seq.*

14. *The Law of the Constitution*

1. James M. Beck, *The Constitution of the United States* (Doubleday, 1933), p. 35
2. *The Complete Madison*, p. 16
3. Adams, p. 87
4. *The Federalist*, pp. 37, 299
5. Beloff, p. 68
6. Commager, p. 65
7. *Ibid.*, p. 105
8. Koch and Peden, pp. 242–243
9. Hyneman and Lutz, Vol. I, p. 627
10. *Elliot's Debates*, p. 332. Madison made essentially the same argument, at p. 335.
11. *The Federalist*, p. 337

12. *Ibid.*, p. 320
13. *The Debate on the Constitution*, Vol. I, p. 64
14. *The Federalist*, pp. 534, 249
15. *Ibid.*, p. 303
16. *Ibid.*, p. 200
17. *Ibid.*, p. 269
18. Koch and Peden, p. 573

15. *An Establishment of Religion*

1. Rice, p. 9
2. Rene Williamson, *Independence and Involvement* (Louisiana, 1964), pp. 213 *et seq.*; Solberg, pp. 388 *et seq.*; M.E. Bradford, *A Worthy Company* (Plymouth Rock Foundation, 1982), *passim.*
3. Ralph Ketcham, "James Madison and Religion—A New Hypothesis," *Journal of the Presbyterian Historical Society*, July 1960
4. *Elliot's Debates*, p. 203; John Miller, *Alexander Hamilton and the Growth of the New Nation* (Harper, 1964), p. 572
5. James McClellan, "The Making and Unmaking of the Establishment Clause," in McGuigan and Rader, eds., *A Blueprint for Judicial Reform* (Free Congress, 1981), p. 303; Rice, p. 174
6. William H. Marnell, *The First Amendment* (Doubleday, 1966), pp. 124, 122, 104–105, 121
7. McClellan, p. 303; Marnell, p. 123
8. Robert Cord, *Separation of Church and State* (Lambeth Press, 1982), pp. 216 *et seq.* See also Robert Healey, *Jefferson on Religion and Public Education* (Yale, 1962), p. 135
9. W.W. Sweet, *Religion in the Development of American Culture* (Peter Smith, 1963), p. 50
10. Rice, p. 28
11. Sweet, p. 52
12. Rice, p. 65
13. *Ibid.*, p. 30
14. Cord, p. 71
15. *Gales & Seaton's History of Debates in Congress*, June 8, 1789
16. *Ibid.*, August 15, 1789

17. *Documentary History of the First Federal Congress* (Johns Hopkins, 1977), pp. 228, 232
18. Richardson, ed., *Messages and Papers of the Presidents* (Government Printing Office, 1896), p. 64
19. Cord, pp. 156–157
20. Koch and Peden, p. 341
21. *The Writings of Thomas Jefferson* (Jefferson Memorial Association, 1903), Vol. XI, p. 428

16. The Economics of Freedom

1. Arthur R. Hogue, *Origins of the Common Law* (Liberty Fund, 1966), pp. 216 *et seq.*; Pound, pp. 140–141
2. Hill, pp. 29–33
3. Pound, pp. 146–147
4. Samuel Eliot Morison, *The Oxford History of the American People* (Oxford, 1965), p. 52; Bradford Smith, *Bradford of Plymouth* (Lipincott, 1951), p. 188
5. Murray Rothbard, *Conceived in Liberty*, Vol. I (Arlington House, 1975), p. 263; see also Gary North, "Medieval Economics in Puritan New England, 1630–1660," and "From Medieval Economics to Indecisive Pietism in New England, 1661–1690," *The Journal of Christian Reconstruction*, Winter 1978–79 and Summer 1979
6. Burke, p. 123
7. Adams, p. 148; *Self-Government with Union*, pp. 453–455
8. *The Federalist*, p. 512
9. Jacob Viner, *Essays on the Intellectual History of Economics* (Princeton, 1991), pp. 208–209
10. *The City of God*, pp. 366, 368, 348
11. *Ibid.*, p. 692; Pegis, p. 618
12. Adam Smith, *The Theory of Moral Sentiments* (Arlington House, 1969), pp. 345–347
13. Frederic Bastiat, *Economic Harmonies* (Foundation for Economic Education, 1968), p. 19
14. A.C. Crombie, *Medieval and Early Modern Science* (Doubleday, 1959), Vol. II, p. 69. As to the pronounced Christian theism of Newton himself, see Burtt, pp. 207 *et. seq.*

15. *Science and Creation*, pp. 276 *et seq.*; Giorgio de Santillana, *The Crime of Galileo* (Chicago, 1955), *passim*; Burtt, pp. 72 *et seq.*

17. *The Need for Limits*

1. F.P.G. Guizot, *General History of Civilization in Europe* (Appleton, 1896), p. 52; McIlwain, *The Growth of Political Thought*, p. 217
2. Richard Vetterli and Gary Bryner, *In Search of the Republic* (Roman and Littlefield, 1987) p. 70
3. *Ibid.*, p. 1
4. Tocqueville, Vol. II, p. 336

Bibliography

REWRITING WESTERN INTELLECTUAL history turned out to be more difficult than I thought; throw in a revamp of American political history as well, and it gets to be a time-consuming business.

The rewriting of which I speak, of course, has been done by others, not by me. What I have attempted is to harvest the work of many excellent scholars in different disciplines, and then see what the composite looks like. Since the result is in many ways so different from conventional notions, the extent and nature of these sources deserve some further comment. I accordingly cite the main ones I have used, both to pay my intellectual due bills and to suggest, for those inclined that way, some candidates for further reading.

Most of the volumes I have consulted are mentioned at one place or another in the text, or notes, but not all of these have been created equal. Some are quoted as sources of specific information, others in adversarial fashion, still others to clarify some esoteric matter. There are certain books and articles, however, that are critical to understanding the basic issues, or at least have proved so in my case, including several not expressly cited. Certain of these concern the overarching thesis, and the general standpoint from which the evidence is examined; others are invaluable for the light they shed on a given period, controversy, or institution.

Wherever possible, I have tried to cite editions that are readily available to the public, though this isn't always a realistic option. I have done this as a convenience for myself, since more modern versions of these works are generally easier to carry around and handle, and also for the reader, since the edition I am citing can usually be obtained without excessive trouble. Thus, to take an obvious case, I generally quote the Modern Library edition of Jefferson's works, supplemented here and there by other popular versions. In most instances such editions are quite satisfactory; only when these have failed me have I resorted to the more comprehensive, but more cumbersome and less accessible, twenty-volume edition of his writings. Similar methods have been used with Madison, Adams, Wilson, and others among the founding fathers.

Likewise, I have had to rely on a very antiquarian edition of Hallam, whose famously balanced treatment of English constitutional history contains many details important to our discussion. Unfortunately, and suggestively, there is no modern commercial edition of Hallam that I know of, so the version I have had to use is more than a century old, making it hard for readers to follow up citations. My references to Macaulay and Hume are also from very old collections, but these have been reprinted in newer formats, and in this bibliographical survey the reader is referred to the more recent products.

In resorting to these sources, I have tried to use them for hard factual information, and/or direct statements by major actors in the drama, rather than for hypothesis or opinion. Indeed, in nine cases out of ten, my interpretation varies from the usual histories, including some whose data I rely on. The object is not to argue from authority, but to assemble evidence on the points at issue. Even so, as should be apparent in numerous places, my attitudes have been influenced by, and thus resemble, the views of people being cited.

In terms of general outlook, the affinities of my position, and also my source of data on crucial points, will be fairly plain. To begin with one of the most obvious and important, the writings and speeches of Burke are an education in themselves. Again, while there are many different editions out there, the handiest are the Modern Library volume, *Selected Writings of Edmund Burke* (1960), edited by Walter Bate, and Burke's *Selected Writings and Speeches* (Doubleday, 1963), edited by Peter Stanlis. Also, Professor Stanlis' *Edmund Burke and the Natural Law* (Ann Arbor, 1965), is highly recommended. If one wanted to compress the best advice about studying politics (and writing) into a single phrase, it would be: Read Burke.

Not far behind, in style or substance, is Tocqueville, whose insights into our political system, and Western freedom generally, remain as cogent today as when they were written in the 1830s. *Democracy in America* (two vols., 1955) is available in the Vintage Books edition, and is obligatory reading for students of these issues. On the other side of the question, *The Old Regime and the French Revolution* (Doubleday, 1955) and *The European Revolution* (Doubleday, 1959), are also recommended; the latter is fragmentary and uncompleted, but full of wisdom nonetheless.

Among expositors of my central theme concerning the unity of our freedom and our religion, the greatest by far, as most readers doubtless know, is Acton. *Essays on Freedom and Power* (Gertrude Himmelfarb, ed., Meridian, 1955) is an excellent compendium, as are his *Lectures on Modern History* (Meridian, 1951). For those who want to delve further into Acton's fabled erudition, Liberty Fund of Indianapolis has brought out a handsome three-volume set, edited by Rufus Fears (*Selected Writings of Lord Acton*, 1986). He who has read Burke, Tocqueville, and Acton will know most of what is worth knowing on these topics.

To get the full range of disagreement on libertarian/conservative issues, among precursors to twentieth-century thought, there are many volumes that might be cited. For the full-blown traditionalist-paternalist position, *The Works of Joseph de Maistre* (Macmillan, 1965) are unsurpassed, and in many respects have much to teach us. Conversely, Herbert Spencer's *Principles of Ethics* and *Social Statics* give us a "classical liberal" reading, replete with the Darwinian metaphysics. (The former is also available from Liberty Fund, with an excellent introduction by Tibor Machan.) Many readily available editions of Mill's works give much the same perspective. My view, of course, is that each side of this argument had it half right: Maistre on issues of religion and tradition, Mill and Spencer on state power and personal freedom. Combine these halves and you have, essentially, Lord Acton.

In the erudition department, among more modern writers, few can compare with Eric Voegelin, whose four-volume *Order and History* (Louisiana, 1957–74), is a monument of scholarship and analysis. Voegelin's effort was to trace the idea of transcendence, its origins and applications, from ancient societies to Israel to the modern era, providing a unique comparative study in philosophy and religion. For those who prefer a briefer sampling of Voegelin's thesis, *The New Science of Politics* (Chicago, 1952), and *From Enlightenment to*

Revolution (Duke, 1975) are considerably shorter and more compactly written, though for that reason not the easiest of reading.

Among other twentieth-century writers, the affinity of my views will be evident to many. Closest in many ways was Frank S. Meyer, a good friend who approached these subjects in more theoretical/metaphysical fashion than do I, but emerged with much the same conclusions. His *In Defense of Freedom* (Regnery, 1962) and *The Conservative Mainstream* (Arlington House, 1969) are essential reading on these subjects—the prototype of the (mislabeled) "fusionist" position. Frank arguably did more to straighten out these matters than anyone since Acton, and our debt to him is accordingly immense.

Our obligations are equally large to Russell Kirk, the founding father of the modern conservative intellectual movement. While Frank and Russell were early on at swords' points, I think their positions were more congruent than at first appeared; likewise, while Kirk was the traditionalist *par excellence*, and had many harsh things to say about the libertarians, I think his position was libertarian in effect, for reasons set forward in Chapter V. *The Conservative Mind* (Regnery, 1953) is a classic, and I would rate *The Roots of American Order* (Open Court, 1975) not far behind. These books, and indeed the whole corpus of Kirk's writing, are essential to understanding conservatism in this country, and the broader tradition from which our institutions were derived.

Also important to comprehension of these issues are the works of Richard Weaver, whose *Ideas Have Consequences* (Chicago, 1948) not only exposed the solecisms of liberal thought, but also contributed a memorable tag line to our discourse. To grasp the full import of Weaver's critique of modern error (and to see its divergence from the Burkean position) one should also read his *Ethics of Rhetoric* (Regnery, 1953) and *Visions of Order* (Louisiana, 1964). Weaver's concern throughout was to show the fallacy of relativist theory in all its many guises, a task performed with an incomparable gift of language. My thoughts about these questions are but a pale reflection of his pages.

To cite a few writers on these subjects is, of course, to leave out many. Others who must be mentioned are Gerhart Niemeyer, Stanley Parry, Frederick Wilhelmsen, Eliseo Vivas, Thomas Molnar, L. Brent

Bozell—all of whom have written cogently on the issues from a religious/traditionalist perspective. Among those contributing to my understanding of our traditions and legal institutions have been Ernest van den Haag, Willmoore Kendall, M. E. Bradford, Forrest McDonald, John Willson, George Carey, William Dennis, Otto Scott, and James McClellan. While few if any of these would endorse my thesis in its entirety, all helped to shape it in one fashion or another.

Bridging the gap between traditionalist views and libertarian economics was the great F. A. Hayek, Nobel laureate and tireless exponent of free markets. Like others mentioned, he produced an enormous body of work, which at many places has informed my treatment of the issues. Among many volumes that might be cited, *The Road to Serfdom* (Chicago, 1944), *The Constitution of Liberty* (Chicago, 1960), and *Individualism and Economic Order* (Routledge & Kegan Paul, 1949) are indispensable. Hayek expounded the connection between the grown institutions of tradition and the spontaneous order of the market, and also provided a withering criticism of rationalist systems (see below).

One cannot mention Hayek, of course, without thinking of his colleague and mentor, Ludwig von Mises, with whom I had the honor of studying almost forty years ago. His *Human Action* (Yale, 1953) and *Socialism* (Yale, 1951) are critical to a comprehension of the market, and have been fully vindicated by the fall of collectivist systems around the world (for exactly the reasons Mises and Hayek so often stated). Mises never received the Nobel Prize for economics, but should have done so, and perhaps someday one will be posthumously awarded. For those who would prefer a shorter introduction to his works, *Planning for Freedom* (Libertarian Press, 1952) and *The Free and Prosperous Commonwealth* (Ralph Raico, ed., Van Nostrand, 1962) are recommended.

Combining like Hayek an appreciation of free markets and the cultural setting required for their survival was Wilhelm Roepke, whose *A Humane Economy* (Regnery, 1960) and *The Economics of the Free Society* (Regnery, 1963) present a well-argued case that virtue and liberty must go together, and that free markets are essential to other forms of freedom. Making similar points, in a somewhat different way, is Murray Rothbard, inveterate foe of the traditionalists. I think it instructive that Rothbard's libertarianism is axiomatically based, virtually Thomistic in its nature—thus, up to a point, congruent with my thesis. His *Man, Economy and State* (two vols., Van Nostrand, 1962) and *Power and Market* (Institute for Humane Studies, 1970), are cogent statements of his uncompromising libertarian position.

While many others could be cited in the realm of economics, I shall confine my further references to as brief a space as possible. No discussion of these issues could possibly leave out Milton Friedman, whose *Capitalism and Freedom* (Chicago, 1962) and *Free to Choose* (with Rose Friedman, Harcourt Brace, 1980), have perhaps done more to educate the public to free market economics than anything since *The Road to Serfdom*. Likewise, Thomas Sowell's *Knowledge and Decisions* (Basic Books, 1980) is a brilliant exegesis of the view that only the market can bring together the multitude of factors required for intelligent decision-making on economic questions.

Others who have contributed to my understanding of libertarian principle, and market economics, make up a considerable list, and their writings should be consulted by readers interested in these topics. Among them are Yale Brozen, James Buchanan, Ben Rogge, Martin Anderson, Hans Sennholz, William Peterson, Walter Williams, Paul Craig Roberts, Alan Reynolds, George Reisman, John Chamberlain, Henry Hazlitt, and my colleagues and teachers of long ago at the Foundation for Economic Education and *The Freeman*: Leonard Read, Frank Chodorov, Ivan Bierly, F. A. Harper, Dean Russell, Paul Poirot, Bettina Bien, W. M. Curtiss, Charles H. Wolfe, and Edmund Opitz.

On the general themes I have addressed, I must acknowledge the important work of R. J. Rushdoony, who has written an entire library of books about the biblical basis of our freedom; several of these are cited in the text, and in the specific categories addressed below. Likewise, the polymathic Gary North, whose books and articles I have relied on in several places, and whose *Journal of Christian Reconstruction* is a repository of valued information on many topics covered in this essay. Both Rushdoony and North are in the tradition of the great Reformed theologian, Cornelius Van Til, of whom more shall be mentioned in a moment.

Others who have sought to trace our freedoms to their religious roots, from many different angles, should also be mentioned: Michael Novak, *The Spirit of Democratic Capitalism* (Simon and Schuster, 1982), Edmund Opitz, *Religion and Capitalism: Allies, Not Enemies* (Arlington House, 1970), John Courtney Murray, *We Hold These Truths* (Image Books, 1964), and George Gilder, *Wealth and Poverty* (Basic Books, 1981). Others whose views should be consulted on these questions include Don Feder, Douglas Bandow, Dennis Prager, Benjamin Hart, Leonard Liggio, Father Robert Sirico, Ronald Nash, Richard Vetterli, William Campbell, Salim Rashid, and George C. Roche. Special mention should also be made of Stephen Tonsor, arguably the closest of any contemporary writer to the thought and style of Weaver.

On the specific matters under discussion, readers will recognize my reliance on many authors of distinction. Concerning the transition from pagan thought to biblical conceptions, with all the resulting cultural and political changes, one should of course go to original sources—the Scriptures themselves and such of their expositors as Ambrose, Augustine, Aquinas, and the great Reformers. Similarly, on the other side of the divide, there is no substitute for reading Plato, Aristotle, and the pre-Socratics, whose message in many cases is remarkably different from the notions promoted in our histories.

Among secondary sources that I have used, several in particular should be mentioned. Among the most important are Charles N. Cochrane, *Christianity and Classical Culture* (Oxford, 1957); Henri Frankfort, *Kingship and the Gods* (Chicago, 1969); Mircea Eliade, *Cosmos and History* (Harper, 1959), and *The Sacred and the Profane* (Harper 1961); Will Herberg, *Judaism and Modern Man* (Meridian, 1953); Lev Shestov, *Athens or Jerusalem* (Simon & Schuster, 1968); Fustel de Coulanges, *The Ancient City* (Doubleday, 1956); T. R. Glover, *The Conflict of Religions in the Early Roman Empire* (Beacon, 1960), E. K. Rand, *Founders of the Middle Ages* (Dover, 1957); Van Til, *A Christian Theory of Knowledge* (Presbyterian and Reformed Press, 1969); and Rushdoony, *The Foundations of Social Order* (Craig Press, 1968). The reader of these volumes will not be left in doubt about the difference between pagan and biblical ways of viewing things, the political order in particular.

On the medieval period, my sources are evident enough in the citations. Otto Von Gierke's *Political Theories of the Middle Age* (Beacon, 1960) is standard, though the original sources of his assertions must be dug out from the notes. Equally essential are Marc Bloch's *Feudal Society* (two vols., Chicago, 1964 and 1966), Etienne Gilson, *The Spirit of Medieval Philosophy* (Scribners, 1940), Harold Berman, *Law and Revolution* (Harvard, 1983), C.H. McIlwain, *The Growth of Political Thought in the West* (Macmillan, 1950), and Brian Tierney, *The Crisis of Church and State* (Prentice-Hall, 1964). Many works of Christopher Dawson might be cited, but three in particular may prove useful by way of introduction: *The Making of Europe* (Meridian, 1957), *The Historic Reality of Christian Culture* (Harper, 1965), and *The Formation of Christendom* (Sheed and Ward, 1968). I found Edward F. Cheyney's *The Dawn of a New Era* (Harper, 1962) helpful on many matters of detail, while Hilaire Belloc's *The Servile State* (Constable, 1927) contains a notable vindication of the Middle Ages.

For the English historical passages, as noted, I have chiefly consulted the classic historians—Hume, Hallam, and Macaulay. Hume's history is now available in paperback from Liberty Press, while Macaulay has been recently reprinted by Penguin. For details on the Great Charter, I have relied on J. C. Holt's *Magna Carta* (Oxford, 1960), and *Magna Carta and the Idea of Liberty* (John Wiley, 1972). On the unique persistence of the British common law, Maitland's works are canonical. Popular versions include *Domesday Book and Beyond* (Norton, 1966) and *Selected Historical Essays* (Beacon, 1959). I have also drawn on J. G. A. Pocock's *Ancient Constitution and the Feudal Law* (Norton, 1967), Roscoe Pound's *Development of Constitutional Guarantees of Liberty* (Yale, 1967), and Arthur Hogue's *Origins of the Common Law* (Liberty Fund, 1966). On the growth of Parliament, G. L. Haskins' *The Growth of English Representative Government* (A. S. Barnes & Co., 1960) is an excellent summary, while the Oxford compilation, *English Historical Documents* (1969) is a valued resource. May McKisack's *The Fourteenth Century* (Oxford 1992) should be consulted for detail about the depositions of Edward II and Richard II.

For the transition of feudal-medieval conceptions into modern argot, nothing is more instructive than simply reading the *Vindiciae Contra Tyrannos* (Peter Smith, 1963), while Motley's *Rise of the*

Dutch Republic (Harper, 1858) gives us, with Whig flourishes, the details concerning the Act of Abjuration. J. W. Allen's *History of Political Thought in the Sixteenth Century* (Methuen, 1960) provides particulars about these matters that are neglected in other histories, and Figgis' *Political Thought from Gerson to Grotius* (Harper 1965) supplies background on the Catholic side of this development. Ralph Roeder's *Catherine de Medici* (Vintage, 1964), G.R. Elton's *Reformation in Europe* (Harper, 1963) and *England Under the Tudors* (Routledge, 1991), and Sir Ernest Barker's *Church, State and Education* (Ann Arbor, 1957) help establish needed context.

On the Tudor and Stuart periods, and the battle over the "reception" of the Roman law, Maitland, Pound, and McIlwain are all instructive. McIlwain's *Constitutionalism: Ancient and Modern* (Cornell, 1958) provides significant detail about the Tudors. Other sources I have relied on include David Lindsey Keir, *The Constitutional History of Modern Britain* (Norton, 1967), J. E. Neale's *Elizabeth I and Her Parliaments* (Norton, 1966), G. Constant's *Reformation in England* (Harper 1966), and F. E. Hutchinson, *Cranmer and the English Reformation* (Collier, 1962). On the reigns of James I and Charles I and the burgeoning clash with Parliament, I have used G. M. Trevelyan, *England Under the Stuarts* (Barnes and Noble, 1965), J. R. Tanner, *English Constitutional Conflicts of the Seventeenth Century* (Cambridge, 1962), Christopher Hill, *The Century of Revolution* (Norton, 1966) and G. W. Gooch, *English Democratic Ideas in the Seventeenth Century* (Harper, 1959). Otto Scott's *James I* (Mason and Charter, 1976) is especially interesting on the relationship of Buchanan to King James.

For the Glorious Revolution, as indicated in the notes, I have chiefly followed Macaulay, with an assist from Hume and Hallam. On the theories of resistance and social contract that accompanied this last uprising against the Stuarts, Sidney's *Discourses Concerning Government* (Liberty Press, 1986) and Locke's *Treatises on Government* (Everyman, 1993) are the obvious sources. As mentioned, Locke's argument is best understood if the first and second treatises are read together; however, the Regnery Gateway reproduction of the *Second Treatise* is valuable for its introduction by Kirk.

Reams of data are available on the settlers of our country, but for reasons noted these are much ignored. On the covenantal precepts of the early settlers, the reader is especially referred to Perry Miller's *Orthodoxy in Massachusetts* (Beacon, 1959), Samuel Eliot Morison's *Builders of the Bay Colony* (Houghton Mifflin, 1964), Edmund Morgan's *The Puritan Dilemma* (Little Brown, 1958) and Daniel Wait Howe's *The Puritan Republic* (Bowen-Merrill, 1899). For the history of the Pilgrims, I have used Bradford Smith's *Bradford of Plymouth* (Lipincott, 1951). The Virginia history is taken from Jefferson and Richard Bland (see below), Alf Mapp's *The Virginia Experiment* (Open Court, 1974), and C.M. Andrews, *Our Earliest Colonial Settlements* (Cornell, 1959). On the Puritan-covenantal influence, Rushdoony's *This Independent Republic* (Craig Press, 1964) is full of relevant information, as are many numbers of North's *Journal of Christian Reconstruction*. On the later seventeenth century, David Lovejoy's *The Glorious Revolution in America* (Harper, 1974) is excellent, while the identically titled volume edited by Michael Hall, *et al.* (North Carolina, 1964), is a valuable compilation of documents from the era.

The American Revolution proper is among the most controverted issues addressed herein, and I have tried to canvass the major schools of thought before arriving at my conclusions. David Ramsey's contemporaneous *History of the American Revolution* (two vols., Liberty Press, 1990) should be read to get an idea of the colonists' conservative views about the issues. Lawrence H. Gipson's *The Coming of the American Revolution* (Harper, 1962), Andrews' *The Colonial Background of the American Revolution* (Yale, 1961), and John Miller's *Origins of the American Revolution* (Stanford, 1966) should also be consulted; though each has a thesis to propound, all contain much needed information. Anthologies edited by Esmond Wright, *The Causes and Consequences of the American Revolution* (Quadrangle, 1966), Jack P. Greene, *The Reinterpretation of the American Revolution* (Harper, 1968), Carl N. Degler, *Pivotal Interpretations of American History* (Harper, 1966), and Richard Morris, *The Era of the American Revolution* (Harper, 1965), all contain highly useful essays, several of which are cited in the text.

As most students of the revolution are aware, the works of Bernard Bailyn are essential reading on this subject. *The Origin of American Politics* (Vintage, 1965), *The Ideological Origins of the American*

Revolution (Harvard, 1973), and *The Ordeal of Thomas Hutchinson* (Harvard, 1974), are invaluable sources on the era, though my findings vary from those of this distinguished scholar. Much the same may be said of Gordon Wood, a Bailyn disciple, whose *Creation of the American Republic* (Norton, 1972) and *Radicalism of the American Revolution* (Knopf, 1993) are impressive feats of scholarship, though governed throughout by the author's "radicalism" thesis.

Among the most striking and influential interpretations of the revolution is that of Daniel Boorstin, as set forward in *The Genius of American Politics* (Vintage, 1958) and *The Americans* (Vol. I, Vintage, 1964). Boorstin is the mirror image of Wood and Bailyn; he argues for a type of conservatism among the Founders, but does so on the grounds that they were pragmatic problem-solvers without pronounced conviction. While his formulations are thought-provoking and his insights many, the reader will recognize that my conclusions are quite different from this reading.

The most useful surveys of the era, in my view, are Bernard Knollenberg's *Origin of the American Revolution* (Collier 1962), and the Morgans' study of *The Stamp Act Crisis* (Collier, 1965). These focus, refreshingly, on what the British and their colonial cousins were actually *doing* in the prerevolutionary period, rather than fixating on purely theoretical statements. Read in conjunction with these histories, C. H. McIlwain's *The American Revolution* (Cornell, 1962) and Rossiter's three-volume compilation of revolutionary notions— *The First American Revolution* (1958), *Six Characters in Search of a Republic* (1964), and *The Political Thought of the American Revolution* (1963)—all Harcourt Brace—are extremely useful.

Among many productions of the Liberty Fund that have been cited in these pages, none is more valuable than the anthology assembled by Charles Hyneman and Donald Lutz, *American Political Writing During the Founding Era* (two vols., 1983). This contains many statements from the revolutionary epoch, including election sermons, philosophical writings, and political manifestoes. It is instructive not only for the insights it provides about the revolutionary era, but also for many essays presaging the constitutional settlement that would follow. Among those appearing in its pages are Thomas Tucker, Richard Bland, Josiah Tucker, and several other forgotten worthies.

On the Declaration of Independence, my completely heretical reading is based initially on the medieval, Reformation, and English background, thereafter on such sources as are available on the Declaration itself. These include Jefferson's and John Adams' notes and recollections, Burnett's study of *The Continental Congress* (Norton, 1964), Niles' *Chronicles of the American Revolution* (Harper, 1965), Commager's *Documents of American History* (Appleton, 1963), Commager and Morris, *The Spirit of Seventy-Six* (Harper, 1967), and Hyneman and Lutz. The construction that comes closest to my own is Gary Amos, *Defending the Declaration* (Wolgemuth and Hyatt, 1989). Variant readings are provided by Carl Becker, *The Declaration of Independence* (Vintage, 1958), Harry Jaffa, *How to Think About the American Revolution* (Carolina Academic Press, 1978), and Garry Wills, *Inventing America* (Vintage, 1979). Fawn Brodie's *Thomas Jefferson: An Intimate History* (Norton, 1974) offers interesting data on Jefferson's ill-timed absence from the Continental Congress.

On the philosophical outlook of the Founders, the best sources are of course the leading actors themselves. The reader is referred to collected editions of Jefferson, Madison, Hamilton, Wilson, et. al., various of which are mentioned in the notes. The popular versions I have used are the *Life and Selected Writings of Thomas Jefferson* (Modern Library, 1944), *The Political Writings of John Adams* (Liberal Arts Press, 1956), *The Complete Madison* (Harper, 1953), *The Washington Papers* (Harper, 1955), excerpts from Wilson in Beloff and Hyneman and Lutz, Dickinson in *Empire and Nation* (Prentice-Hall, 1962). Also extremely valuable are Zoltan Haraszti, *John Adams and the Prophets of Progress* (Harvard, 1952), and Lester Cappon, ed., *The Adams-Jefferson Letters* (North Carolina, 1959). All of these are useful in tracking the opinions of the Founders during the revolutionary/constitutional era.

My reading of the constitutional settlement as an effort to bind down governmental power by every possible means is based, initially, on such sources: The views of Sam Adams and James Otis, *e.g.*, in Beloff, and also in Wilson Clough, *Intellectual Origins of American National Thought* (Corinth, 1961); Jefferson's comments in *Notes on Virginia*; Madison's many statements on the subject; Thomas Tucker in Hyneman and Lutz. I have used two versions of the debates at the convention, McClellan and Bradford, *Elliot's Debates* (James River Press, 1989) and Winton Solberg, *The Federal Convention and the Formation of the Union of the American States* (Liberal Arts Press, 1958). For the debates on ratification, *The Federalist* is obviously basic, and Bailyn has recently edited a handsome two-volume compilation of discussions in the state conventions and popular press, entitled *The Debate on the Constitution* (Viking, 1993). Good sources on the anti-Federalists are J.T. Main, in a study of that title (Quadrangle, 1964), Merrill Jensen, *The Articles of Confederation* (Wisconsin, 1959) and *The New Nation* (Vintage, 1965), A.T. Mason, *The States Rights Debate* (Prentice Hall, 1964), and essays by Cecilia Kenyon *e.g.*, in Greene.

As to the centrality of conventions, this had to be pieced together from several sources: The Adamses, Jefferson, Tucker, Madison, Mason at the Constitutional Convention. The most detailed treatment I have found is Wood's *Creation of the American Republic*, but while he mentions the idea of limits in passing, he mainly stresses the sovereignty-of-the-people aspect, somewhat losing the major point as I construe it. A useful corrective to this is Andrew McLaughlin's *Foundations of American Constitutionalism* (Fawcett, 1961), where the idea of fixed and certain limits is brought out very clearly.

If any part of this manuscript is more outrageous than my treatment of the Declaration, it is undoubtedly the chapter on the First Amendment. Again, my sources are obvious from the notes. On the religious views of the Founders and general outlook of the era, Sweet's *Religion in the Development of American Culture* (Peter Smith, 1963) is essential. Likewise, an excellent conspectus of the subject is provided in hard-to-come-by volumes edited by Verna Hall (with introductions by Felix Morley): *The Christian History of the Constitution* and *Self-Government With Union* (American Christian Constitution Press, 1962). The great value of these books is the vast amount of original material that they reproduce.

For particular information on individual founders, I have in large measure (but not entirely) followed René Williamson, *Independence and Involvement* (Louisiana, 1964), M. E. Bradford, *A Worthy Company* (Plymouth Rock Foundation, 1982), and biographical notes in

Solberg, as well as the treatments of specific people cited in my notes. As to the practices and attitudes of the era, Robert Cord's *Separation of Church and State* (Lambeth Press, 1982) is extremely useful, containing a wealth of much neglected information. Likewise, James McClellan, "The Making and Unmaking of the Establishment Clause" in *A Blueprint for Judicial Reform* (Free Congress, 1981), William Marnell, *The First Amendment* (Doubleday, 1966), and Charles E. Rice, *The Supreme Court and Public Prayer* (Fordham, 1964). The reader of these volumes will discover that I have barely skimmed the surface of compelling data that many learned authors have assembled.

Concerning my view that free market economics derive from biblical notions of natural harmony, as opposed to pagan theories of top-down power, I don't know of anyone who has argued the point in quite this fashion. Viner's *Essays on the Intellectual History of Economics* (Princeton, 1990) contains many valuable insights, as do the works of Berman, Hill, and Pound. Also suggestive are Elie Halevy, *The Growth of Philosophic Radicalism* (Beacon, 1955), Kingsley Martin, *French Liberal Thought in the Eighteenth Century* (Harper, 1963), and Lewis Haney, *History of Economic Thought* (Macmillan, 1955)—touching such matters as, *e.g.*, the influence of Malebranche on the Physiocrats, and their association in turn with Smith. *The Wealth of Nations* is available, of course, in many editions, while *The Theory of Moral Sentiments* was republished in 1975 by Arlington House.

Oddly enough, the scientific side of this development is much better documented, thanks chiefly to the Herculean labors of Stanley Jaki. Two of his works are cited in the text—*Science and Creation* (Scottish Academic Press, 1974), and *The Road of Science and the Ways to God* (Chicago, 1978)—but many others should also be consulted: *The Relevance of Physics* (Chicago, 1970), *The Origin of Science and the Science of its Origin* (Regnery, 1979), *Chance or Reality* (Intercollegiate Studies Institute, 1986), and half-a-dozen more. The astounding erudition of these works, and the importance of the subject, make them imperative reading for anyone remotely interested in such matters.

Second only to Jaki in this regard is A.C. Crombie's *Medieval and*

Early Modern Science (two vols., Doubleday, 1959), which contains many specifics on medieval economic and scientific practice. William C. Bark, *Origin of the Medieval World* (Doubleday, 1960), is briefer but an excellent discussion. Burtt's *Metaphysical Foundations of Modern Science* (Doubleday, 1954) is also useful for its treatment of Copernicus and Newton, while de Santillana, *The Crime of Galileo* (Chicago, 1955), is a standard reference on this topic. George Sarton, *The History of Science and the New Humanism* (Indiana, 1962), contains some helpful passages, as does Landon Gilkey, *Maker of Heaven and Earth* (Doubleday, 1965), discussing the importance of the *ex nihilo* doctrine. The reader is also referred to surveys of these issues by Charles Dykes and E. L. Hebden Taylor in the summer 1979 issue of *The Journal of Christian Reconstruction*.

Thus, in brief compass, the sources I have used in tracing the development of our ideas and institutions. This listing is but a selection of many titles that could be mentioned, and doubtless there are many important sources I have neglected. Also, the reader may have noted that I give short shrift, or none, to several writers included in the "canon"—Machiavelli, Hobbes, Montaigne, Voltaire, Kant, and numerous others. The reason for this should be evident on its face. I am trying to track the development of *our* political tradition, and it is by this standard that various writers and political actors have been considered. The notion that Machiavelli or Hobbes had any positive role to play in this respect—though frequently suggested—seems to me absurd. Typical references to such writers in the literature of our founding are completely hostile, for reasons that by this point should be apparent.

Something does need saying, however, concerning this aspect of the subject, and my treatment of it. Given the usual praise heaped on the Renaissance, for instance, my negative view may strike some readers as surprising. For those who think this was an era of individual freedom, some handy references are suggested: Burckhardt's *Civilization of the Renaissance in Italy* (Modern Library, 1954), J. C. L. de Sismondi, *A History of the Italian Republics* (Doubleday, 1966), and J. A. Symonds, *The Age of the Despots* (Capricorn, 1960), are three that may be easily consulted. Though these authors are all inclined to favor the Renaissance, they leave no doubt that

Symonds' title (which I have borrowed for Chapter III) is entirely accurate.

As to the transition of Renaissance conceptions into the French Enlightenment and Revolution, there are countless works to be considered. Those of Tocqueville, already cited, are highly recommended. So are James H. Billington, *Fire in the Minds of Men* (Basic Books, 1980), and Simon Schama, *Citizens* (Vintage, 1989), among more recent studies. On the contrast between the French and American revolutions, the various commentaries of Burke are of course first rate, and Friedrich Gentz's *The French and American Revolutions Compared* (Regnery, 1955) is also instructive.

Finally, on the conversion of all this into the authoritarianism of the modern era, the sources are as usual many. Oakeshott's *The Social and Political Doctrines of Contemporary Europe* (Cambridge, 1949) contains numerous statements and manifestoes from the offending parties, and his *Rationalism in Politics* (Liberty Press, 1991) is a brilliant exposition of the subject. Among several studies on the fallacies of utilitarianism, A. V. Dicey's *Law and Public Opinion in England* (Macmillan, 1962) is the standard. Other important sources on the general topic are Hayek's *The Counter-Revolution of Science* (Free Press, 1952), Henri de Lubac's *The Drama of Atheist Humanism* (Meridian, 1966), Hannah Arendt's *The Origins of Totalitarianism* (Meridian, 1961), and Voegelin's *From Enlightenment to Revolution*, already mentioned. A particularly valuable recent study, which makes many of the points considered in this essay, is Gene Veith, *Modern Fascism* (Concordia, 1993).

Index

Page numbers followed by n indicate references to footnotes.